# Harrington on Hold 'em

## Expert Strategy for No-Limit Tournaments; Volume II: The Endgame

*By*

DAN HARRINGTON
1995 World Champion

BILL ROBERTIE

**A product of Two Plus Two Publishing LLC**

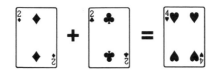

FIRST EDITION

THIRD PRINTING
AUGUST 2007

*Printing and Binding*
Creel Printers, Inc.
Las Vegas, Nevada

*Printed in the United States of America*

# Harrington on Hold 'em: Expert Strategy for No-Limit Tournaments; Volume II: The Endgame COPYRIGHT © 2005 Two Plus Two Publishing LLC

For information contact:      **Two Plus Two Publishing LLC**
**32 Commerce Center Drive**
**Suite H-89**
**Henderson, NV 89014**

ISBN: 1-880685-35-3

*The Man*: To the true gambler,
money is never an end in itself,
but simply a tool;
as language is to thought.


From *The Cincinnati Kid* (1965)

# Table of Contents

# About Dan Harrington

Dan Harrington began playing poker professionally in 1982. On the circuit he is known as "Action Dan," an ironic reference to his solid but effective style. He has won several major no-limit hold 'em tournaments, including the European Poker Championships (1995), the $2,500 No-Limit Hold 'em event at the 1995 World Series of Poker, and the Four Queens No-Limit Hold 'em Championship (1996).

Dan began his serious games-playing with chess, where he quickly became a master and one of the strongest players in the New England area. In 1972 he won the Massachusetts Chess Championship, ahead of most of the top players in the area. In 1976 he started playing backgammon, a game which he also quickly mastered. He was soon one of the top money players in the Boston area, and in 1981 he won the World Cup of backgammon in Washington D.C., ahead of a field that included most of the world's top players.

He first played in the $10,000 No-Limit Hold 'em Championship Event of the World Series of Poker in 1987. He has played in the championship a total of 13 times and has reached the final table in four of those tournaments, an amazing record. Besides winning the World Championship in 1995, he finished sixth in 1987, third in 2003, and fourth in 2004. He is widely recognized as one of the greatest and most respected no-limit hold 'em players, as well as a feared opponent in limit hold 'em side games. He lives in Santa Monica where he is a partner in Anchor Loans, a real estate business.

# About Bill Robertie

Bill Robertie has spent his life playing and writing about chess, backgammon, and now poker. He began playing chess as a boy, inspired by Bobby Fischer's feats on the international chess scene. While attending Harvard as an undergraduate, he became a chess master and helped the Harvard chess team win several intercollegiate titles. After graduation he won a number of chess tournaments, including the United States Championship at speed chess in 1970. He also established a reputation at blindfold chess, giving exhibitions on as many as eight boards simultaneously.

In 1976 he switched from chess to backgammon, becoming one of the top players in the world. His major titles include the World Championship in Monte Carlo in 1983 and 1987, the Black & White Championship in Boston in 1979, the Las Vegas tournaments in 1980 and 2001, the Bahamas Pro-Am in 1993, and the Istanbul World Open in 1994.

He has written several well-regarded backgammon books, the most noted of which are *Advanced Backgammon* (1991), a two-volume collection of 400 problems, and *Modern Backgammon* (2002), a new look at the underlying theory of the game. He has also written a set of three books for the beginning player: *Backgammon for Winners* (1994), *Backgammon for Serious Players* (1995), and *501 Essential Backgammon Problems* (1997).

From 1991 to 1998 he edited the magazine *Inside Backgammon* with Kent Goulding. He owns a publishing company, the Gammon Press (www.thegammonpress.com), and lives in Arlington, Massachusetts with his wife Patrice.

# Introduction

In Volume I of *Harrington on Hold 'em,* I explained some of the basic (and not-so-basic) concepts you needed to be a successful no-limit hold 'em player. We saw how to evaluate a hand in the context of all the information available at the table, how to take into account the different playing styles you might encounter in your opponents, how to analyze hands and evaluate pot odds, and how to play before and after the flop, as well on later streets.

My emphasis in Volume I was playing in the early stages of tournaments, when most of the following conditions apply:
1. The tables are mostly full, with 9 or 10 players.
2. The stacks are large relative to the blinds.
3. The stacks sizes are roughly the same.
4. The money is still far off in the distance.

In this book, I'm going to show you what happens when we reach the ending stage of a tournament, and some (or all) of these conditions break down. Be warned: Ending play is very different from early play, and I'll introduce many ideas that you've never seen explained in a poker book before. But as in Volume I, I'll introduce them slowly and carefully, with plenty of hand examples along the way.

To be consistent with Volume I, the parts of the book will be numbered starting where Volume I left off.

## Organization

Part Eight, "Making Moves," is really the last chapter of Volume I, but space considerations forced us to move it here to Volume II. In contrast to the discussions in Volume I, which were mostly concerned with betting for value, here I'll discuss bets that

1

don't reflect the true value of your hand. We'll look at bluffs, delayed bluffs, check-raises, and the various forms of slow-playing. Most important, I'll show you the preconditions required to give your moves a high percentage of success.

Part Nine, "Inflection Points," is probably the most important chapter of the two volumes. Here I'll show you how to play when the blinds become a larger and larger portion of your stack size. I'll introduce the M and Q ratios, as well as my "Zone" concept, and show you how different types of hands become more or less playable as you move from zone to zone.

Part Ten covers the play at tables where stack sizes and inflection points are wildly different, so that each player is operating under a different agenda. Once again, you have to consider how the table appears to each possible opponent before making your moves.

Part Eleven, "Short Tables," shows you how to play when the table size shrinks to six, five, four, or even just three players. Starting hand and playing requirements change dramatically at these tables, and of course inflection points play a major role as well.

Part Twelve, "Heads-Up," shows you what to do when only one other player remains with you. This phase of the tournament doesn't usually last very long, so you have to be alert and decisive to squeeze out an edge.

Part Thirteen is our miscellaneous catch-all chapter, where I'll talk about some loose ends that didn't really fit anywhere else, like making deals and playing in tournaments with multiple qualifiers, as well as some final insights on the psychology of the game.

# Thanks to the Forums and Others

The Two Plus Two Online Forums (www.twoplustwo.com) are an excellent source of poker discussions and commentary. We'd like to thank all the contributors who submitted comments and suggestions following the release of Volume I. All were appreciated, and we used some of the ideas to improve the layout of Volume II.

In addition, I want to thank David Sklansky and Mason Malmuth for their comments throughout this manuscript, and Ed Miller for his help in creating the index.

# Part Eight
# Making Moves

# Making Moves

# Introduction

In Volume I focus for the most part was on "value bets," bets that more or less accurately reflected the true strength of your hand. When you play poker, however, you can't simply bet when you have a hand and throw your cards away otherwise. If you do, even the most perceptually challenged opponents will eventually figure you out. Instead, you'll have to mix in some moves with your value bets, pretending to be strong when you have nothing, and pretending to be weak when you really have a hand.

Moves break down into two broad categories. Bluffs, where you pretend to have a strong hand when in fact you don't, and slow-plays, where you pretend to have a weak hand when in fact you are strong. Both can be powerful and effective tools. Both techniques can be underused, and both can be overused.

In this chapter I'll look at the various forms these moves can take. I'll show you what conditions provide a favorable situation to make a move, and when moves should be avoided. Remember that while moves can be used to set up your value bets, they can generate a profit on their own if properly employed.

# Bluffing

Bluffing is a pretty straightforward idea. You have a weak hand, but you bet anyway, pretending to have a strong one. If your opponent believes you, you take down a pot.

In this section I'll outline some very specific bluffing moves that have a better-than-average chance of success. First, however, let's talk about some general characteristics of all bluffs.

**How many players should you bluff?** The fewer, the better. One is better than two, and two are better than three. Bluffing more players creates the appearance of a stronger hand, but increases the chance that someone may have a hand that's strong enough to call or raise your bet.

**Who to bluff?** The ideal opponent is the weak-tight player. He thinks every glass is half-empty and every rising market is a bubble. The only hand he really wants to play to a showdown is the nuts. The weak-tight player looks for an excuse *not* to play a hand. A big bet by you could be just the encouragement he needs.

**What kind of stack to bluff?** Medium-sized stacks are better targets than either small or large stacks. The danger with a small stack is that the player may be getting desperate, and decide that his hand is just good enough for an all-in move. The large stack may feel he's in a comfortable enough position to look you up and see what you're doing. The medium-sized stack is probably more concerned about the danger of shrinking to a small stack than the opportunity of growing to a large stack, and is therefore more likely to fold a moderate hand in the face of apparent strength.

These are all very general guidelines, of course, and you'll encounter many exceptions. Now let's look at some specific types of bluffs.

# Bluffing Pre-Flop

I won't say that bluffing before the flop is entirely a beginner's move. There's a place for pre-flop bluffing in poker, especially as the blinds rise relative to the chip stacks. However, beginners certainly get too involved trying to steal the blinds. Usually this occurs because beginners don't yet have the patience to endure the long runs of bad cards that prevent them from making any solid bets, so periodically they'll take a couple of worthless cards and make a move at the pot. (We saw a few examples in the problems in Volume I.)

While these random moves can certainly work from time to time, eventually they will become an expensive habit. Keep in mind that the starting hand requirements that I outlined in Part Five of Volume I *already include the equity of bluffing.* When you raise with something like

on the button, your move has a big bluff component already. You're not rooting for someone to stand up to you; you just want to pick up the pot when the blinds fold. But when someone does call, you still have a hand to play.

By using your starting hand requirements to generate your bluffs, you achieve an additional goal: randomizing your play. The shuffle will ensure that your bluffing hands arrive on a random time schedule, thus making your play harder to read.

# The Continuation Bet

Continuation bets, which we discussed briefly in Volume I, are the most basic sort of post-flop bluff. A continuation bet occurs when you took the lead in the betting pre-flop, indicating strength, you missed the flop, and now you are in position to make the first bet after the flop, either because you're first to act or because the players have all checked to you. In this situation, you lead out with a bet. The bet "continues" your pre-flop action, and indicates to the table that you're still strong. Since it's consistent with your previous play, the bet has a reasonably high probability of success unless the flop really hit your opponent.

Here are a few ideas to keep in mind when making continuation bets:

1. **Bet size is important**. While you'll need to vary the size of your continuation bets to keep your opponents guessing, the basic continuation bet should be about half the size of the existing pot. That's both large enough to give you a good chance of winning the pot, while small enough to create favorable odds for yourself. A half-pot bet only requires you to win one time in three to break even.

2. **The number of opponents is important**. The ideal number of opponents when making a continuation bet is one. The more opponents, the smaller the chance of success. I might on occasion try a continuation bet against two opponents, but if I'm facing three or more players, I need to hit the flop to keep playing.

3. **The quality of your hand is important**. Did you completely miss the flop, or do you have a draw to a good hand? Completely missing the flop is a good indicator for a

continuation bet, since it costs you nothing extra to walk away from your hand when your move fails. If, however, you have a draw to a big hand, then a continuation bet could be a big mistake, giving your opponent another chance to chase you out of the pot. This advice particularly applies if you act last in the hand and have already seen your opponent check. Now taking a free card with a drawing hand is likely to be better than making a continuation bet. (Notice that this concept is the opposite of good strategy in limit games.)

4.    **The texture of the flop is important**. A dangerous flop is one with several high cards, which are likely to have hit the holdings of the other players. You don't want to bet into a dangerous flop with nothing, for the obvious reasons. While a weak-tight player will fold, no one else will. Good flops for continuation bets have low cards, or a medium card and a low pair, or three widely separated cards. Flops of three different suits are always a plus as well.

When these criteria aren't in place, a continuation bet becomes a low-equity play that often just takes you off a hand that you'd really like to play. Here's a concrete example:

**Example 1. You're at the final table of a major event, in the big blind. Your stack is $65,000, and the small blind has $83,000. Other stacks range from $60,000 to $180,000. The small blind is an experienced and tenacious player who likes to set traps. The blinds are $600 and $1,200, with $200 antes, and the starting pot is $3,000.**
     **You pick up**

**The first four players fold around to the small blind, who puts in $600 more to call.** *What do you do?*

Answer: King-jack suited is a pretty good hand heads-up, so you might as well find out if the small blind is serious about playing. Put in a raise about the size of the pot. Most of the time, this will end the hand right here.

**You raise $3,600, and the small blind calls. The pot is now $10,800. The flop is**

**The small blind checks.** *Should you now make a continuation bet, and if so, how much?*

Answer: This is not a good spot for a continuation bet. You've missed your hand, but you have some good draws. A queen will almost certainly win for you, while either a king or a jack might also be an out. If you bet and your opponent check-raises, you'll have to throw your hand away, wasting your draws. His check might have indicated weakness, but he's certainly capable of checking a strong hand as well. You have position, so your opponent will have to make the first move on fourth street, giving you a little extra information. Preserve your draws and check. Note that if the flop had missed you completely and you had no draws, a continuation bet would make much more sense.

**You check. The pot is still $10,800. Fourth street is the Q♥. Your opponent checks.** *What do you do?*

**Answer:** You've made your straight but there are now three hearts on board. Your opponent probably doesn't have a flush, but you can't let him draw at a flush for free. A bet of at least half the pot will require him to take 3-to-1 odds on a 4-to-1 flush draw, so that's good enough to push him out if he has a small heart. It's also small enough to allow him to call if he's just made a pair of queens or perhaps two pair.

**You bet $5,000, and the small blind folds.**

Players who have moved to no-limit from limit hold 'em will recognize the continuation bet as a variation of a limit move called the lead bet. In limit play you almost always (if you were the pre-flop aggressor) make a lead bet after the flop, because so often your opponent will just throw his hand away, and the cost of discovering that information is very cheap. But in no-limit the cost is not nearly so cheap; you're making a bet that, when it fails, will cost you half the pot instead of something like one-quarter to one-sixth of the pot.

# Defending Against the Continuation Bet

Since continuation bets are a powerful part of no-limit strategy, what can you do when you're on the other side of what may be a continuation bet? What's the best defense?

The first part of a successful defense is *knowledge*. As you study the table when you're not directly involved in the action, one of the most important things to observe is how players behave when they're in situations where a continuation bet is a possible strategy. How often, after taking the lead pre-flop, do they make bets after the flop? How many of those bets are in the neighborhood of half the pot? (The optimal size for a continuation bet.) Are most of their bets in this range, or do they like pot-sized bets instead? Or do they prefer making little probe bets? (One-quarter to one-third of the pot)

As you're watching, keep one key fact in mind: *Most flops miss most hands*. If you notice that when a particular player took the lead before the flop, he almost always bets after the flop, you know that a lot of the bets are simply bluffs, since he couldn't have hit his hand that often. (On the other hand, a player who rarely bets after the flop but who makes pot-sized bets when he does bet is just a super-tight player who wants the nuts before he commits his money. Play at him when he doesn't bet and stay away from him when he does.)

A tough player will by definition be hard to read after the flop. If he showed strength before the flop, he'll probably be taking the lead 50 to 60 percent of the time after the flop. He can't be filling his hand quite that often, but you're going to have a hard time deciding when he's got a strong hand and when he doesn't. And his bets won't all be around half the pot. There will be some pot-sized bets, some probe-sized bets, and some overbets in the mix as well. Against such a player, you'll need to use your best judgment, but for the most part you're going to need a real hand to continue to play.

One further fact to consider: Continuation bets are a good tactic against a single opponent, or two at the most. If a (competent) opponent led out before the flop and was called by three or four players, and now leads out again after the flop, he's almost certainly got something and he's making a value bet, not a continuation bet. Stay out of the pot unless you too have a good hand.

Now let's consider the interesting cases. Your opponent, who took the lead before the flop, makes a continuation-type bet after the flop. You are his only opponent. From your observations, you know that this player makes continuation bets with some frequency after he misses his hand. How should you proceed? We'll break our analysis down into a few cases.

**Case 1: The flop gave you a monster**. This is the most pleasant case to analyze, since your options are all good. You've flopped a set, or a straight, or the nut flush. (The non-nut flush is a little different. We'll look at that in a bit.) How do you extract the most money from your great hand?

The standard play is to simply call the continuation bet, hoping that your opponent already has something and will lead out again on the turn, or that he will catch something on the turn so he will call a bet by you later on. If he does lead out on the turn, you'll win at least that bet, plus possibly much more if he's willing to go to the end with you.

The other play is to raise his continuation bet. If he has nothing, he'll throw his hand away right there. (This looks like a bad result for you, but keep in mind that if he had nothing at this point, you most likely weren't going to make any more money on the hand anyway.) If he has something, either a pair or a draw, he may call this bet; whether you make any more money depends on just how much of a hand he has and what comes on fourth street.

Of the two plays, simply calling is the technically "better" play against most opponents, in the sense that it will win more money, on average, if your opponents aren't watching what you're doing. Since unfortunately they will be watching, you'll need to vary between the two plays on occasion. I'd recommend a mix of two-thirds calls and one-third raises on a random basis, to keep them guessing. Note one important exception, however: If an ace has come on the flop, there will be a better than average chance that your opponent is betting with a pair of aces. In this case, you should simply raise his bet, and be prepared to get all your money in the pot on the flop or the turn.

The case where your monster is a flush that's not the nuts is a little trickier. Let's look at an example.

**Example 2. Blinds $50/$100. A solid conservative player in middle position puts in $300. From past observations, his most likely holding is two high cards, but he would bet a high pair the same way. You elect to call on the button with T♥9♥. (It's a bit unusual for you, but you're varying your play to keep the table guessing.) The blinds fold. Just the two of you are in the pot, which is now $750. You each have about $8,000 remaining. The flop is Q♥7♥3♥. He bets $400. *What should you do?***

**Answer:** You've made a flush, but it's not the nut flush. Should you slow-play and just call? It's an idea, but there are some problems.

You may already be beaten if your opponent raised with A♥K♥ or A♥J♥ before the flop. (Ace-small of hearts is pretty unlikely from a solid opponent.) That's unlikely, but must be considered.

Your opponent willingly bet into that board. That fact makes the high-card hands containing a single heart much more likely than the high-card hands without any heart. Now you must confront the possibility that your opponent has a draw to a flush that will not only beat you, but which might win all your chips.

On balance, slow-playing with a call is too dangerous here. I would assume that my opponent held a single heart, and make a bet that they couldn't call if they saw my hand. In this case, suppose my opponent holds A♥Q♣. Now six hearts are accounted for, and seven remain in the deck, out of 45 unseen cards. My opponent's odds of drawing a heart on the turn are 38-to-7, or about 5.5-to-1. With the pot now containing $1,150, you should call his bet (making the pot $1,550) and raise him about $750 more. Now he'll be getting 3-to-1 odds to call, not enough if he knew that the flush was his only out. If he calls anyway, he's made a mistake, which is what you want no matter how the hand turns out.

**Case 2: The flop hit your hand, but you don't have a monster**. Sometimes the flop will hit your hand and give you middle pair or bottom pair. Your hand certainly isn't a lock, but it is worth something. In general, if your opponent now makes a continuation-type bet, you should call it. Your game plan is to see what happens on fourth street, and take the pot away if he shows weakness.

Remember that a continuation bet contains a weakness: When you bet around half the pot, you're offering about 3-to-1 calling odds to your opponent. (If the pot contains $20,000, and your opponent makes a $10,000 continuation bet, you have to put in $10,000 to see a $30,000 pot — 3-to-1 odds.) Those are good odds when you already have something and you probably have some number of outs as well. So call, and if your opponent checks on fourth street, be prepared to move at the pot. In many cases, a continuation bet represents a player's last attempt to win a pot cheaply. If it doesn't work, they're prepared to throw their hand away rather than lose a lot of money. For your part, you're willing to pay some money (at good odds) to see if they were making a continuation bet or not.

**Example 3: In the middle of a multi-table tournament. Blinds are $300/$600 with $50 antes. At a 10-player table the player in fifth position with a stack of $35,000 raises to $1,500 pre-flop, and you, with a stack of $40,000, call on the button with**

**It's a weak holding, but you're varying your play. The blinds fold behind you. The pot is now $4,400.**

**The flop comes**

**You've hit bottom pair. Your opponent bets $2,000. *What do you do?***

Answer: Your pair of fives aren't worthless, so don't be in a hurry to throw your hand away. It costs you $2,000 to see a pot of $6,400, so you're getting pot odds of 3.2-to-1. You could easily have the best hand now, and the fives and sixes are probably all outs even if you don't. Call, and see what happens on the turn.

**You call. The pot is now $8,400. The turn comes 4♦. Your opponent checks. *What do you do?***

Answer: That was a good card for you. You added eight more outs to the five you already had, and your opponent checked besides. You should bet about $5,000 to $6,000.

You may hold the winning hand now, and you have many ways to get a big hand on the river.

**You bet $5,500, and your opponent folds**.

**Case 3: The flop missed you**. Your opponent bet before the flop, and you called. The flop missed you, and your opponent bets again with a continuation-sized bet. *What should you do?*
  **Answer:** Absent any specific information, you should mostly just fold. There's no shame in avoiding the loss of a lot of money on a hand when you don't have anything and you don't know where you stand. You should only play here under certain (somewhat rare) circumstances.

1.  Although you missed your hand, you have a draw with close to the right odds.

2.  You've seen this player make many continuation-type bets in the past, so you know there's a reasonable chance he does not have a made hand.

3.  On occasion, you've seen him fold to a bet on fourth street after making a continuation-sized bet on the flop.

4.  You haven't seen him check good hands after his flop bet was called

  Put all of these circumstances together, and it's reasonable to call his bet with the idea of taking the pot away from him on the turn. Remember, many players who make a continuation bet on the flop will surrender the hand on the turn if they encounter resistance.
  Be cautious, however! The money odds for stealing the pot on the turn are not particularly favorable. For example, suppose the pot has $2,000 after the pre-flop betting, you

miss the flop, and now your opponent makes a continuation-sized bet of $1,000. The pot now contains $3,000. At this point you can fold your hand, losing nothing more. If you decide to wrestle the pot away from him, you'll need to invest $1,000 to call now, plus a $2,000-$3,000 bet on the turn, assuming he checks. That's an investment of $3,000 to $4,000 to win a pot that's currently $3,000. You'll need to think that you're an actual favorite to get away with this play in order to make it. While that can be possible, you need to know your opponent very well. It's not a move that's suitable for a table of strangers.

# Probe Bets

A probe bet is a cross between a bluff and an informational bet. It's a lead-out bet of somewhere between one-quarter and one-third of the pot. The bluff part comes from the fact that it is, after all, a bet. Sometimes your opponent will just lay his hand down to any bet, and in that case you scooped the pot without risking much. But mostly the probe bet has an informational function. It's a way of asking two questions:

1.  Please tell me a little something about your hand?

2.  Wouldn't it be nice if the two of us could just see the next card cheaply? (Can't we all just get along?)

When confronted with a probe bet, I like to employ the Travis Bickel Defense. "You wanna know somethin' about my hand? You talkin' to me? You talkin' to ME?!!," and then toss in a big raise. This usually takes the pot, and when it doesn't, I'm gone. (I don't actually start screaming, it's just a metaphor.)

While probe bets may look like a cheap, low-risk way to gain information, they contain a potential hidden downside. Consider the next example.

**Example 4. Late in a minor tournament. Blinds are $600/$1,200, antes are $75. There are 10 players at the table, so the starting pot contains $2,550. You have $13,600, and are in sixth position holding 8♦8♠. The player in first position, who has $24,000 but who plays tight and weak, calls. The intervening players fold to you.** *What do you do?*

> **Answer:** A raise is certainly reasonable. A weak-tight player would almost certainly raise with a high pair, so you're probably facing two high cards or a low pair, in which case

your hand is best right now. You also want to be sure to chase out the players behind you so you have position during the hand.

**You raise to $5,000. The players behind you and the blinds fold. The first player calls. The pot is now $12,550. The flop comes A♣7♣7♥ and your opponent bets $1,200.** *What do you do?*

Answer: Your opponent, who has a much bigger stack, bets 10 percent of the pot. You probably have the best hand right now, but you can't be sure and you don't really want to lose your whole stack on this hand if he's trapping. Just call.

**You call. The pot is now $14,950. The turn is the J♥. Your opponent bets another $1,200.** *What now?*

Answer: There are two overcards to your pair on board, but he's giving you 12-to-1 odds, so you can't fold.

**You call. The pot is now $17,350. The river is the 9♥. He checks.**

There are three overcards to your pair and a heart draw on board, so don't even think about betting. Just see his hand.

**You check, and he turns over 4♠4♣. You win a nice pot.**

You did nothing wrong, and won a nice pot for your effort. But look at what happened to your opponent. His call of your raise before the flop was weak. Then he made two probe bets, to prevent you from raising. He succeeded, but in this particular case he actually would have been better off just checking after the flop and throwing his hand away if you bet (which you would have). His plan worked, but cost him an extra $2,400. A series of probe bets with a very weak hand aren't necessarily an improvement on folding — they just look more active.

# The Squeeze Play

The squeeze play is an advanced and elegant bluff. You make a large reraise after two players have already entered the pot, the first with a raise and the second with a call. The first player is trapped between you and the second player (the "squeeze"). While he may believe he has the pot odds and cards to play against you, he can't be sure what the second player will do. Hence he throws his hand away. The second player felt he had enough equity to play against one raiser, but not against a reraiser. So he mucks his hand as well, and you take the pot.

A successful squeeze play is a delight when it works, but to make the play several preconditions are required.

1.   You need some reason to believe that the first player does not quite have the hand he's representing with his initial raise. Some sort of tell is nice, but usually you're looking for a player who's been aggressive for some period of time, and who's clearly been pushing some marginal raising hands.

2.   The second player has to just call, not reraise. If he reraises, he has an excellent hand and you can't play. If he just calls, he could be on any number of drawing hands that he's willing to play against one raiser but not two.

3.   You should have a reputation for at least solid play, if not outright conservative play. Don't try this move if you've been caught bluffing lately. If you've shown down any hands in the past couple of hours, they should have been good hands.

4.   Don't try this move if you've already made it once at the session (even if you actually had a hand that time). It's a big move and people will remember, so don't overdo the play.

If all the pieces fall in place, the squeeze play is a powerful weapon that can win a lot of chips. Here's a good example from last year's World Series.

**Example 5. Final table of the 2004 World Series of Poker. Seven players remain, with chip count and positions given below.**

| Sm Blind | Glen Hughes | $2,375,000 | |
|---|---|---|---|
| Big Blind | David Williams | $3,250,000 | A♠Q♣ |
| 1 | Josh Arieh | $3,890,000 | K♥9♠ |
| 2 | Al Krux | $2,175,000 | |
| 3 | Greg Raymer | $7,920,000 | A♣2♣ |
| 4 | Matt Dean | $3,435,000 | |
| 5 | Dan Harrington | $2,320,000 | 6♥2♦ |

**The blinds were $40,000 and $80,000, with $10,000 antes, so the pot was $190,000 to start.**

**Josh Arieh.** Josh opened the betting with a raise to $225,000, a little less than three times the big blind. So far, Josh had been active at the final table, and his bet looked to the other players like a pretty standard raise on his part. Actually king-nine offsuit is a little weak for an opening raise even at a seven-handed table. I like raising for value at seven-handed in opening position with hands like ace-ten, ace-nine, and king-queen.

**Al Krux.** Folded his hand.

**Greg Raymer.** Greg had been crushing the table for a long time, although in the last hour his cards had cooled off a bit, and some of his lead had been trimmed away. He elects to call with ace-deuce suited. That's another aggressive play, although as the cards lie he's actually a favorite over Josh.

If Josh had been playing a conservative game, the gap concept would apply and Greg would need an even stronger hand to call than the minimum hands Josh would need for opening. Since Josh has been playing aggressively, Raymer doesn't need hands of that strength. In Raymer's position I would call with the same hands I might use for opening in third position — ace-seven, ace-six, king-queen, and any pair. With medium pairs, I would actually be raising to try to win the hand pre-flop. I wouldn't, however, make a call with ace-deuce, a hand which is just too vulnerable to being dominated.

**Matt Dean**. Folded his hand.

**Dan Harrington.** Of course I could throw the six-deuce away, but Raymer's call has created the perfect conditions for a squeeze play. My sense from Arieh was that he had a good hand, but not a premium hand. (Raymer may have picked up on this as well). If I was right, then it would be nearly impossible for him to call a big raise with Raymer still to act behind him. Raymer's call, on the other hand, probably indicated a hand that was not strong enough to raise. It might also indicate a hand that Raymer felt was adequate for calling a bet from Arieh (who had been playing loosely) but not me (who had been playing conservatively). In any event, it was clear that a big raise on my part had an excellent chance of winning the whole pot immediately.

The next question was — how much to raise? Here I thought back to how the table had been playing over the last couple of hours. In general, the table had been loose, and players had shown a willingness to call raises, based on their good pot odds. (This varies from final table to final table. In 2003, the final table had played somewhat tighter.) I thought it was likely that a normal-sized reraise, to perhaps $450,000 or $500,000, stood a better-than-usual chance of being called. As a result, I made an unusually big bet for me: $1,200,000. I wanted both Arieh and Raymer to know that by betting more than half my chips, I was committing myself to the pot, so they couldn't have any notion about calling and then maneuvering me out of the pot after the flop.

**Glen Hughes**. Folded his hand.

**David Williams.** Williams picks up the best hand at the table, ace-queen offsuit! Unfortunately, the action in front of him has been raise, call, and big reraise, and ace-queen just can't stand that kind of action. He correctly (given what he knows) folds his hand.

**Josh Arieh.** He has no interest in playing king-nine offsuit with two players active behind him, so he folds.

**Greg Raymer.** At this point, he has to assume that either his ace is dominated by a bigger ace, or he's facing a medium-to-big pair. In either case, he's not getting close to the pot odds he needs, so he folds.

# The No-Limit Semi-Bluff

A semi-bluff is a post-flop bet that's partially a bluff and partially a value bet. The flop gave you something, or perhaps a combination of little somethings — say a medium pair plus a straight or flush draw. You doubt that your hand is the best one at the table right now, but it might be. If you hit your draw, it almost certainly will be. In that case, you might lead out with what we call a semi-bluff. It's a bet which will probably be profitable because it offers multiple ways to win:

1.  You might win right away if your opponent folds his hand.

2.  You might get a call, but win because your hand is actually best.[1]

3.  You might get a call, but win because of your draw.

In addition, since your bet represents strength, you may get to see both the turn and river cards for free, as your opponent may interpret a future check as a trap and refuse to bet.

The semi-bluff works best against a tight opponent, of course. But if you think there's as much as a 30 percent chance that your opponent will lay down his hand right away, then the semi-bluff is usually a profitable move, even if your plan is to fold to an immediate raise.

The no-limit semi-bluff is frequently made with an all-in move. You usually don't want to go all-in with your very strong hands, since you want people to call, not go away. A semi-bluffing hand, where you have for example a pair and a flush draw, is a

---

[1] The traditional definition of a semi-bluff, as defined by David Sklansky in *The Theory of Poker* discounts this option.

more likely candidate for an all-in move. Now you'd really like your opponent to go away, you have outs based on the flush draw, while the pair may generate a few outs on its own. The multiple ways to win will make the move profitable.

Good players understand this point, while beginners and intermediates often do not. When the board shows two of a suit and their opponent makes a big bet or moves all-in, most top players would think that a semi-bluff flush draw is now the most likely hand they're facing.

Between experts, a cute variation on the no-limit semi-bluff is a play which simply *represents* the no-limit semi-bluff. Consider the next example carefully.

**Example 6. Final table of a major tournament. Five players remain. You are in the big blind with an average-sized stack of $100,000. The button, an imaginative and aggressive player has slightly more chips than you, with about $110,000. Blinds are $600/$1,200, with $200 antes, so the starting pot is $2,800. The first two players fold, the button raises to $5,000, and the small blind folds. Your hand is A♥3♠.** *What should you do?*

Answer: With plenty of chips, you're under no pressure to get involved in marginal situations. However, here your situation looks pretty good. The button bet more than four times the big blind, a larger-than-usual raise which looks like he'd prefer that you go away quietly. You have to put up $3,800 to see a pot of $7,800, so you're getting more than 2-to-1 odds. And finally, you do have an ace, although it's not a strong ace. It's reasonably likely you have the best hand at the table right now, so you have a very easy call.

**You call, and the flop comes A♠T♣3♣. You act first. The pot is now $11,600.** *What do you do?*

Answer: Under the circumstances, top and bottom pair rates to be a very strong hand. If your opponent was trying to steal the pot in the first place, a bet may chase him away, but a check may induce him to try and steal again. Check, and see if you can make a little extra money.

**You check and the button bets $12,000.** *What do you do?* **Answer:** You could call, but the combination of your call before the flop and your call after the flop with an ace showing is going to make even the dullest opponent a little suspicious. If he's not holding an ace, you're not going to make any more money in the hand.

You could raise him another $12,000. He'll probably fold his hand now, but he might stick around with a pair of aces. With smaller pairs he should go away and concede you the pot.

Or you could go all-in! With the two clubs on board, one explanation for this play is that you're pulling a semi-bluff. You're representing a hand with two clubs, where you just want your opponent to go away and give you this sizeable pot, but you'll have a few outs if he doesn't. Mostly, of course, this play will just win the current pot like your other options. But occasionally the button will call your apparent bluff only to discover it wasn't a bluff after all!

**You go all-in, and your opponent folds**.

# Back-Alley Mugging
## Betting When a Big Card Comes on a Late Street

Another nice bluff to have in your arsenal is what I call the back-alley mugging. A scary card arrives on fourth or fifth street, a card that could swing the hand. It missed your hand, but your opponent doesn't know that; you make a big, scary bet, and he folds.

This is a nice play when you can make it, but a number of preconditions are required.

1. **The card has to plausibly fit some hands that you might have been playing.** If a king or a queen hits a board of mostly low cards, *review the betting* and make sure that holdings like ace-king, ace-queen, or king-queen would fit the bets you've made thus far.

2. **Make this move against a player of medium strength.** Weak players pay much more attention to their own cards than to whatever their opponents might hold (a big reason they're weak). Your subtle trap may simply go unnoticed. A very strong player, on the other hand, has seen it all before. He'll wonder if you're making a move and he might spot something in the betting sequence that you didn't. A medium-strength player is a good target; he'll see what you're representing and worry about it.

3. **Make this move against a player who has shown he can lay down a hand.** Mentally review what you've seen him do. Has he been able to lay down a hand once he's committed some chips to the pot? Some players can't lay a hand down after they've made a couple of bets with it. Make sure your opponent can give up a hand.

4.  As with most bluffs, bluffing a tight opponent is better than bluffing a loose one.

# The Dark Tunnel Bluff

Hollywood cranks out a lot of cheap horror films which revolve around a pretty simple formula. A demented lunatic, armed to the teeth with axes and hatchets, stalks about committing mayhem. A bunch of supporting characters decide this would be a really neat time to start wandering around caves, tunnels, and abandoned houses, looking for clues. While the audience shrieks, the maniac dispatches them in ever-more-gory fashion.

This scenario often reminds me of how many beginners and intermediate players approach poker hands. They find themselves making bets which aren't really bluffs, but which aren't value bets either. They're just — bets. I call these "dark tunnel" bluffs. You don't know where you stand, you don't really know what you're doing, but it feels more active to bet than not, so you put more money in the pot. Eventually you've lost a big pot where you never really had much of a chance.

The cure for this syndrome is simple: stay out of dark tunnels. Always know why you are making a bet, and what you expect to gain. Every good bet should either give you a chance to win the pot right there, or provide you with information about your opponent's cards that you can act on through the rest of the hand.

**Example 7. First day of a major tournament. Blinds are $100/$200, no antes yet. You are in the big blind with $17,000 in chips. The small blind, a well-known world-class player, has $22,000. Everyone folds to the small blind, who calls. You have**

31

*What do you do?*

   **Answer:** The pot is $400, and you very likely have the best hand, so you have no reason not to bet. Your opponent's call most likely means he has a little bit of a hand and he's looking to see a cheap flop. Just bet $300 or $400, and you will most likely win the hand right here.

**You actually raise $1,000, and your opponent calls.**

   $1,000 is an unusual bet size. If your opponent is going to fold, he would probably have folded to a $400 raise.

**The flop comes**

**The small blind checks. The pot is $2,400.** *What should you do?*

   **Answer:** The flop missed you, but it may have missed your opponent as well. The shape of the flop isn't great for you; the queen and the ten are certainly danger cards. However, his most likely holdings at this point are ace-x or a medium pair, so you may still have the best hand. Since you led before the flop, it's worth thinking about taking a stab at the pot with a continuation bet to see if you can take the hand down. Even if your bet is called, you may have ten outs. A jack gives you an inside straight, and either aces or kings may be outs as well.

   On the other hand, as in the previous example, you could just take a free card. With ten draws to what should be the winning hand, do you want to give your opponent a chance to take you out of the pot?

The play I actually like here is the *delayed* continuation bet. Check to take a free card now, then bet on fourth street if your opponent checks. Daniel Negreanu is a specialist at this play, and he's worked it to perfection on many occasions.

**You bet $1,500 and your opponent calls. The pot is now $5,400. The turn comes an 8♥. Your opponent checks. *What now?***

**Answer:** You didn't improve your hand, but you still have outs and your opponent gave you a chance for a free card on fifth street. Check and take the free card.

**You actually bet $2,000, and your opponent calls.**

The "dark tunnel bluff" rears its ugly head! You bet before the flop and got called, and you bet after the flop and got called. Your opponent says he has something and he's not going away. Your last bet was reasonable, but this tiny bet is just blind aggression. What can the bet accomplish, aside from sweetening a pot you are almost certainly losing right now? If your opponent raises, you will have to drop, and you'll have taken yourself right out of the pot.

Players who bet like this are usually thinking that a failure to bet will show weakness. Their pre-flop bet showed strength, their continuation bet showed strength, and now they're afraid that not betting here will reveal that they don't have anything yet. That's all true, but it's not a reason to blow another $2,000 *if that bet can't win the pot.*

**The river is a J♣, giving you a straight. Your opponent checks, you go all-in, and after long thought he calls. You show your straight and he shows J♦9♠.**

You're saved by some great luck, and you win a nice pot.

# Slow-Playing

Slow-playing is just the opposite of bluffing. You have a strong hand, but you want to represent a weak hand, to lure more money into the pot. Slow-playing is a powerful weapon that can either win a big pot or knock an opponent out of the tournament. The great danger of slow-playing is that you may lose a big pot by allowing someone to catch free cards that eventually make a hand stronger than yours. It also has the problem that it sometimes results in winning a smaller pot than a non-slowplay would.

I'll look at specific examples of slow-playing in the following sections. Meanwhile here are some guidelines to slow-playing in general.

**Who should you slow-play?** The loose aggressive player is the best target because he will often actually make a bet. He likes to take pots away from players who seem weak, so checking to him is likely to induce the bet you need. Slow-playing the weak-tight player is likely to be both a waste of time and dangerous. By giving him free cards, you're allowing him a chance to make money from you, but you have no chance to make money from him, since he won't bet with a weak hand. (If you're slow-playing a real monster, of course, this reasoning doesn't apply since he has no outs.)

**What kind of stack should you slow-play?** Big and small stacks are the best targets, while medium stacks are the worst.

Note that these criteria are the exact opposite of our bluffing criteria. The best situations for bluffing are the worst for slow-playing, and vice-versa.

# Slow-Playing Before the Flop

Very few hands are legitimate candidates for slow-playing before the flop. You might, for instance, choose to call rather than raise with a hand like ace-queen suited, but what you're doing is varying your play so your opponents can't detect your betting pattern. The same holds true with a hand like a pair of tens in early position when you're first in the pot. You could raise five times the big blind, or three times the big blind, or you could just call, but the point of calling is not to draw more players into the pot but just to disguise your hand so you can't be read so easily.

The only hands that are really candidates for a legitimate slow-play are aces, kings, and sometimes queens. Even with hands this strong, I need several preconditions in place before I'm tempted to slow-play the hand.

1. I'm at a full or nearly-full table — 9 or 10 players.

2. I'm in early position, and no one has entered the pot before me.

3. The table has been generally loose and aggressive, with lots of raising and reraising pre-flop. The loose and aggressive players are on my left.

What I'm seeking is a situation where I can call with a strong likelihood that someone behind me will raise. I need a full table and early position so that as many people as possible are eligible to raise. Obviously I want loose and aggressive players to be doing the raising. Less obvious but equally important is that I be first to act. If someone has raised or called in front of me, a call on my part will tend to dampen action (even at a loose table) since two players have already shown strength. The right play after a raise or call is just to raise with my high pair. Remember that a series of limpers is a disastrous result for the high pair. As always in this case, your eventual goal is to get heads-up against one opponent with as big a pot as possible.

Note that David Sklansky advocates an unusual play which is worth mentioning here. He sometimes likes to limp with aces in middle position after a limper has entered the pot, the players are somewhat loose, and the stacks are large. A series of limpers may cause a late player to put in a big raise, or it may enable you to play a completely disguised set of aces when an ace falls on the flop. The occasional massive wins from these situations more than compensate for the loss of equity when you're forced to play an unraised pot against several limpers. In order to make this play, however, you must be skilled at letting your aces go when the post-flop betting shows you're in trouble.

# After the Flop: General Considerations

Slow-playing after the flop is much more common. In fact, I think it's *too* common. Many good players, perhaps trying to live up to their tricky, trappy image, overuse the slow-play concept. My natural move is to bet good hands for value. When I do slow-play, I'm careful about picking my spots and I'm looking for very specific criteria.

**An aggressive opponent**. When I check my strong hand, I want my opponent to bet out. A loose, aggressive player is most likely to do just that. A tight player, obviously, is a poorer candidate for slow-playing.

**A single opponent**. Slow-playing works best against a single opponent. With a very strong hand, you can consider slow-playing two opponents. I would only slow-play three or more opponents with a real monster, something close to the nuts. The problem with multiple opponents is twofold: there are more chances that someone is drawing to a hand that can beat you, and it's more likely that someone has a hand that could actually call (or raise) your value bet. Remember that there's no need to slow-play if a straight value bet is likely to be called.

Always bear in mind that the immediate goal of slow-playing is to win an extra bet. Instead of the sequence "bet, fold," you're hoping for the sequence "check, bet, raise, fold." Some beginners get carried away by the idea of setting an elaborate trap which slowly causes the opponent to lose all his chips. That certainly can happen, but only when your opponent has a strong hand of his own which he's inclined to keep pushing. If he has a weak hand and thinks, from your check, that you have a weak hand too, then it's only his first bet that you'll win. Once he realizes that you actually have a hand, he's not going to put more money in the pot.

# After the Flop: Candidate Hands

What hands are strong enough to slow-play after the flop?

**Full house or four of a kind**. Not only are these obviously good enough to slow-play, you *must* slow-play them. When you flop a full house, for example, there are very few cards left in the deck that can fit with the board. If you hold

and the flop comes

there are only two aces and one queen remaining. You've gobbled up all the oxygen in the room, and now you have to wait and hope that someone bluffs or hits a card on the turn or the river and can play with you.

**Flushes and straights**. These are also strong slow-play situations, although you have to be careful when you flop a flush which is not the nut flush. The danger here is that a player with a high card which matches the board will stick around and draw to a flush that beats you. Slow-playing a flush when the ace of the suit is on the board is the safest situation; good players will often play ace-x suited but are much less likely to play two lower suited cards. If the ace is on the board, your chances of facing a draw to a better flush go down. (Online, weak players love to play two suited cards pre-flop, so this logic doesn't apply there.) Straights are excellent slow-playing hands since the danger is not as obvious to your opponents.

**Trips**. These are good slow-playing hands, and are much more common than the stronger hands. Some authors tell you to be careful when you flop middle or bottom trips, because you might lose to higher trips. Nonsense. If you get knocked out of the tournament because you lost in a set-over-set confrontation, then it just wasn't your tournament. When your set gets outflopped, you're supposed to lose a lot of money. When I hear someone telling a story about how he shrewdly laid down middle set after some intricate chain of reasoning convinced him he was beaten, my quick (but silent) reaction is "Idiot."

**Two pair**. Top two pair are a candidate for slow-playing. The other two pair combinations are weak. The bottom pair, especially if it's a very low pair, is too often counterfeited when high cards appear on the board. I prefer to just bet out for value and win the pot.

**Top pair**. Even a lowly top pair can be slow-played under certain very specific conditions. Here's what I like to see.

1.  The best situation is to hold ace-king and flop king-x-x, with three different suits and no connecting straights. You're not afraid of an ace flopping since you have one, and you're not afraid of the pair being outdrawn since you have top pair. Your only fear is that one of the two low cards on the board has paired someone, and they might now hit trips or pair their other hole card. But those are small risks, worth taking to pick up an extra bet.

2.  The second-best situation is to flop queen-x-x when you hold ace-queen or king-queen. Again you hold top pair and a higher kicker, but now there is one overcard that can appear and beat you.

3.  The final situation is to flop jack-x-x when you hold a jack with an ace, king, or queen. This is a very marginal slow-playing situation at best, but against the right opponent and under perfect circumstances I might try it.

For the top categories of hands, the straights, flushes, and full houses, a more interesting question is "When *don't* you slow-play the hand?" If you believe from his betting before the flop that your opponent may have started with a high pair, or made one on the flop, then just bet. There's a good chance you will be raised. Remember, your primary goal is not to trick him, but to get his money in the pot. Many players lose sight of that simple fact in the heat of battle.

A betting sequence I particularly like when I have a monster hand is one where I make my continuation-sized bet and get called. Then I check on the turn and he checks behind me. Now I've created the impression that I had nothing, I made my one stab at the pot, and gave up after I got called, but now just maybe I can steal the pot on the river. When I make one final good-sized bet, it's almost impossible for my opponent not to pay me off if he has anything at all!

# After the Flop: The Check-Raise and The Check-Call

The check-raise can be a very powerful move. Good players usually employ it after the flop, or in some cases, after the turn. You make a big hand, but instead of betting you just check, indicating that you've missed the flop. Your opponent bets. Now you raise, revealing the strength of your hand. If your opponent throws his hand away, you've made one more bet than presumably you would have had you bet out straightaway. If he calls, you've gotten significantly more money in the pot.

While the check-raise can make you some extra money with a good hand, it does come with associated risks. Here are a few things to consider when contemplating a check-raise:

1.  **Is your opponent aggressive?** If he's not aggressive, then checking with the idea of check-raising may just be a tactical error. A tight or weak-tight player may just check behind you and take a free card, and you haven't succeeded in getting any more money in the pot.

2.  **Can you stand to give a free card?** If there are draws on board that can beat your strong hand, you may well be better off taking the pot right there, or at least giving your opponent the wrong odds for drawing.

3.  **Do you have the table persona of a straightforward value bettor or a tricky trappy guy?** If you've been playing straightforward poker, your check-raise is more likely to work. If you've been shucking and jiving through the session,

your opponents have probably started to assume that your plays mean the opposite of what they appear to mean, and will give you a wide berth.

Here's an example showing a good check-raise situation:

**Example 8. Eight players remain at your table. Blinds are $400/800 with $50 antes. $1,600 in the pot to start. You are the big blind with A♣Q♣. The first five players fold, and the button, a very aggressive player who routinely bets at pots no one has opened, and who makes continuation bets after the flop, raises to $3,000. The small blind folds. Both you and the button have large stacks at this point. You have played solidly throughout the tournament.** *What do you do?*
   Answer: The normal play is to reraise with a hand this good, but you need to call occasionally for variety. The button may be stealing, but you don't know that and he will have position on you in subsequent rounds. I would use a mixture of 70 percent raises and 30 percent calls in this situation.

   **You actually call and the pot is $6,800. The flop comes A♥9♠2♦. You act first.** *What do you do?*
   Answer: All conditions are right for a check-raise. Your opponent is aggressive and has moved at pots in the past, you seem solid and straightforward, and the board isn't offering any dangerous straight or flush draws. Your pair of aces with a queen kicker is very likely to be good at this point.

   **You check. He bets $3,500.**

   A good amount for a raise is something between double and triple his bet, but closer to triple than double. Drawing out on you should be a very expensive proposition.

   **You raise to $9,000, and he folds.**

Check-calling is a riskier but potentially more profitable play than check-raising. Here you are going to voluntarily give your opponent a free card, with the idea of winning more money later in the hand. The next example shows some of the issues involved.

**Example 9. Final table of a major tournament. Six players remain. The blinds are $1,000 and $2,000, with $200 antes. The starting pot is $4,200. You are second to act before the flop. The players and their chip counts are as follows:**

| | |
|---|---|
| Sm Blind | $80,000 |
| Big Blind | $210,000 |
| Player 1 | $240,000 |
| You | $250,000 |
| Player 3 | $110,000 |
| Player 4 | $90,000 |

**You are known to be a very smart, experienced player, capable of making moves at any time. Player 3 is also smart and very experienced, with a reputation for aggressive play. Player 1 folds. You pick up**

**and raise $7,000, slightly more than three times the big blind. It's been the standard opening raise during this round of blinds. Player 3 calls. The button and the blinds fold. The pot is now $18,200. The flop comes**

**You're first to act.** *What should you do?*

**Answer:** You've flopped a monster, trip nines, and your hand is obviously strong enough to slow-play. You should mostly elect to check here. I say "mostly," because you will occasionally have to put out a bet in these situations, so your opponents can't simply peg you as someone who checks when he's strong and only bets when he's weak. Good players have a tendency to fall into that pattern, especially in short-handed situations at the end of tournaments. But let's assume you've been mixing up your play well recently, so now you are free to check and set a trap.

Here's the really interesting question. Suppose you check and your opponent makes a good-sized bet, say $10,000. Do you then raise, or just call?

Deciding between slow-playing with a check-raise and slow-playing with a check-call is one of the toughest decisions in poker. Often there will not be a clear-cut answer. You have two goals:

1. Extract as many extra bets as possible from your opponent, and

2. Avoid losing the hand.

Here are some of the issues that bear on the decision:

**Is your opponent weak and/or tight?** Will he put in extra bets down the road, or not? A weak-tight player might make one stab at the pot, but if he meets resistance, he's done with the hand unless he catches something big down the road. Check-calling an opponent with this profile is wrong since he won't put any more money in the pot unless the free card you gave him actually improves his hand in a way that may beat you. Here you check-raise, and expect to win the hand immediately.

**Is your opponent known to be aggressive?** An aggressive player presents different problems. He'll certainly interpret your check-call as representing some sort of hand, but if he puts you on a drawing hand (in this case a flush draw), he may be inclined to test you with another bet on fourth or fifth street. If he's holding a medium or low pair (say eights or fours) he may simply believe that he still has the best hand and bet on that basis. A check and a call makes the most sense against this player. That play represents two high cards, and if a small card comes on fourth street and you check again, he may bet again.

**Do you need to establish some defense?** There's yet another reason for check-calling against an aggressive player — a defensive reason. You'll find yourself in plenty of situations where you check after the flop and don't want anyone to bet at you. To get some respect and free cards, you need to demonstrate occasionally that you're capable of checking a very strong hand all the way down to the river while waiting for your opponent to bet at you. Once your opponents realize you can do this, they'll be a little more reluctant to toss out routine bets after you miss the flop and check. If your opponents have been betting at you relentlessly, this hand could be useful for that purpose.

**How likely are you to lose the hand if you give free cards?** I emphasized in Volume I that giving free cards was potentially one of the worst mistakes you can make. For each hand, you need to ask "What's the chance that a free card will beat me?" In this hand, that chance is clearly very small. The 9♥9♠3♠ flop can't fit very many hands, especially when you hold the third nine. The two spades are a small threat, but the spade flush draw is sufficiently unlikely that you're going to have to pay off to it for now, given how strong your hand is.

**Conclusion:** Given your opponent's known aggressive nature and the relatively safe flop, your plan is to check and call.

**You check and your opponent checks as well. Fourth street is the 5♠.**

You didn't induce a bet, and a third spade appeared on the board. Both are bad signs for continuing to trap. It doesn't look like your opponent had anything, and you could lose the hand to a spade on the river. (It's highly unlikely he has a flush now. If he had four spades after the flop, he was in a good semi-bluff situation after your check, and probably would have bet.) Time to make a bet and take the hand down.

**You bet $10,000, and your opponent folds.**

His actual holding was J♦T♠, and he made a fairly loose call preflop. Afterwards, the situation was just too dangerous for him to make a move.

# Massaging the Pot

The classic error that most beginners make with a monster hand is an obvious eagerness to get all their chips in the pot. With the security of a big hand behind you, focus on getting your chips in the pot gradually. We call this *massaging the pot*, and it's a key skill for winning extra bets and larger bets. Keep these ideas in mind when you're betting with a big hand:

1.  **Build the pot gradually**. Use smaller bets rather than larger bets, because they're easier to call. The more money you can lure into the pot, the more tempting a prize it becomes.

2.  **Let him go all-in**. You can't win all your opponent's money unless he somehow thinks he can win all *your* money. Try to pick bets that are smaller than half his stack. That leaves him feeling that he can call your bet and still be in pretty good shape. Don't raise him all-in, let *him* raise *you* all-in.

3.  **Sit on your hands**. (Your real hands, not your cards.) I got this good advice from an old chess coach, but it applies just as well to poker. Don't ever give the impression you're in a hurry. If you must, count to 15 before you put in a raise. Let him wonder what you're thinking about. Who knows what reasons his fevered imagination might invent?

# The Check-Raise Bluff

As we move into the more arcane forms of move-making, we need to mention the check-raise bluff. This operates just like a check-raise, except that now you don't really have a hand at all. You're just representing one by first checking, and then raising.

Some of the more adventurous pros love the check-raise bluff, and try to pull a couple in every session they play. Others of us are more skeptical. The trouble with the check-raise bluff is simple: It's a very expensive play when it fails. You've allowed your opponent to bet at the pot, then you come over the top with a big raise, probably about the size of the new pot. You're hoping that either your opponent's bet was a bluff, or that he had a medium-strength hand but will lay it down in the face of your apparent monster. Most of the time, one or another of these conditions will be true, but when he does have a real hand you've cost yourself a lot of money.

To see the problem clearly, imagine that the pot contains $2,000 after the pre-flop betting. You're first to act against one other player. The flop arrives and misses you. For whatever reason, you're unwilling to give up on the hand. You contemplate two moves: a straight continuation bet/bluff, or a check-raise bluff.

1.   The continuation bet will cost you about $1,000. (Let's say that if your bet doesn't win the pot, you will go away and commit no more money.)

2.   The check-raise bluff will cost you about three times as much. You check, he makes a continuation-sized bet of $1,000, and you come over the top for a pot-sized reraise of $3,000. You've invested much more of your stack to discover if your opponent has a real hand or not.

The check-raise bluff isn't one of my favorite moves. I'll make it occasionally, but I'll need to have seen this opponent lay down some hands even after committing significant chips to the pot.

# The Post-Oak Bluff

"Post-Oak Bluff" is Doyle Brunson's term for a particularly sneaky sort of play that you can make on the turn or the river. (I don't get the reference — it must derive from those legendary old Texas road games.)

To understand the idea, imagine that you have made the nuts on the river and you're first to act. You know you're going to win the pot, and you'd like to win as much money as possible. You think your opponent has a little something, but you're also pretty sure that he thinks he's second-best at this point. If you shove in a pot-sized bet, he'll just throw his hand away. So instead you make a luring bet, a small bet amounting to perhaps 20 percent or 25 percent of the pot. You're giving him pot odds of 5-to-1 or 6-to-1, and these odds are so good that he'll toss in a little more money on the off chance you're bluffing. It's not much, but it's a little extra profit in your stack. You've made these bets from time to time, as has everyone else.

The post-oak bluff turns that idea on its head. You don't have anything on the turn or river, but your play to that point represented a good hand. Now you make a small bet, hoping your opponent will think you're trying to lure him into the pot, and throw his hand away.

It's a brilliant play when it works, but unlike some other moves it requires extensive preconditions. Before I make the move, I need to be sure of several things:

1.  I must have seen my opponent make the luring bet himself in the past, so I'm sure he's familiar with the basic idea.

2.  My opponent must have seen me make luring bets, so he knows they are in my repertoire.

3.   I must have seen my opponent fold to a small bet, so I know he won't routinely call with great odds to keep me honest.

   Those are a lot of preconditions, but if all are in place the move is worth trying. The post-oak bluff has the advantage of being a cheap and clever way to try to win a lost hand.

# BSB Play

When everyone folds to the button, an interesting dynamic develops between the three remaining players in the pot. I call this "BSB Play," since the remaining players are the button, the small blind, and the big blind.

The button has seen most of the players at the table get out, and he'll have position on the remaining two players for the rest of the hand. Logic dictates that he's entitled to call or raise with much weaker hands than normal, since the chance of his winning the blinds is so great. In Volume I the hands I like to play on the button were listed. Summarizing quickly, raise with any pair, any ace, any two cards jack-nine or higher, and suited connectors down to six-five. That's a lot of hands.

The small blind, of course, knows that the button could be raising with a wide range of hands, so his calling or raising requirements are much less as well.

And the big blind knows what the button and the small blind are doing, so he may also move with hands that aren't so strong.

When all three of these players start moving on the pot, the result is a poker version of three-card monte: Who's really got a hand? The key idea to remember is simply this — don't get too caught up in your own cleverness. Suppose you're on the button, you raise with a pair of sixes, the small blind reraises you, and the big blind reraises him! Yes, they might both be raising with trash. In many cases, they both *will* be raising with trash. But the simple fact remains that your hand is weak and your real goal, to take down the blinds without resistance, didn't happen. Let the hand go and move on. I've seen many ingenious players lose all their chips when their intricate chain of logic bumped into an unexpected pair of kings. (It's perfectly legal for the blinds to get dealt good cards.) Keep it simple and move on.

# Smallball Versus Longball

In baseball, smallball refers to a style of play that scores a lot of runs, one base at a time. The manager blends speed and alertness with bunts, stolen bases, hitting behind the runners and other such stratagems to keep the runs coming without the benefit of power hitting. Many of the great National League teams of the 60s, 70s, and 80s were exemplars of this style.

The opposite style in baseball is longball, exemplified by the raw power of the 1927 Yankees (Ruth and Gehrig) or the 1961 Yankees (Mantle and Maris) or even today's technological marvels. Just pound the stuffing out of the ball and keep the runs coming in huge clumps.

Poker has its own equivalents to these approaches. In poker, smallball is a style based on making small moves at pots, blending probe and continuation bets, or calls followed by small raises, or bets based on position, to pull down pots cheaply without much of a hand. The key word here is "cheap." Since not all of these moves will work, don't invest a lot of money in any particular move. Just keep bobbing and weaving, jabbing and dancing, stealing small pots while you wait for the big hand that will double you up.

The opposite approach I'll call longball (although I've never actually heard the term used before for poker). Here you construct big, outrageous bluffs, representing a big hand from the beginning, moving at the pot again and again until finally your last bet makes your opponent lay his good hand down. If you have the courage, longball-type moves will win the pot a very high percentage of the time. When they do fail, however, you'll lose all your chips.

Longball can't be overdone, for the obvious reasons. Here's an example of longball in action, from the 2003 World Series of Poker.

**Example 10. Final table of the 2003 World Series of Poker. Six players remain, with chip count and positions given below.**

| | | | |
|---|---|---|---|
| Sm Blind | Jason Lester | $1,035,000 | K♥Q♦ |
| Big Blind | Dan Harrington | $985,000 | A♥J♣ |
| 1 | Chris Moneymaker | $3,205,000 | |
| 2 | Amir Vahedi | $560,000 | |
| 3 | Tomer Benveniste | $495,000 | |
| 4 | Sam Farha | $2,055,000 | A♦5♣ |

**The blinds were $15,000 and $30,000, with $4,000 antes, so the pot was $69,000 to start.**

**Chris Moneymaker**. Folds his hand.

**Amir Vahedi**. Folds his hand.

**Tomer Benveniste**. Folds his hand.

**Sam Farha**. On the button, Farha raises to $70,000 with his ace-five offsuit. A reasonable play with a good chance of taking the pot immediately.

**Jason Lester**. Lester picks up king-queen offsuit, an excellent hand for the situation. It's stronger than many hands Farha might have elected to play from the button. However, his position will be poor after the flop, so he just calls.

**Dan Harrington**. I have a good hand, ace-jack offsuit, so I'm happy to play the hand. It's likely that I have a better hand than Farha at this point. However, the fact that Lester was willing to call despite poor position indicates that he may have a strong hand. Under the circumstances, I elect to just call.

The alert reader will ask "Why didn't you try the squeeze play after a raise from late position and a call?" It's a good question. The answer is simply that my hand is too good! A squeeze play is basically just a bluff, and I don't like to use my hands that have genuine value on bluffs. I'd much prefer bluffing with a hand that's worthless, which I can cheerfully dump when someone plays back at me.

Notice that in this position it costs me $40,000 to call a pot which is currently $194,000. I'm getting almost 5-to-1 odds with my ace-jack, which are wonderful odds, so I'm content to just call and see what happens.

**The pot is now $234,000. The flop comes K♠T♠T♣.**

**Jason Lester**. Jason has flopped top pair, and could reasonably make a strong bet. Instead he elects to check. He may be planning on trapping Farha later in the hand after seeing what I do.

**Dan Harrington**. I have nothing except an inside straight draw, and the high cards out there make it likely that this flop has helped at least one of my opponents. I took my shot, but the hand hasn't panned out, so I'm not planning to get involved. I check, hoping for a free card.

**Sam Farha**. The flop is dangerous and Farha has nothing yet. Despite the dangerous flop, neither of his opponents has taken the lead in the betting. So Farha decides to lead out, betting $120,000. It's a gutsy move, typical of Farha. Note that at this point he has twice as many chips as either Jason or I, so he'll be able to threaten us with elimination later in the hand, a threat we can't make.

**Jason Lester**. Jason only calls after some thought. The obvious question is — "Why not raise with top pair?" I think that was probably Jason's intention when he first checked the hand. But now he's seen Farha bet into an obviously dangerous board, and he's wondering just what Farha could be holding to justify that move.

Before the flop, Farha could have raised from the button with just about anything. But to bet here, Farha must have something. If he has a ten, Jason has very few outs. If he has a king, what kings can Jason beat? King-queen is a tie, and ace-king and king-ten are winning for Farha. Ace-queen, ace-jack, and queen-jack are all losing, but would Farha bet with those hands? Jason decides to just call and see another card. On the tape, the play looks strange because we know Jason is way out in front right now. But he's clearly puzzled by Farha's bet, and decides to be cautious. He just calls.

**Dan Harrington**. No deep think required for me. I'm gone.

**The pot is now $474,000. The turn is the 9♣.**

**Jason Lester**. The card didn't help Jason, and it turned one of Farha's possible holdings (queen-jack) into a straight. Jason checks.

**Sam Farha**. Lester isn't showing any strength — he's turned down three opportunities to bet or raise. Although Farha doesn't have anything, he has plenty of reason to believe that this pot is winable. He bets $250,000.

**Jason Lester**. After some thought, Jason folds. Farha bet before the flop, after the flop, and after the turn. Few players can make those bets with nothing, and if Farha has something, Jason is likely to be beaten. What's more, he's probably going to have to risk his whole stack on the river to find out if Farha is bluffing. Jason finally decides that a bluff here is just too unlikely, and he gives up the hand.

Farha fired three volleys at the pot, and finally pulled it down. He made a profit of about $280,000 on the hand, but remember that he had to put almost one-quarter of his stack (nearly $500,000) at risk to do so. Longball is a high-risk, high-reward approach to bluffing, requiring iron nerves and a willingness to ride out huge swings of fortune.

For another more subtle and ingenious example of longball, take a look at the last hand in the book, at the end of Part Thirteen.

# Blending Moves and Styles

What kind of moves you make and how often you make them should be guided to a large extent by your personal style and how you are perceived at the table. Each style has some built-in advantages and disadvantages at the table. Be aware of them, and your overall play will benefit. Disregard them and you will suffer.

## The Conservative Style and Bluffing

Conservative players are perfectly situated to execute the occasional well-timed bluff with little or no hand. A good example was my squeeze play against Arieh and Raymer described earlier in this chapter. The play stands on its own merits once I saw that Arieh was entering the pot from early position with less-than-optimal hands. But my tight image enabled me to make the play with any two cards; my sense was that I had a high enough probability that I would win the pot without any further play that I didn't need to care what my cards were. Hence I was quite comfortable going in with the six-deuce. If a loose player had sat in my seat with the same read I had, he would have needed some sort of hand to make the same move, because Arieh and Raymer would both have been suspicious that he was just making a play.

The key question for the conservative player is: "Just how often should I bluff?" My quick (and very general) answer here would be this: Given an average table and pretty much average cards (no extended runs of either hot or cold hands), about one bluff every hour and a half seems about right. That works out to about six bluffs in the course of a nine-hour playing session. If the table is moving along at 30 to 40 hands per hour, that's about one bluff every 50 to 60 hands. Note too that I'm not talking here about gigantic bluffs where you put your whole tournament at risk, but just your run of the mill moves where you pick up the blinds and antes, plus perhaps an extra bet or two.

That may not sound like much, but it's probably all you can really do before your bluffs start to alter your image. The rest of your plays will be made from solid values, and since you're very unlikely to have to show any bluff hands down, the occasional steal simply won't be noticed.

Since a real table won't be average in all respects, you'll have to stay alert and see just what is happening, and adjust your play accordingly. Here are some more tips for the conservative player:

1.  If you're catching a lot of cards, don't bluff. Your increased action will be generating suspicion, and bluffs are more likely to get called.

2.  If your cards are very cold and you're in very few pots, you're in an excellent position to bluff. A player who sits out 20 hands and then raises a couple of limpers from the big blind will not be seen as stealing.

3.  At a loose table, don't bluff. You're more likely to get called, and your value bets are more likely to get paid off well.

4.  At a tight table, bluff more often. The players are waiting for good hands and are comfortable laying down weak or marginal hands. If your bluff meets resistance at a tight table, you're dead. Don't push it.

5.  You should bluff much less in online poker than in live poker. Projecting a conservative image doesn't count for much against opponents who are playing three tournaments at once and watching TV besides.

# The Conservative Style and Slow-Playing

Slow-playing is a less effective tactic for a player who is recognized as conservative. When such a player gets in a hand, he's presumed to have something. Passive calls or other indications of weakness will be viewed with suspicion. Given his more limited range of starting hands, putting him on a draw isn't as plausible as with an aggressive player. As a result, his slow-plays don't get the action he might like.

**Example 11. You are known to be a solid player who mostly plays good cards. At a full table early in a tournament, you open for three times the big blind in second position with**

**A tight, conservative player in seventh position calls your bet. Everyone else folds. The flop comes**

**You make a continuation bet of half the pot. The conservative player calls. Fourth street is a J♣. *What do you do?***
    **Answer:** You check and fold if he bets. What could a conservative player reasonably have in this position? If he

held aces, kings, or queens he would have raised before the flop. He would almost certainly have folded deuce-deuce. If he held a pair lower than eights, he might have folded after your bet on the flop. If he had a pair of nines or eights he just made a set and you're dead. If he had a pair of tens or jacks he has you beaten and you only have six outs at best. There are no unpaired hands that justify both the pre-flop call and the post-flop call from a hand in early position (although a very loose player might make both calls with an ace-king like yours).

Since most good players can run through an analysis like this fairly quickly, you can see why slow-playing doesn't work that well for the tight player. When he makes a call with a pair of eights in this situation and hits his trips, he can't really fool anyone into thinking he has nothing. An aggressive player might have decided to call with jack-ten suited and now be drawing at a straight, but a conservative player will respect the Gap Concept and throw his jack-ten away.

# The Super-Aggressive Style and Bluffing

The super-aggressive style works in just the opposite way from the conservative style. The super-aggressive style doesn't need to bluff before the flop; in a sense, the whole style *is* a bluff. When you play low suited connectors or cards like ten-eight or jack-nine in early position, you're generating all the action you need or can handle. Put another way, *you're already playing the hands that other players use to bluff!* You don't need any extra hands in the mix.

# The Super-Aggressive
# Style and Slow-Playing

Slow-playing, however, is a natural money-making tool for the super-aggressive player. Super-aggressive players play lots of pots and as a result miss lots of flops. A slow-play simply looks like any other hand where the super-aggressive player played a couple of middling cards and either missed the flop or hit bottom pair or a draw.

Go back to the previous example and substitute a super-aggressive player for the conservative player in seat 7. After the flop, you can't be nearly as certain what cards he's holding or what you should do. That's the strength of the super-aggressive style which partially compensates for the risks taken: It's a difficult style to play, but also a difficult style to play against.

# The Hidden Linkage
# Between Bluffing and Slow-Playing

Although many players are unaware of it, there is a linkage between the frequency of your slow-playing and the effectiveness of your bluffs. The more you slowplay, the less effective your bluffs will be. This is only partly a result of the table's perceiving you as a generally trappy player, whose every play must be viewed with suspicion. The main reason is that you aren't making enough value bets to establish credibility with your bluffs. The logic works as follows:

1. You only get so many high-value hands.

2. In order for your bluffs to be credible, players have to see you bet for value, then turn over strong hands.

3.  The more you slowplay your strong hands, the less often (2) will happen.

4.  Therefore, the more you slowplay, the less credible your bluffs will be.

If you're a super-aggressive player, whose real goal is to win big pots with your legitimate hands, this shouldn't bother you very much. You will be perceived as a trappy player, and you will make big profits on your legitimate hands. But if you're a conservative player who wants to make the occasional effective bluff, make sure your slowplaying frequency doesn't get too high.

# The Problems

Problems 8-1 through 8-3 show some examples of bluffing and stealing. For some advice on when not to steal, look at 8-4. Techniques for defending against bluffs and steals are examined in 8-5 and 8-6.

Problems 8-7 through 8-9 cover other forms of bluffing: continuation bets, overbets, and semi-bluffs. The ever-popular steal from the big blind position is the focus of 8-10.

The intricacies of BSB play are covered in Problems 8-11 through 8-13. Problems 8-14 and 8-15 deal with miscellaneous types of bluffs.

Problems 8-16 through 8-19 show examples of slow-playing. The last two problems, 8-20 and 8-21, show the pros and cons of check-raising.

## Hand 8-1

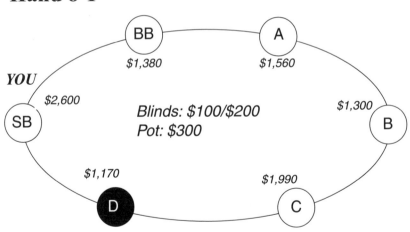

**Situation:** Single table online tournament, paying three places. The initially loose table has turned tight.

**Your Hand: 8♦5♠**

**Action to you:** Players A, B, C, and D all fold.

**Question:** *Do you fold, call, or raise?*

**Answer:** While your hand isn't much, the situation at the table is exceptionally favorable. Let's see why.

Note that while you are the big stack right now, *there are no small stacks.* That's very important. Everyone is still in the hunt. There are six players left and only three places get paid, so no one wants to be the next player eliminated. Usually at this point there will be a micro-stack or two, ready to go all-in with anything. But not here. This arrangement tends to make for the most conservative play you will see, and hence the very best stealing opportunities for the aggressive player. Right now, you want to be as aggressive as possible, so you should be quite happy to play your 8♦5♠, especially with four players already out.

Next question: What's the more appropriate move here — a call or a raise? Here I recommend just a call. If the big blind has a real hand, he'll raise you right here and you can get out cheap. If he doesn't have a hand, he'll just check. Then you can look at the flop and bet unless the texture of the flop is really bad. The combination of a call followed by a post-flop bet is less likely to be interpreted as a blatant steal than a simple raise from the small blind.

**Action: You call. and the big blind checks. The pot is now $400.**

**Flop: Q♦9♥8♥**

**Question:** *What do you do now?*

**Answer:** The shape of the flop is what I would call medium bad, with cards that could fit into a number of holdings, plus two hearts. However, you actually got a little piece of that flop yourself. Just the bottom pair, but it's better than nothing, and some compensation for the unfavorable shape. Now continue your play by making the standard bet of half the pot.

**Action:** You bet $200, and the big blind folds.

The approach in this hand is more effective against weak players than strong players. At a table of strong players, a call is more likely to be interpreted as some sort of trap play. Weak players simply think that a call shows a weaker hand than a bet.

# Hand 8-2

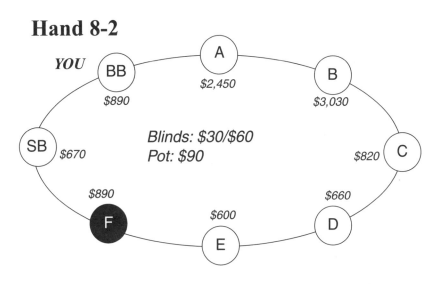

**Situation:** Player A limps into a lot of pots and has been lucky. He tends to fold to a big bet after he limps. Player D is tight. The blinds increase to $50/$100 next hand.

**Your Hand:** 8♦3♠

**Action to You:** Player A calls $60. Players B and C fold. Player D calls. Players E and F fold. The small blind calls. The pot is now $240.

**Question:** *Do you check or raise?*

    **Answer:** Our hand is worthless, but our position at the table is not. Let's look at the possibility of stealing this pot.

    We know that Player A limps into a lot of pots, but will then fold to a big bet.

    Player D is tight, but he didn't raise. His hand isn't worthless, but will he call a big bet with it?

    The small blind was offered huge pot odds. The pot was $210 when he called for $30. Most players will call with almost anything in that situation.

    If we make a large bet, I think A and the small blind are almost sure to go out. We can't be sure about D, but we know that most limpers fold to most large raises, so we're surely a substantial favorite to win the pot right here. If we're called, we're about a 2-to-1 underdog to two overcards, so we have some winning chances later. That's good enough for me; I'm making a move here!

    Next question: *How much to bet?* Some players would go all-in here, for two reasons.

1.    They think an all-in bet is more likely to steal the pot than a smaller bet.

2.    They don't like their prospects if they bet a few hundred now, get called, fold after the flop, and then watch the blinds go to $50/$100, when they'd only have enough chips for three or four rounds.

    I understand that point of view, but I don't agree. If my hand were a little more substantial, say ten-nine suited or something like that, where I felt I had reasonable chances if

I were called, I might go that way. But here my hand is so weak that I want an exit strategy if my move doesn't work.

And while I'm sure not happy if the blinds go up and I have only $500 or $550 in chips, I can still look to make a move in the next round, with almost certainly a better hand than I've got now. So I'm going to raise, but I'm just going to raise to $300. That's big enough to chase my opponents out if they want to go, and leaves me a little extra ammunition if the play doesn't work.

**Action:** You raise to $300. Players A, D, and the small blind all fold. You take the pot.

# Hand 8-3

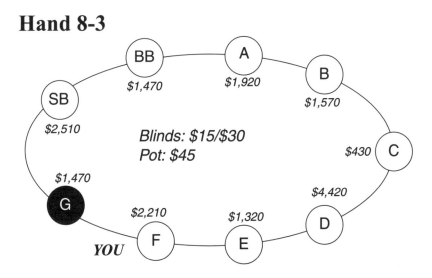

**Situation:** Early in an online tournament. Player D has been loose and lucky.

**Your hand:** 9♦7♠

**Action to you:** Players A, B, and C all fold. Player D calls. Player E folds.

**Question:** *Do you fold, call, or raise?*

**Answer:** I don't mind playing a hand like nine-seven offsuit once in a while, as long as it's cheap and my position is relatively good. While I'm almost always throwing the hand away after the flop (and sometimes before the flop, if there is a raise behind me), there will be rare occasions when I hit the flop solidly, and on those occasions my hand will be very well disguised. Super-aggressive players make this move far more often than I do, and for much higher stakes.

**Action:** You call. The button folds, the small blind calls, and the big blind checks. The pot is now $120.

**Flop:** A♦T♥3♥

**Action:** The blinds and Player D all check. *What do you do?*

**Answer:** You missed the flop, but three players have checked in front of you, indicating weakness. *Is this a good time to try to bluff at the pot?*

No. There are two good reasons for not wanting to bluff at the pot here: the number of your opponents and the flop. Let's take them one at a time.

1.  **Number of opponents**. The more live players in the pot, the less you want to bluff. Ideally, you want to try to bluff a single opponent. A bluff against two opponents is possible but somewhat risky. Three opponents? Forget about it. There's just too much of a chance that someone will elect to stay in the pot against you, or, even worse, that their check was a trap and they'll now raise you. Bluffing when last to act is marginally better than leading out with a bluff, but it's also an obvious bluffing situation, which will arouse suspicion.

2.  **The flop**. When you're looking at a flop to bluff against, there are two cards you don't want to see: an ace or a ten. The ace is obviously a bad card since players tend to play aces more than any other card. The ten is less obvious but also bad; tens are the most common card used in straights. (Tens occur in straights ranging from ace through ten down to ten through six. Except for a five, no other card appears as frequently.) When an ace and a ten both appear on board, you have to ask yourself "What hands could my opponents have that
    1.  Were worth playing before the flop,
    2.  Missed this flop completely?

    You're losing to anyone who played a pair before the flop, or anyone who had an ace or a ten. In addition, any other high card hand like king-queen or queen-jack now has an inside straight draw besides two overcards to your hand.

    You're happy to see three checks, but the flop is too dangerous for a move. Wait for a better opportunity.

**Action:** You check. A jack comes on the turn, and you fold to a bet from Player D who wins the pot.

# Hand 8-4

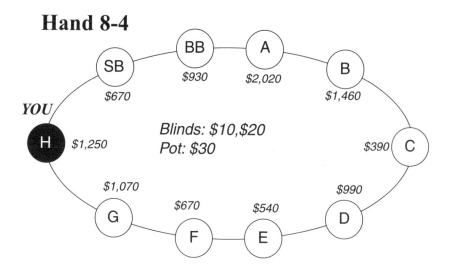

**Situation:** Early in a single-table online tournament.

**Your hand:** A♠2♥

**Action to You:** Player A folds. Player B calls. Players C and D fold. Player E calls. Player F folds. Player G calls. The pot is now $90.

**Question:** Player H decides to make a move to steal the pot and bets $50. *Good play or bad?*

    **Answer:** Many players have the idea that sitting on the button entitles them to steal any pot that comes their way. It's a dangerous notion, and if you believe it, you should disabuse yourself quickly.

    There are advantages to being on the button, of course. Because you act last, you're going to have a better chance of winning any pot in which you're legitimately involved. But notice I said "legitimately." Don't go running into pots you have no business in playing just because you're on the button.

Player H has another problem here. It's nice that he has an ace in his hand, but his other card is a deuce. Unless he catches a deuce on the flop, he's really playing with just one card — a single ace. More often than not, when the hand is played out, the deuce won't even be part of his best five-card hand. It will be trumped by other, higher cards on the board. When you play hands like ace-king, ace-queen, or ace-jack, you're actually giving yourself two ways to win the hand. Your second card could provide your margin of victory. When you play weak hands like ace-deuce or ace-trey, you don't have that possibility. That's why you're quick to throw those hands away.

And here's one last problem: A $50 bet won't chase anyone out. Anyone who wanted to play the pot for $20 will now gladly toss in another $30 because the pot odds will be irresistible.

In online poker, you'll meet a lot of players who will play any ace or any two suited cards. Be glad they're in the game because they're giving you their money.

What would I do here? Folding is far and away my top choice, although just calling isn't hopeless. The pot odds are reasonable, and I'd be hoping to flop some low cards and get a straight draw. Note that I wouldn't particularly be hoping to flop an ace — too much danger that someone else has an ace with a better kicker.

**Action:** You actually raise to $50. The small blind calls for $40, the big blind for $30, and the three original callers all put in another $30 each. The pot is now $300.

**Flop:** K♠9♠4♣

**Action:** Everyone checks to you. *Should you try to steal again by betting $100?*

**Answer:** No. Normally I'd advise checking here, but the right play is to fold, so that you can't get yourself in any more trouble!

This is actually a particularly bad flop for you. With a king, a nine, and a couple of spades, and five callers out there, it's certain that someone either has a made hand or a draw to a strong hand. Anyone who was playing high cards either hit a pair of kings or else has something like queen-jack or jack-ten and a draw to a straight. Someone could be playing two spades and is looking for a flush. Meanwhile, you have absolutely nothing. If you don't want to fold, just check and be glad you got a free card, even though hitting something on fourth street may still just give you the second best hand.

**Action:** You boldly decide to steal the pot by betting $100. Everyone folds except Player E, who calls. The pot is now $500.

## Fourth Street: 5♠

**Action:** Player E checks. *What should you do?*
**Answer:** Just check and be glad that you're getting a free shot at drawing the nut flush. If you're contemplating betting, think about it this way — what could he have that would let him call after the flop, but fold a bet now? If he has a pair of kings he's sticking around to the end. If he was drawing to a flush, he just made it. You might be able to chase him out if he has a pair of nines, but that's about it. Remember, his call on the flop had to mean something. Your hand certainly didn't get better, but he might have a monster hand and be ready to check-raise you.

**Action:** You try to steal the pot again by betting $200. Player E goes all-in by calling your last bet and then raising his last $190. *Should you call?*

**Answer:** He's representing a flush, and given the way the hand has played out, he probably has it. In that case there are only seven spades left in the deck, and you need one to make the nut spade flush. There are now eight cards accounted for: your two hole cards, the four on board, and his presumed two spades, leaving 44 cards in the deck. Your odds against drawing the flush are 37-to-7, or a little over 5-to-1 against. What's the pot offering you? There's $1,190 in there now, and you have to pay $190 to call. That's roughly $200 to win $1,200, or 6-to-1. That's enough, so you can call just based on the odds of drawing the nut flush.

**Action:** You call, and he shows 7♠4♠ for a flush. Fifth street is a J♥, and your ace-high loses to his king-high flush.

If you watch a lot of poker on TV, stealing pots with nothing looks pretty easy. It's not. Sometimes you make off with a few chips, but this hand is a good example of how things can go horribly wrong and half your stack can vanish in a couple of minutes.

# Hand 8-5

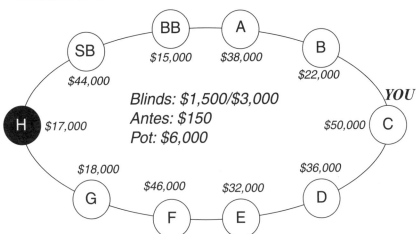

**Situation:** Late in a major tournament. The table is a mix of conservative and aggressive players. Player D seems moderately tight. You have won three recent pots without having to show your hand.

**Your hand:** A♠K♦

**Action to you:** Players A and B fold.

**Question:** *What's your play?*
    **Answer:** Ace-king in an unopened pot is certainly worth a raise. You should raise about three times the big blind here, around $9,000 to $10,000.

**Action:** You bet $10,000. Player D, after a long pause, goes all-in for $36,000. All the players fold around to you. The pot is now $52,000.

**Question:** *What do you do?*
    **Answer:** First, take a deep breath and don't be in a hurry to do anything. This is generally good games-playing advice, but I've always been amazed how often players will go into deep thinks about relatively trivial decisions early in a tournament, then call an all-in bet later on in a split second. Train yourself to be a cool customer, and your results will improve dramatically in the long run.
    The next step is to check out the pot odds. Be sure you do this before you start to think about what hand your opponent might or might not have. I've seen lots of players talk themselves out of playing a hand, and then completely forget to compute the pot odds. Don't fall into that trap.
    In this case, you can fold and have $40,000 in your stack. If you call and win you'll have $92,000, but if you call and lose you'll have just $14,000. Calling means risking

$26,000 to win $52,000, which means you're being offered exactly 2-to-1 odds on your bet.

Now you're ready to think about actual hands. What could your opponent have here? To keep things simple, we'll group his possible hands into three categories.

1.  He has aces or kings. This is the worst possible result for you. Aces is worse than kings by a long shot, but let's group these two disasters together and say that you're about a 4.5-to-1 underdog when this happens.

2.  He has a pair lower than aces or kings. It's probably queens or jacks, although I've seen people make this move with tens, nines, or even lower pairs occasionally. You're about a 13-to-10 underdog here.

3.  He has some other hand, and is putting a move on you with a bluff or semi-bluff, or mistakenly betting for value. With these hands, you're somewhere between a 3-to-2 and a 2-to-1 favorite.

Don't make the mistake of discounting the possibility of Category No. 3. Just because you wouldn't make a move with something like king-queen suited doesn't mean that another player wouldn't do it. He might have 'read' you for a bluff. He might have decided that you'd been pushing him around and it was time to pick a hand and make a stand. Or he might have decided that the blinds were increasing too fast and he couldn't wait any longer to make a move at a significant pot. Over the board, you don't need to figure out which of these possibilities might be true. Just be aware that whenever someone shoves all his chips in the pot, there's a distinctly non-zero chance that he doesn't really have a hand.

I'd estimate the chance of Category No. 3 at a minimum of 10 percent, perhaps as high as 20 percent. If that's the case, how big does the chances of his actually having aces or kings need to be for you to want to fold your hand? Without working through all the calculations here, the answer turns out to be around 50 percent. If you think that there's more than a 50 percent chance that he's holding one of those two hands, you should fold. If less, you should call.

In a tournament, I would almost always call in this situation. In order to fold, I'd have to assess Player D as super-tight, and I'd also have to know that I had been projecting a generally tight image myself, which would discourage people from making loose moves against me when I make a big bet. Here, the problem stipulated that I had picked up a few recent pots without showing a hand, and that increases the chances that someone will move over the top on me with a less-than-premium hand.

By the way, in a ring game where very old-fashioned, conservative play predominates, I would throw away the ace-king in this situation. You're much too likely to find yourself being raised by the hands you fear most, aces or kings. Be aware, however, that cash games have recently loosened considerably with an influx of players accustomed to tournament play, and the old-fashioned conservative style of play is becoming rarer.

**Resolution:** You call, and your opponent turns up a pair of queens. His queens hold up to win the pot.

# Hand 8-6

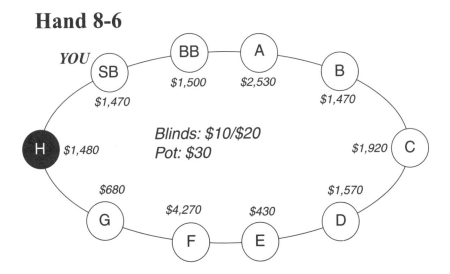

**Situation:** Early in a multi-table online tournament. Players F and G have been loose and aggressive. Player H has been tight.

**Your hand:** 6♦5♦

**Action to you:** Players A, B, C, D, and E all fold. Players F, G, and H all call. The pot is now $90.

**Question:** *Do you fold, call, or raise?*
   **Answer:** Six-five suited is a bit low for a suited connector, but you're being well-paid for your troubles. The pot is offering 9-to-1 odds at this point, so put in another $10 and take a flop.
   Some players like to stick in a big raise here on the theory that everyone has shown weakness by just limping, so perhaps the pot can be stolen easily. That's a legitimate play as long as you don't overdo it, and as long as the table has played tight. It's less good in online play than in live play because the players tend to be looser. It's an especially bad play here. Both Players F and G have been loose in the early

going, and they have extreme stacks. Player F has a big stack and so may feel he has little to risk by taking you on, and Player G is loose and probably desperate. That's two tough targets, and two too many for me. Just call.

**Action:** You call for another $10, and the big blind checks. Five players are in the pot, which now totals $100.

## Flop: 6♠3♣2♦

**Action:** You are first to act. *What do you do?*
   **Answer:** All in all, a very good flop for you. You have top pair, an inside straight draw, and you need two running cards for a flush. It would be silly to hold back; this isn't a hand you want to waste any time on. Just put in a bet of around two-thirds of the pot, and see what happens. Hopefully you may take the hand down right here.

**Action:** You bet $60. The big blind and Player F fold. Player G calls. The button folds. The pot is now $220.

## Fourth Street: 2♥

**Action:** What do you do?
   **Answer:** Three good pieces of news. You eliminated three players, the player who remains is loose and has a short stack, so he can't hurt you much, and the deuce on fourth street is unlikely to have helped his hand.
   You should make a solid bet here. You're not really worried about preventing a draw, as the board makes a flush impossible and a straight highly unlikely. You just need to charge him for the privilege of hanging around. An amount around half the pot looks about right.

**Action:** You bet $100 and he calls. The pot is now $420.

**Answer:** At this point you should be wondering just what your opponent has. Presumably he's not drawing to a flush or straight. If he has an overpair to the board he could have raised at two different points but didn't. If he does have a six, it's almost certainly a better six than ours. Conceivably he stuck around with ace-trey suited and now has middle pair.

**Fifth Street: K♦**

**Question:** *What do you do?*
**Answer:** The king wasn't helpful, but it probably wasn't a disaster either. Players are much less likely to hang around with king-x than with ace-x. However, you don't have anything more than you have represented from the beginning, top pair.

There are two ways to handle the situation now. You could make a defensive bet of about $150 or so, with the idea of heading off any bet on his part. Or you could just check and see what happens. If he has nothing, your check might even goad him into doing something stupid.

My top choice is to check. I don't have a strong hand, and would be quite happy to just check the hand down and see what happens without getting any more chips involved. If that induces him to bet, then we'll decide at that point what we want to do.

**Action:** You check. He goes all-in for his last $500. The pot is now $980. *What now?*
**Answer:** We talked a lot about bluffing in this chapter, and now it's time to decide if we're being bluffed or not!

Let's first check the pot odds. We have to put in $500 to call a pot of $980, so we're getting almost 2-to-1 odds on our money. Under the circumstances (an all-in from a short stack) that creates a strong presumption in favor of calling. You'll need to be convinced you're beaten before folding here.

If his last bet was a value bet, what does he have and does his play of the hand make sense? There are really only two possibilities here:

1.  He has king-x and called to the end with it.

2.  He has an overpair to the board and refused to bet before the flop, after the flop, or after the turn.

A loose, desperate player just might call down with a king, although players are much more likely to make that play with an ace. Would a loose player have refused to bet the whole way with an overpair? Sorry, I'm not buying that. There's plenty of doubt about how this hand was played, so I think there's a solid chance that he's bluffing. Combined with the excellent pot odds, you have an easy call here.

**Action:** You call, and he turns up ace-seven offsuit. You win the pot.

It's always nerve-wracking to call when you don't have much of a hand, but if the betting scenario is suspicious and the odds are good, you have to make him show you the cards. This is doubly true online, where the players don't have as much invested in the tournament and bluffing is much more common.

# Hand 8-7

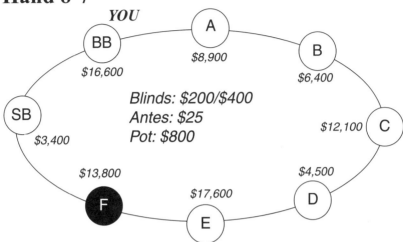

YOU

BB
$16,600

A
$8,900

B
$6,400

SB
$3,400

Blinds: $200/$400
Antes: $25
Pot: $800

C
$12,100

F
$13,800

E
$17,600

D
$4,500

**Situation:** In the middle of a multi-table online event. Player E has been aggressive.

**Your hand:** K♣T♠

**Action to you:** Players A through D all fold. Player E raises, putting in $800. The button and the small blind fold. The pot is now $1,600. It costs you $400 to call.

**Question:** *Do you fold, call, or raise?*
  **Answer:** Your hand certainly isn't strong enough to raise, but it's plenty good enough to call given the 4-to-1 pot odds.

**Action:** You call. The pot is now $2,000.

**Flop:** J♦7♥4♠

**Action:** You act first. *What do you do?*
  **Answer:** This is a textbook scenario for a good probe/steal bet. You missed the flop, but it's a flop that could easily have

missed your opponent as well. If you don't bet, the pot will almost surely be taken away from you. If you bet half the pot, will you win the bet one time in three? In my experience, the answer is certainly "yes." So toss in $1,000 and see what happens.

**Action:** You bet $1,000, and Player E folds.

Were you afraid to go up against the big stack? Remember, you're the second-biggest stack, so you can hurt him almost as much as he can hurt you. In a balance of mutual terror, whoever acts first has the advantage.

# Hand 8-8

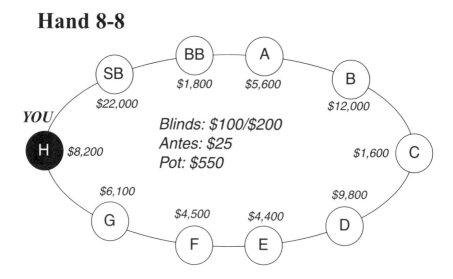

**Situation:** Middle of the first day of a major tournament. The small blind has been playing strong, perceptive poker.

**Your hand:** K♠K♦

**Action to you:** Players A through G all fold.

**Question:** *Do you call, raise $600, raise $1,800, or go all-in?*

**Answer:** Wow. Nice situation. You have a big pair of kings, and just two players to act behind you. The typical play is to make a solid raise to $600 here. That's three times the big blind, but not so much that someone behind you who has some kind of hand can't call. With a great hand and position, you want action. But you don't want to let anyone in for free, in case someone has ace-small. Then an ace on the flop would crush you. So $600 is a good, solid play with your hand.

What kind of hand would bet $1,800 here? Well, that's an overbet, a scared bet, from a hand that's not very good but wants to steal the pot anyway, using the advantage of the button.

If you were the big stack in the small blind, what would you think of a $600 bet? You wouldn't be able to tell much. Might well be a steal, but it could also be a bet from a reasonable hand looking for action.

And in that position, what would you think of an $1,800 chip bet? You'd probably think, "That little creep is trying to steal the pot from me. If I've got any two decent cards, I'm going to step on him like a bug."

That's why you should bet $1,800 here (or some similar amount). It's the perfect bet against a perceptive player, given your stack and the small blind's stack. It's a stealing situation, it looks like you're trying to steal, and a $22,000 stack might see this as a great time to come over the top and take your bet away from you. Moreover, your bet is small enough in relation to your own stack ($8,200) so that (from his point of view) you could walk away and still have a very significant pile of chips. And the big stack is big enough so that, in a worst-case scenario, it could lose an all-in bet and still be doing well.

**Action:** You raise to $1,800. The small blind puts you all-in. The big blind folds. You call. The small blind turns over Q♠T♥. Your pair of kings hold up.

A great hand, and worth repeated study. *Remember that the best way to execute a trap is to imagine the hand you're representing, then play the hand exactly as you would play the imaginary hand.*

Note again that this play only works against a strong and perceptive player, one who would understand why you were overbetting the pot. A weak player with an average-plus hand would just see the big bet and throw his hand away.

# Hand 8-9

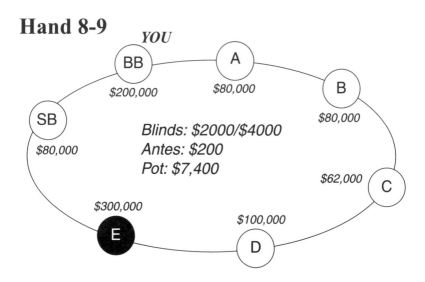

**Situation:** Late in the second day of a major tournament. Thirteen players remain at two tables. Only 11 places will be paid. Player C is a solid player who has recently lost a couple of key hands.

**Your hand: 9♣6♣**

**Action to you:** Players A and B fold. Player C raises to $19,000. Players D and E fold. The small blind folds. The pot is now $26,400, and it costs you $15,000 to call.

**Question:** *Do you fold, call, or raise?*
> **Answer:** Fold. Your pot odds are okay, but your hand is very weak. There's no reason at this point to think that Player C is making a move. He's simply put in a reasonable raise from middle position. It could mean anything, but in the absence of any other information you should assume it means what it appears to mean — a good hand.
>
> Also, don't assume you can somehow muscle Player C out of the pot with a fancy move or a bigger stack. He just put one-third of his chips in the pot, so you have to give him credit for being willing to go all the way with this hand.

**Action:** You actually call for another $15,000. The pot is now $41,400.

**Flop:** K♣5♣3♠

**Question:** It's your move. *What should you do?*
> **Answer:** Some hands have a moment or two when it's possible, with a shrewd bet, to win a hand that might otherwise be lost. This is such a moment. At the table, you need to develop a sense of these moments; all good players have it.
>
> Let's consider the possibilities here.

1.  **If you check,** Player C will assume you missed the flop and bet. Since his stack and the pot are right now the same size, any reasonably big bet on his part will commit him to the pot. You will either have to fold his bet or be prepared to go all-in to win it.

2. **If you go all-in,** he will interpret your bet as weakness. After all, if you had a king in your hand and had just hit top pair, would you try to chase him out? No. You'd try to squeeze a little more money out of him with a smaller bet. An overbet practically screams that you have a flush draw and would like him to go away quickly. If you go all-in and he has anything at all, he'll deduce that he has the best hand and will call.

3. **If you lead out with a medium-sized bet,** you just might win the pot. That's a bet that makes sense for a player that had just made a pair of kings, and will scare him more than any other play. It's also a typical no-limit hold 'em semi-bluff. You might win the pot right now, and if you get called, you'll still have some outs with your club flush draw.

Once you've decided to make a bet, you need to decide how much to bet. Since your stack is very large compared to Player C, you'll need to take your cue from the size of Player C's remaining stack. So far, Player C has bet $19,000, leaving him with $43,000. You need to bet enough so that your opponent has to think about folding. You also need to consider what would happen if your opponent decides to go all-in after your bet. Would you have a call or a fold at that point? Let's look at some candidate bets and see how they stack up.

1. **Suppose you bet $10,000**. Your opponent will need to put in $10,000 to call a pot of over $50,000. The 5-to-1 pot odds will make a call almost mandatory if he has any hand at all.

2. **Suppose you bet $15,000**. Now he needs to put in $15,000 to call a pot of about $55,000. He's getting

almost 4-to-1 odds, so again he can call with almost anything. If he comes back with an all-in raise, you'll be faced with a $95,000 pot and $25,000 to call. You'll be less than a 2-to-1 underdog to make your flush in two cards, and you'll be getting just under 4-to-1 odds from the pot, so you'll have to call his all-in raise.

3. **Suppose you bet $20,000.** Now he needs to put in $20,000 to call a pot of about $60,000, so he's only getting 3-to-1 odds. He'll still call with most hands, but if he's missed his hand entirely he should fold. If he raises you all-in instead, you'll be faced with a $95,000 pot and $20,000 to call. Again, an easy call on your part.

Any bet will allow you to call the all-in raise, so bet the amount that is most likely to get him to fold: $20,000.

**Action:** You actually go all-in, and Player C quickly calls. He turns over K♥9♠, and his pair of kings hold up to win the pot.

As the hand played out, there actually was no play that could have won the pot or chased him away. But remember this principle for the future: *A small bet can be much scarier than a big bet, especially to a strong player.*

# Hand 8-10

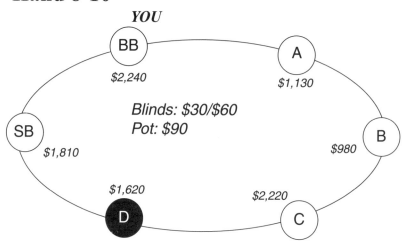

**Situation:** Late in a single-table satellite. Player C and the small blind are very aggressive.

**Your hand:** 4♣4♦

**Action to you:** Players A, B, C, and D all call. The small blind folds. The pot is now $330.

**Question:** *Do you fold, call, or raise?*
> **Answer:** Although the standard play here would be to check and see a cheap flop, this is actually a great stealing opportunity. Think about it. Four players, one of whom is known to be very aggressive, have just limped into the pot instead of raising. The requirements for raising are smaller than usual since the table is down to just six players. What could they have? It looks like you're facing perhaps one or two players with unpaired high cards, or maybe ace-x where the "x" is a low card, or some hands with suited connectors or connecting cards, drawing at flushes or straights.

I'd put in a good-sized bet here, at least $600, and see what happens. Most of the time, all four players will lay down their hand rather than call a big bet and face a presumably strong hand heads-up. If you make a bet like that and you do get called, at least you have a pair, so although you're out of position, you still have some chances to win from that point.

This is a pretty elementary move and an easy one to spot, so don't overdo it. Most of the time I would just check with this hand, even in this position, but occasionally I'll trot out the "Big Blind Steal" move to swipe a pot.

**Action:** Actually you check. The pot is still $330.

**Flop:** T♥8♠7♠

**Question:** *What do you do?*

**Answer:** You didn't flop a four, there are three overcards to your hand, and a spade draw. Since you didn't bet before the flop, you can't plausibly try to steal now. The texture of the flop is particularly bad for you. Too many possible hands either got hit by this flop or now have strong draws at straights or flushes. With four opponents, at least one player has to have you beaten right now. I'd check, then fold after someone bets.

**Action:** You check. Player A goes all-in for $1,070. Players B, C, and D all fold. You fold as well.

# Hand 8-11

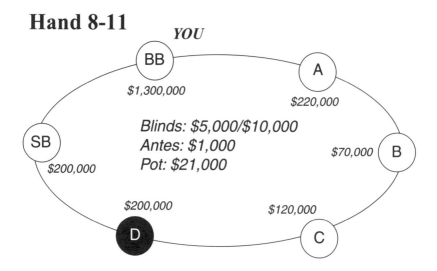

*YOU*

BB
$1,300,000

A
$220,000

Blinds: $5,000/$10,000
Antes: $1,000
Pot: $21,000

SB
$200,000

$70,000  B

$200,000

$120,000

D

C

**Situation:** Major tournament, final table. You are an experienced pro with a solid reputation. Player A is a daring and feared player. Players B, C, D and the small blind are all amateurs, some at their first major tournament. The final table has just gotten underway and the TV cameras are rolling.

**Your hand:** T♠9♠

**Action to you:** Players A, B, and C all fold. Player D raises, putting in $30,000. The small blind calls, putting in $25,000. The pot is now $76,000.

**Question:** *Do you fold, call, or raise?*
> **Answer:** Before you make a move, remember to take the whole position into account. In poker, your position includes everything you know: about your hand, about the players at the table, the chip counts, the situation — anything that can provide a clue about how the people you're facing will behave.

What you're seeing here is a good example of what I called BSB play. We have a bet from the button, which might be an attempt to steal the pot, and a call from the small blind, which doesn't necessarily indicate any strength. Your first thought should be that a big bet here might work. Then you need to consider what's unique about this situation, and see if those factors make you more or less eager to make your play.

The really unique aspects of this particular position are the relative stack sizes, the fact that your opponents are amateurs rather than experienced pros, and the TV coverage. Here's how I would weigh these factors:

1. **TV coverage**. Being on television tends to make people nervous, and most people, when they get nervous, get cautious. Above all, they don't want to look foolish in front of millions of people.

2. **Amateurs rather than pros**. They are less likely to see your play as part of a move, and more likely to see it as just a strong play from the big stack.

3. **Relative stack sizes**. This factor cuts both ways. A big bet offers them a chance to double up and get back in the tournament, but it also offers a chance to exit quickly in sixth place, with a smaller prize payout. Even amateurs react differently to this situation. Some are just happy to be in the money and feel the pressure is now off, while others are calculating the value of moving up the ladder a rung or two.

On balance, it seems to me that the situation presents an even stronger case for betting here than normal, so I would put the two players all-in with a $200,000 bet.

**Action:** You bet $200,000, and both players fold.

# Hand 8-12

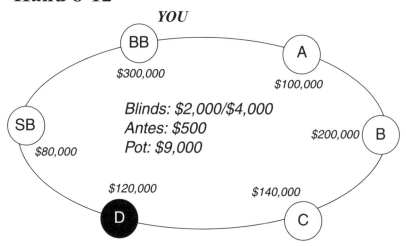

**Situation:** Major tournament, working its way down to the final table. At this point 12 players remain at two tables. Player D is aggressive and in the past has moved at the pot from the button.

**Your hand:** J♦2♦

**Action to you:** Players A, B, and C fold. Player D raises to $15,000. The small blind folds. The pot is now $24,000. It costs you $11,000 to call.

**Question:** *Do you fold, call, or raise?*
   **Answer:** Despite your weak holding, you should often raise here — perhaps $30,000 to $40,000. The raise is good for two reasons:
   There's a significant chance (probably as much as 60 percent) that Player D was stealing and will now fold. If he calls, your hand will catch some flops and win some pots. If he reraises, you are definitely beaten and you can lay down

your hand. Any bet that can win immediately 50 to 60 percent of the time is a profitable bet to make.

In the latter stages of a tournament, you must defend your blind and let the other players know that you are not to be trifled with. They'll get the message and pick on someone else at the table. Much of poker psychology harkens back to lessons that boys learn in schoolyards. "Stand up to a bully." "Don't let anybody push you around." "Show you're willing to fight, and the other kid will back off." What worked on a playground works at a poker table as well.

**Action:** You raise to $50,000. Player D folds.

# Hand 8-13

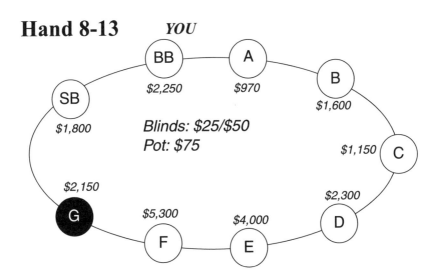

**Situation:** Early in a major tournament. Player G has seemed moderately tight.

**Your hand:** K♣Q♦

**Action to you:** Players A through F all fold. Player G raises, putting in $100. The small blind folds. The pot is now $175.

**Question:** *Do you fold, call, or raise?*

    **Answer:** Here's an example of typical button — small blind — big blind play. The button raises, which could be anything from a pure value bet to a blatant steal attempt. You have a much better than average hand in the big blind, so you're entitled to make a substantial reraise. Not raising is a clear mistake. The button will have position on you throughout the hand, and you'd like to eliminate that disadvantage as quickly as possible. So raise now and try to end the hand.

**Action:** You reraise to $400. The button goes all-in for his last $2,050. *What do you do?*

    **Answer:** You asked a question and got a clear answer. He says he has a real hand, probably a high pair. It's early in the tournament, his stack was solid, and there wasn't any obvious reason for him to jeopardize all his chips with nothing. So believe him and go away.

    Two more points to remember here:

1.   Never be afraid to let a move go if it doesn't work. Strictly speaking, our raise with a king-queen can't be considered a "move." We had plenty of value given that the raise came from the button. Still, we hoped to take the pot down or at least set our opponent back on his heels a bit, and we failed. There's no disgrace in admitting a bet didn't work and just letting the money go. Remember that going all-in with a king-queen offsuit was not our intention when we bet.

2.   Even online, an all-in bet usually means something. It's very rarely just a complete bluff. There aren't that many players who have the stones to take a seven-three and
   A.   Make a move with it, then
   B.   Go all-in against someone who's shown strength.

**Action:** You fold.

# Hand 8-14

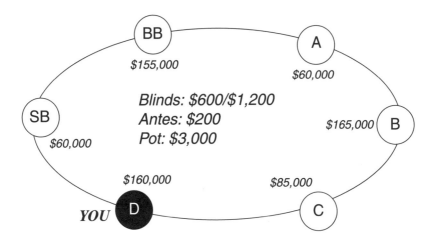

**Situation:** Final table of a major tournament. The big blind has been generally tight. On a couple of occasions you've seen him make a move at a pot, then back down after a sizeable reraise. You are known to be aggressive.

**Your hand:** J♥T♣

**Action to you:** Players A, B, and C all fold.

**Question:** *Do you fold, call, or raise?*

> **Answer:** Jack-ten on the button is good enough to make a move at the blinds, especially since the small stack is in the small blind, and the big blind is known to be tight. Just put in the standard pre-flop raise (at this table it's been $5,000 during this round) and see what happens.

**Action:** You raise to $5,000. The small blind folds but the big blind calls.

**Flop:** The flop comes 9♣7♠7♦

**Action:** The big blind checks. The pot is now $11,800. *What do you do?*

**Answer:** What could the big blind have at this point? He was offered very favorable odds to call before the flop. The pot was $8,000, and it cost him $3,800 more to call, so he had better than 2-to-1 odds. Even a tight player would have called with most pairs or a couple of high cards. A high pair would mostly have prompted a reraise pre-flop, especially from a tight player. Unless he called with a pair of nines or a high card and a nine, this flop shouldn't have helped him, so there's nothing mysterious about his check after the flop. Your best guess at this point should be that he has either

1.  A low to medium pair,
2.  A high card and a nine, or
3.  Two high cards.

If he has two high cards, a bet should chase him off the hand.

Should you bet? The answer is clearly yes. The shape of the flop is very good, with all cards lower than yours. If your opponent was holding two high cards, the flop has missed him completely. If you bet and are called, you have ten probable outs: three jacks, three tens, and four eights for a straight. The final (and important) argument for betting is that your opponent is known to be tight.

If you're going to bet, should you make a continuation-sized bet (about half the pot) or a pot-sized bet? Either bet should chase him away if he holds two high cards, and neither bet will chase him away if he holds nine-x. A low pair will probably stick around in either case as well. I would go with the continuation-sized bet simply because it should accomplish the same goal with less risk.

**Action:** You bet $12,000. The big blind calls. The pot is now $35,800.

**Fourth Street: K♦**

**Action:** The big blind bets $20,000. *What do you do?*

> **Answer:** After calling pre-flop and checking on the flop, the big blind now bets half the pot after a king appears. If the big blind is representing a king in his hand, what king could he have? Ace-king or a pair of kings would have reraised pre-flop. King-queen, king-jack, or king-ten would have thrown the hand away after your bet last round. K-9 or K-7 would probably still be slow-playing, since you are known to be aggressive. A king just doesn't seem like a plausible holding at this point.
>
> A more likely holding is something like a medium or low pair, in which case this bet represents a last stab at winning the pot. In addition, you've seen this player make a couple of such stabs in the past and then back away when raised. The right move here is pull out the back-alley mugging play and come over the top, representing that the king helped you (reasonable from your previous strong betting) with a bet large enough to show that your opponent may eventually have to commit all his chips to the hand. Note also that even if your bet is called, the king has given you four more outs, as now queens fill your straight.

**Action:** You raise to $48,000. The big blind folds.

At this point some readers may be asking "Wait a minute. How do you know that those previous times you saw the guy fold after a late bet weren't just a set-up? Perhaps he knows you remember those plays and now he's sprung a trap on you, getting ready to take all your chips?"

Well, you don't of course. In poker you always have to make these judgments based on what statisticians would consider an inadequate sample size. But unless you play with the same people over and over again for weeks and months at a time, that's all the evidence you're ever going to have. In the final analysis, it's just a matter of going with the best evidence you have, sketchy though it may be, while combining it with common-sense reasoning and pot-odds analysis.

# Hand 8-15

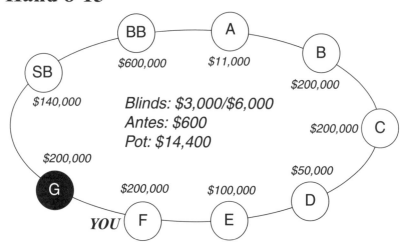

**Situation:** Final table of a major tournament.

**Your hand:** 5♥5♦

**Action to you:** Player A goes all-in for $11,000. Player E calls. The pot is now $36,400.

**Question:** *Do you fold, call, or raise?*
   **Answer:** Here's a chance to make a play that every good player knows by heart.

The all-in move from Player A doesn't necessarily mean anything. He's about to be gobbled up by the blinds in the next two hands, so he might go into the pot with almost anything.

Player E's call is more interesting. He presumably knows that Player A went into the pot with a random hand, and may be trying to pick up a few cheap chips with a hand that's just slightly better than random.

The right move here is to come over the top with a good-sized bet, about $40,000. If Player E lays his hand down, you can take back $29,000 of your chips and you'll be heads-up against Player A, but with plenty of dead money from the blinds, antes, and Player E still in the pot. Of course you need some kind of hand to make this play, but a small pair is good enough.

**Action:** You raise to $40,000. Player G and the blinds fold. Player E folds. The pot is now $47,400, of which you contributed just $11,000. Player A shows J♦4♦. Your pair of fives holds up to win the pot.

This is a great money-making move, but it doesn't arise that often. Player E made a beginner's mistake. If he was going to play, no matter what his hand was, he should have put in some kind of a raise, just to head off this move.

# Hand 8-16

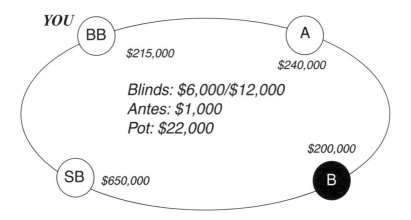

**Situation:** Final table of a major tournament. You're playing in your first big event. The small blind is a tricky, super-aggressive player, recognized as one of the best in the world.

**Your hand: J♦8♥**

**Action to you:** Players A and B fold. The small blind raises to $30,000. The pot is now $46,000. It costs you $18,000 to call.

**Question:** *Do you fold, call, or raise?*

   **Answer:** Most players correctly think of jack-eight as a relatively weak hand. At a full table it certainly is. But heads-up, it's just a little below average. When you couple this fact with a raise from a super-aggressive player, which he might have made with any two cards, and the huge pots odds you're being offered (better than 2.5-to-1), and your positional advantage, it's clear that a call is mandatory.

   When you play against super-aggressive players, remember that all your hands are stronger than they look. Against a conservative player at a full table, J♦8♥ looks like trash because all the hands your opponent might play are better than that. But a super-aggressive player in the small blind could easily be making a move with four-trey offsuit, in which case your hand is a solid favorite. In these situations the pot odds and your position, not your cards, are the best guide to when you want to play.

**Action:** You call. The pot is now $64,000.

**Flop:** J♠8♣2♦

**Action:** The small blind checks. *What do you do?*

**Answer:** You've hit top two pair on what would otherwise be a mediocre flop, so you have a tremendously strong hand. Your real problem now will be trying to figure out how to make the most money from a great situation.

Your opponent checked, which from a super-aggressive player probably means he has something. Super-aggressive players have a tendency to check strong hands and bet weak ones after the flop, especially against players they consider weak. Right now he'll be trying to deduce what you have from how you respond to his check.

1.  If you check, he'll conclude you have nothing, because that's what first-timers do when they have nothing.

2.  If you bet, he'll put you on a pair, probably jacks. He'll figure
    A.  You couldn't have had a pair before the flop, since you didn't reraise,
    B.  You wouldn't bet here with just a pair of deuces, and
    C.  You'd be a little scared to bet with just a pair of eights. If whatever he's holding is lower than jacks

(which is likely), he won't get too involved with the hand.

Your best bet to make some money here is to slow-play, starting with a check. If he does have something, he'll deduce that you have nothing and start betting on fourth street to take down the pot.

**Action:** You check. The pot remains $64,000.

## Fourth Street: 3♣

**Action:** The small blind bets $30,000. The pot is now $94,000. *What do you do?*

**Answer:** The temptation here for most players is to stick in a big raise, in effect saying "Ha! I outsmarted you!" Resist this temptation. Your objective when you play poker is to win your opponent's money, not to demonstrate how clever you are.

Instead, you should employ the rope-a-dope strategy and just call. The 3♣ probably didn't help your opponent's hand, but it did put two clubs on the board. When you call, your opponent will try to figure out what you have. Here's what his reasoning will look like:

1. You didn't have a pair before the flop, because you didn't reraise.

2. You didn't pair your jacks on the flop, because you just checked after him.

3. You called a bet after the 3♣ appeared, putting two clubs on the board.

The most reasonable guess of a hand that fit all these facts is two clubs, one of them high. You were getting 3-to-1 pot odds to call, which is not quite enough to call based on just the flush, but if you held a card like the K♣, you might think that the three remaining kings were all outs.

By calling here you've provided your opponent with a plausible but incorrect scenario for your hand. That's a great play when you can make it, because if a blank comes on fifth street and you bet, he'll be convinced that you missed your hand and are now bluffing him.

Note that you can only be this tricky against a very good player. A dope won't know what you're doing and won't try to figure it out either.

**Action:** You call. The pot is now $124,000.

**Fifth Street: A♠**

Good and bad news. Your opponent may be afraid you paired aces. On the other hand, it's not a club, so if he thought you were drawing at a flush, he knows you missed it.

**Action:** The small blind checks. *What do you do?*
**Answer:** You're almost certainly best, so it's time to spring your trap and bet something. You can't bet too much, however, because you don't want to chase him away. A good number is a little less than half the pot. He'll be afraid of the ace, but he'll know you missed your draws, and the pot odds will be a big incentive to call.

**Action:** You bet $50,000, and your opponent calls. He shows T♣T♦, and your two pair win the pot.

When you have a great hand against a super-aggressive player, let him take the lead in the betting. Try to combine slow-playing with the rope-a-dope. You often only need to put in one bet, on fifth street.

# Hand 8-17

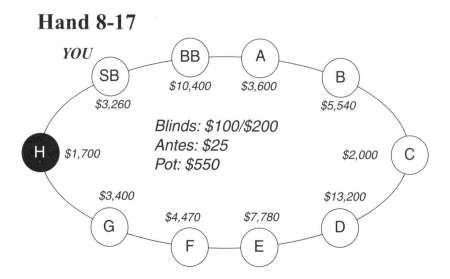

YOU

SB $3,260

BB $10,400

A $3,600

B $5,540

H $1,700

C $2,000

Blinds: $100/$200
Antes: $25
Pot: $550

G $3,400

F $4,470

E $7,780

D $13,200

**Situation:** Major tournament, early on the second day. The big blind is a very aggressive player who likes to come over the top and raise people out of pots.

**Your hand:** A♠A♦

**Action to you:** Players A through H all fold. It's just you and the big blind.

**Question:** *How do you handle your aces?*
    **Answer:** While slow-playing a hand like aces before the flop can be a poor play, there are situations where the move makes sense, and this hand shows one of them.
    The only question here is the best way to bet so as to get all your chips in the pot, and his as well. If you raise and your aggressive opponent on the big blind has any kind of hand, he'll interpret your raise as a small blind trying to steal the

pot, which no true bully would ever permit. But if he has absolutely nothing, even a bully will throw his hand away. A call, on the other hand, signifies a pretty feeble hand in this position (not even worth making a half-hearted attempt to steal), and will get reraised by anything. So I vote for just a call.

**Action:** You call for $100, and the big blind raises you $400. Pot is now $1,050.

**Question:** *What's the best way to proceed?*
   **Answer:** That was obviously a good result. Now what? If possible, we want to get all our chips in the pot before the flop comes. If he's raising on a medium-strength hand, and the flop misses him completely, and we've shown resistance, it becomes hard to justify continuing to play, even for the most certifiable lunatic. So we want to make one more raise, to keep the pot alive and give him one last chance to push us out. But it can't be too big a raise — we don't want to scare him. We just want to act like a mouse with a little swagger still left.
   I'd settle on calling his $400 and then raising an additional $600. That will put $2,050 in the pot and give him over 3-to-1 odds on his call, probably an irresistible number. In addition, an all-in bet at that point might start to look good to him. Consider the situation from his point of view. We started the hand with $3,260 and have so far put in $1,200, leaving us with $2,060. If he puts us all-in, we can (he thinks) still retreat with about two-thirds of our original stack. We're not committed to the pot yet, so he could still push us out with a big bet. If we bet more than $1,000 right now, it will be obvious that we're committed to the pot, and that might hold off a semi-bluff on his part. So putting in $1,000 right now looks pretty good.

**Action:** You put in $1,000, and he puts you all-in for $2,060. You call.

Perfect! Now we just have to win the hand.

**Resolution:** He shows down A♣6♣. The board comes T-8-6-5-3 with no clubs, and we double up.

# Hand 8-18

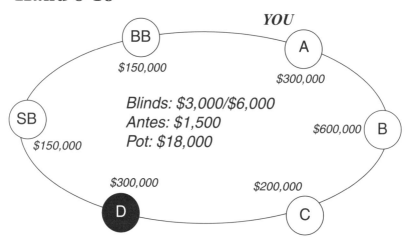

**Situation:** Final table of a major tournament. Player D is an aggressive player who has shown that he will try to steal pots with a positional advantage.

**Your hand:** A♠T♠

**Action to you:** You are first to act.

**Question:** *Do you fold, call, or raise?*
    **Answer:** At a full table, ace-ten suited would be a little weak for opening the pot. In a six-handed table, it's a perfectly good opening hand. You should make a solid raise here.

**Action:** You actually raise to $25,000. Players B and C fold. Player D calls on the button. The blinds fold. The pot is now $68,000.

**Flop:** K♣T♥3♠

**Question**: *Do you check or bet?*
  **Answer:** You've made middle pair, but with a king and a ten on board, you're vulnerable to a lot of plausible holdings. Any king has you beaten, but other high card combinations could be drawing to a straight.
  There are a couple of ways to play this hand. The straightforward way is to just bet out for about half the pot, perhaps $35,000. This might win the hand right here, and will certainly give you some solid information about your opponent's hand if he chooses to call or raise.
  A second way is to check and allow your aggressive opponent to try to steal the pot. This is both more dangerous and potentially more profitable. Given what you know of your opponent, there's a high probability that most of his bets from this position will be made with hands that you can beat.

**Action:** You actually check. Player D bets $40,000. *What do you do now?*
  **Answer:** There's $108,000 in the pot and it costs you $40,000 to call. Since Player D is very aggressive, there's a good chance he's just on a steal and you have him beaten. Easy call.

**Action:** You call. The pot is now $148,000.

**Fourth Street:** 6♥

**Question**: *Do you check or raise?*
  **Answer:** The six didn't help you, but it probably didn't help your opponent either. Having picked a strategy for the hand, you should continue with it and just check.

**Action:** You check. Player D checks as well.

**Fifth Street: 6♣**

**Question**: *Do you check or raise?*
  **Answer:** If the first six didn't help your opponent, then the second six didn't help him either. Unless your opponent has a king in his hand, you are winning right now. His check on fourth street was a mistake if he had a king, unless he's running a trap that's really deep. There's a move that some very strong players occasionally employ, which I call the "bet-check-bet" move. Here's how it works. You're holding a hand like ace-king, and you get a flop like the one we have here, king-x-x. You make a bet of half the pot on the flop, which might indicate strength or might be a standard continuation bet. Your opponent calls. On fourth street you check, indicating that your first bet was just a continuation bet and now you've given up on the hand. On fifth street you bet again, indicating that you decided the pot could be stolen, and you're making a stab at it. When this play works, your opponent calls or raises you on the end with a medium or small pair, figuring you missed your hand, and you win a big pot.
  Is this move likely to be happening here? Probably not. But be aware of it. It's a tool in the arsenal of all top players.
  Meanwhile, what should you do here? Betting out might take the pot, but checking could induce a desperate attempt to steal on the end. Having checked thus far, you should be consistent and check on the end as well.

**Action:** You check. Your opponent bets $80,000. The pot is now $228,000. It costs you $80,000 to call. *What do you do?*

> **Answer:** The call is clear, of course. The pot is offering you almost 3-to-1, and there's an excellent chance that your tens are good.

**Resolution:** You call, and your opponent shows 7♦5♦. You take the pot.

You had a good but not great hand, against an opponent who liked to steal pots. The rope-a-dope approach netted much more money from the hand than any straightforward betting could.

# Hand 8-19

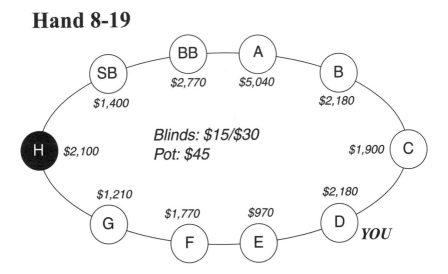

**Situation:** Early in an online tournament. The big blind has been aggressive. Player F has just arrived at the table, and you have no information on him.

**Your hand:** 9♠7♠

**Action to you:** Players A, B, and C all fold.

**Question:** *Do you fold, call, or raise?*
    **Answer:** The purely conservative play is just to throw your hand away, of course. Super-aggressive players are very comfortable playing hands like this in middle position. (If you watch some tapes of tournaments that Gus Hansen has won, you'll notice that he displays great skill handling these mid-sized suited cards.) The idea is to see a cheap flop with a hand that might amount to something, in a situation where the strength of your hand is likely to be well-concealed. I like to make this play myself, but on rare occasions.

**Action:** You call. Player E folds and Player F calls. The other players fold and the big blind checks. The pot is now $105, and you are second to act among three players.

**Flop: T♦8♣6♣**

**Action:** The big blind checks. *What do you do?*
    **Answer:** You flopped your straight, which is the best possible result for your hand. It's even better than flopping a flush, since the hand is so well concealed. Now the problem is to make some money. Obviously the hand is a perfect candidate for slow-playing, but what's the right way to slow-play? Let's look at three different approaches.

**The full slow-play: You check**. This gets no money in the pot, but guarantees that the hand will continue. You're hoping for one of four outcomes here.

1.  Player F has a little something and makes a value bet.

2.  Player F sees two checks in front of him and decides he can steal the pot with a bet.

3.   Player F checks, but a high card comes on fourth street and pairs one of the two players.

4.   Player F checks, and either he or the big blind decides to steal the pot on fourth street.

The upside of the full slow-play is that it's very likely to win one additional bet even if no one at the table has anything. The downside is that it fails to get any extra money in the pot, and it's easier for your opponents to walk away from a small pot.

**The partial slow-play: You bet $30.** Placing the minimum bet in the pot has the downside that merely by acting, you will chase everyone else away. But if that happens, it was a longshot that you were going to make much money on the hand anyway. The upside is that your bet is so small that it's easy to call (Player F is getting 4.5-to-1 on his money to call), and the larger you make the pot, the easier it is to get more money in on later rounds.

**The continuation bet: You bet $50.** This bet looks like a standard continuation bet, which might be interpreted as a stealing attempt. But if neither of the other players has anything, it won't really matter if they think you're stealing; they're just going to let you steal.

Between these choices, I think the $50 bet is clearly worst. I would only make this play if I had made several continuation bets recently, if I had backed down from a continuation bet in the face of a reraise, and if the other players were known to be aggressive. If all those circumstances were present, there might be a good enough chance that someone would go after me to make the bet worthwhile. Otherwise there's just too much of a chance that I will chase folks away.

The other two choices (check or bet the minimum) are close. Checking is almost certain to get another bet somewhere down the road, and that's my default play. Betting $30 looks like I'm making a probe bet, which is useful since it provides some cover for my real probe bets later. My top choice (by a nose) is to check, but I wouldn't criticize anyone who wanted to toss in a minimum bet.

Beginners tend to go astray in these positions because they feel that the hand is so good, they're entitled to win more than a minimal amount of money. One cruel reality of poker is that your very good hands often don't make much money because no one else at the table has the strength to come in against you. The hidden disadvantage of playing hands like middle suited connectors is simply that flops that hit you very well almost by definition will miss the other players at the table, who are playing high cards.

**Action:** You actually bet $50. Player F and the big blind fold, and you win a tiny pot.

## Hand 8-20

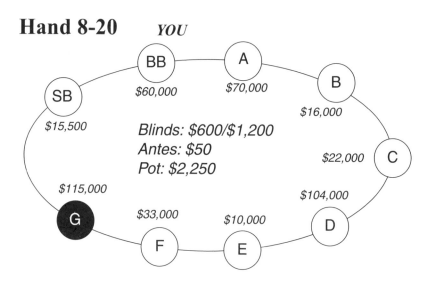

**Situation:** Major tournament, early in the second day. Player A is a savvy tournament veteran with dozens of major prizes under his

belt. He can play any style, and is known to make continuation bets.

**Your hand:** 8♥8♦

**Action to you:** Player A bets $5,000. All others fold around to you. The pot is now $7,250. It costs you $3,800 to call.

**Question:** *Do you fold, call, or raise?*
    **Answer:** You're out of position, but you have a hand, and the pot odds are quite favorable. It costs you $3,800 to take a shot at a pot of $7,250, which represents almost 2-to-1 pot odds. So you call. You shouldn't raise because the original bet came from early position. Against a player in late position who stuck in a bet, you should often put in a nice-sized reraise, since many of those players will just be pot-stealing.
    In general, you don't want to fold medium pairs before the flop if the price is at all reasonable. Your strategy with them post-flop is pretty simple. If you hit your trips (the odds are 7½-to-1 against, a number you should commit to memory), then you're a big favorite to win what will be a big pot. If you miss the flop but the flop is all low cards, you're still all right; your opponent may have been playing two high cards, in which case you're now a big favorite. If the flop comes with a couple of high cards, you'll throw your hand away. Otherwise? Be creative.

**Action:** You call. The pot is now $11,050.

**Flop:** T♦4♠3♣

**Question:** You're first to act. *What's the play?*
    **Answer:** That's a pretty good flop for you. No flush or straight on board, and only one card higher than your eights. Unless your opponent started with a high pair, or had a ten in

114 Part Eight: Making Moves

his hand, you probably have the best hand. But you can't be sure.

This is a hand that calls for some *controlled aggression*. If you have the best hand, you want to find out and make some money. If you have the worst hand, you don't want to lose your whole stack. Your problem is simple: If your opponent has the best hand here, he probably knows it. Suppose you held, let's say, a pair of kings, and the flop came T♦4♠3♣. Wouldn't you be pretty sure you were on top? And wouldn't you be thinking "How can I trap this opponent into losing all his money?" Well, that's what your opponent is now thinking, if he has you beaten.

The normal conservative play here is to lead out with a probe of about half the pot, say $5,000 to $6,000. This play may win the pot right here at minimal risk. If your opponent lays down his hand, you're quite happy to take the pot. If he raises, you're probably beaten and you'll throw away your hand. If your opponent just calls, however, you have some problems. If fourth street comes with a blank, which is likely, do you plan to bet again?

Another and more aggressive move here is the check-raise. Check now, and Player A will almost certainly bet at you. He's done that frequently in the past in response to a check. Then put in a nice raise. If Player A is still in the hand after your check-raise, then you're almost certainly beat, and you won't have to put any more money in the pot. (It takes a great player to play with nothing after a check-raise.) But if Player A is bluffing, the check-raise gives you your best chance to win the pot right here, along with some extra chips, while being able to exit the hand with certainty after any other sequence.

**Action:** You check, and Player A bets $8,000. You raise to $24,000. Player A folds.

# Hand 8-21

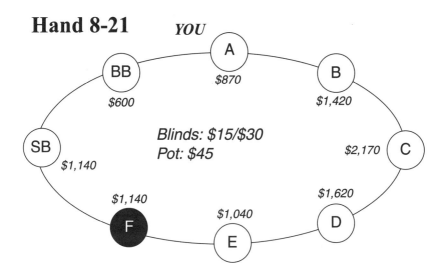

**Situation:** Early in a one-table online tournament. Player F has shown a tendency to raise aggressively in late position.

**Your hand:** K♦J♦

**Action to you:** You are first to act.

**Question:** *Do you fold, call, or raise?*

    **Answer:** A raise would be a little over the top here. Your holding is too weak for a value raise in first position at an 8-player table. There are three big stacks coming up right behind you, and you don't know what they're going to do. Your position at the table really forces you to play tight here.

    It's all right to make a slightly aggressive move; just call and see what you get for action. If there's a big raise behind you, you will fold. If you're lucky, you'll get a couple of limpers, and see a cheap flop. It's also perfectly okay to fold.

**Action:** You call $30. The three big stacks all fold. Player E calls. Player F, on the button, raises to $85. The blinds fold. The pot is now $190.

**Question:** *What's your play?*
> **Answer:** This is a close one. You're in bad position with a weakish hand and two active players behind you. You were playing to see a cheap flop but now you can't. Those are good arguments for folding. But there's a good argument for calling: You're getting about 3.5-to-1 pot odds.

**Question:** *What to do?*
> **Answer:** Despite the generous pot odds, I lean towards folding. Besides my non-premium hand, there are two additional reasons:

1. The two active stacks are both larger than me. They can eliminate me, but I can't eliminate them.

2. When players are active behind you, the pot odds you're seeing aren't necessarily the final odds. You don't really know what it may cost you to play this pot, so the 3.5-to-1 odds have an asterisk attached.

> There's another problem with your hand which is typical of hands with high cards but no ace. Since players tend to stick around with high cards, the very flops which help your hand tend to help other players' hands as well. I call this "The Tragedy of the Commons," and it means you have to be very cautious holding hands like king-queen, king-jack, queen-jack, and so on. The best flop for this hand is actually a draw to a diamond flush, which could give you a winning hand, *and a hand that you were sure was a winning hand.*

**Action:** You in fact call the raise for another $55. Player E now folds. The pot is now $245.

**Flop:** K♠Q♣J♣

**Question:** *You act first. What do you do?*
　**Answer:** You've got top and bottom pair on the flop against a raiser in better position. You should like the flop, but you can't like it that much. Your opponent very likely caught a piece of this flop. He might have a made straight, a flush draw, or some combination of a made hand and a flush draw. Your hand is good enough to bet, but you've got to exercise some caution (since the texture of this flop is very dangerous).

　　Your first choice would be to lead out for about $150 to $160. This might win the pot right here. Your second choice would be to check and call when he bets (which he will).

**Action:** You check. He bets $85. You check-raise to $325, and he calls. The pot now contains $895.

　Your check-raise was very aggressive, but you picked a poor situation. If you had just led out, you'd know exactly what to do now (he has something) but you would have paid much less for the information.

**Fourth Street:** Q♥

**Question:** *What's your move now?*
　**Answer:** You're down to $460, and the pot contains $895 at this point. The arrival of the Q♥ was a disaster — it counterfeited your jack, reducing your hand to basically just a single king. Now any hand that contains a queen has crushed you. In addition, an ace-king holding has taken the lead.

It makes no sense to bet. Given the size of the pot, you can't force your opponent out even if you go all-in, and you have plenty of reason to think you're beaten. Your best possible result is to have the hand checked down, so check and see if that happens.

**Action:** You check, and Player F bets $200. *Should you call?*
**Answer:** No. You should raise.

This looks counter-intuitive since I just explained why everything is going wrong with your hand. Indeed, you're probably beaten right now. But Player F's bet is giving you 5.5-to-1 odds, which are huge given that there's some possibility you're still best right now. The odds force you to call, but if you call now, the odds will force you to call on fifth street no matter what comes. So raise now. It won't cost you anything extra if you're in fact losing, but may make you some money if you're winning and your opponent would give up on the river.

**Action:** You call. The pot is now $1,295.

**Fifth Street: 9♥**

**Question:** *Do you bet?*
**Answer:** No. Your situation just got worse, as now any ten in his hand gives him a straight.

**Action:** He puts you all-in for your last $260. *Do you call?*
**Answer:** Yes. You're getting 6-to-1 pot odds. Call and hope.

**Action:** You call, and he turns over T♣T♥, with a winning straight.

Your opponent's play was completely reasonable throughout. He raised initially with a pair of tens. Then after the flop he called your check-raise with an open-ended straight draw. He had ten outs (four aces, four nines, and two tens) twice, so he was a slight underdog in the hand at that point. But he caught his straight on the river.

You made two small mistakes: Electing to play the hand at all in bad position, and calling rather than raising on fourth street. The second mistake didn't hurt you, but the first mistake ended up costing all your chips. That's why good players are so cautious with these face card hands which look good but just aren't that strong.

# Part Nine

# Inflection Points

# Inflection Points

# Introduction

One of my favorite films on late-night cable is an obscure horror movie from the early 1990s called *The Langoliers*, adapted from a Stephen King novella. In the movie, a small group of strangers traveling on a cross-country flight find themselves in a weird parallel universe where all the other people have disappeared. While everything around them looks real — buildings, plants, fields — it's all curiously inert. Food tastes bad, matches don't light, and sound doesn't echo.

After a few adventures, our heroes realize that they've passed through the usual rip in the space-time continuum and are now trapped in a slice of time past. It seems that as time moves on, it leaves behind dead copies of reality in its wake, and they are stranded in one such copy. More bad news quickly follows. Since nature presumably doesn't like the idea of filling the universe with infinite copies of the dead past, they are soon set upon by armies of piranha-like creatures (the langoliers) whose job it is to gobble up everything in sight. Can our heroes outrace the ravenous langoliers? I won't spoil the finish, but it's a fun movie.

I'm always reminded of this film when I get to the last few tables of a big tournament. No matter how assiduously I've accumulated chips in the early stages of the tournaments, the blinds just keep rising and rising, gobbling up stack after stack. The tournament devolves from a slow battle of subtle bets and bluffs to a breakneck race to the finish, characterized by desperate all-in moves and climactic showdowns. Very entertaining for the spectators, nerve-wracking and frustrating for the participants, who see days of careful effort obliterated in one big showdown after another.

This phase of the tournament is not without strategy, however. Players have to assess their hands in the light of the ever-increasing blinds, which means hand evaluation is constantly changing. Depending on position and the blind sizes, hands that were worthless on the first day can now become strong enough to justify an all-in move before the flop.

My term for the rules that govern this phase of a tournament is the *Theory of Inflection Points*. In this chapter I'll develop that theory for you, and show how the strategy for proper play changes as your stack shrinks in relation to the blinds. *Be advised that playing correctly around inflection points is the most important single skill of no-limit hold 'em tournaments.*

# The Problem
# of Inflection Points

A good way of thinking about inflection points in poker is by using the analogy of a football game. When the score is close and there is plenty of time remaining, a football coach has his whole range of offensive options available to him. He can call for a run into the line, a run wide, a short pass, or a long bomb. He can employ a running game exclusively, if that's his team's strength. He's not constrained in any way by the clock.

But if his team falls behind by a touchdown or two, and the clock starts to wind down into the fourth quarter, his set of options deteriorates. First he loses the ability to play a short running game. Running plays allow the clock to keep moving, gobbling up time he can't afford. Then he loses the ability to call for short passes; they don't gain yards in the clumps he needs. Next he stops calling for passes in the middle of the field; they lose too much time on the clock even when successful. In the last few seconds, his choices are reduced to a single play — the Hail Mary bomb into the end zone.

The problem of inflection points in a poker tournament is very similar to the problem faced by the football coach. As your stack withers, your options shrink. How quickly do they shrink? Before we answer that question, let's take a look at the two key ratios that govern short-stack play.

# The Strong Force
# and the Weak Force:
## Magriel's M and Harrington's Q

The most important single number that governs your play toward the end of tournaments is M, which is simply *the ratio of your stack to the current total of blinds and antes*. This number is crucial, and you must develop a facility for calculating it quickly and easily at the table. You don't need to know it to two decimal places; a rough approximation will work just fine, but you need to know your M at all times. Here are a few examples:

**Example 1. Nearing the end of a major tournament. The blinds are now \$100/\$200, and the antes are \$25. Nine players remain. Your stack is \$1,600.** *What is your M?*
    **Answer:** With nine players left, there are \$225 in antes in addition to the blinds, so the total amount of the blinds and antes is \$525 per hand. Your M is \$1,600/\$525, which is about 3.

**Example 2. Nearing the end of a major tournament. The blinds are \$5,000 /\$10,000. The antes are \$1,000. Ten players remain. You have \$170,000 in your stack.** *What is your M?*
    **Answer:** Each pot now contains \$5,000 + \$10,000 + \$10,000, or \$25,000. Your M is 170,000/25,000, which is a little less than 7. (When I'm doing these figures at the table, I never actually do any divisions; I've always found that multiplication is much easier. Six times \$25,000 is \$150,000, and seven times \$25,000 is \$175,000. So my \$170,000 is between 6 and 7 times the blinds and antes, but closer to 7 than 6. That's good enough for practical purposes.)

**Example 3. Nearing the end of a large multi-table online tournament. The blinds are $3,000/$6,000, with $500 antes. Eight players remain. The four players who will act after you have the following chip stacks:**

> **Player A**    **$150,000**
>
> **Player B**    **$75,000**
>
> **Player C**    **$40,000**
>
> **Player D**   **$225,000**

*What is each player's M?*

Answer: Knowing your own M is good but ideally you'd like to know (roughly) the M of other players at the table, especially the ones behind you, so you have some idea of the pressure they're under from the blinds. In this case the sum of the blinds and antes is $13,000, so the calculation for each player would go as follows: (I'll drop off the thousands to make the numbers easier to use)

> Player A        150/13 = about 12
>
> Player B         75/13 = about 6
>
> Player C    40/13 = a little more than 3
>
> Player D   225/13 = a little more than 17

What M tells you is the number of rounds of the table that you can survive before being blinded off, assuming that you play no pots in the meantime. It's an incredibly important number, and you'll need to be making these simple little calculations constantly at the end of a tournament. As your M drops, your play needs to get more and more aggressive. But your aggression has to be selective, and in fact there are certain hands which are very playable at high Ms but unplayable at lower Ms. I like to refer to M as the "strong force." It's the dominant idea which governs your play at the ending stages of tournaments.

The idea of M had been floating around the poker world for a long time, but players didn't have a simple name for it until Paul Magriel started calling it "M," which sounded right to everyone and the name has stuck. Paul Magriel, for those of you who don't know, is a brilliant backgammon player and former World Champion (1978) whose book, *Backgammon,* revolutionized that game in the 1970s and is still considered the definitive textbook for beginners and intermediates. He turned his attention to poker in the 1990s and became a fine player and thinker, whose advice is prized by many of today's top names.

There's another ratio which I call the "weak force." It's Q, which is the ratio of your stack to the average number of chips left for each player. For example, if you have $60,000 in your stack and the average player left in the tournament has $15,000, your Q is 4.

Calculating Q can be a little tricky since no one is standing around with a sign telling you what the average chip count is. But it's pretty easy to figure if you just remember how many players started the tournament, and how many are left now (information which is usually provided on screen scattered around the tournament hall.)

**Example 4. You have $60,000 in your stack. The tournament began with 650 players, each of whom started with $10,000 in chips. Only 50 players remain. *What is your Q?***

**Answer:** The unimaginative but straightforward way of solving this problem is to multiply 650 by $10,000 (careful, don't lose any zeros) and then divide by 50 to get the average. The easy way is to realize that only one-thirteenth of the field remains, so the average stack must be $130,000. Your stack is about half of that, so your Q is about ½.

Q gives you a measure of your position in the tournament relative to the other players. A high Q is good and indicates you can play a little more conservatively. A low Q is a sign you must step up the pace. When M and Q conflict, go with M; the strong force dominates the weak force.

Q is of less importance in normal, percentage pay-back tournaments, but assumes a greater importance in qualifying tournaments where several players share the same prize (usually advancement to another tournament) and everyone else gets nothing. I'll examine this question some more in Part Thirteen.

# The Zone System

You should think of a no-limit hold 'em tournament as being divided into five zones, depending on how your stack compares to the size of the blinds and antes. As you descend through the zones, your play gets increasingly constrained and you lose the ability to play in certain styles or to make certain kinds of moves. Let's take a look at what the zones are and how they affect your play.

**The Green Zone: You have 20 or more times the pot.** This is where you want to spend as much of the tournament as possible. All styles are open to you. You can be conservative, aggressive, or super-aggressive, and switch back and forth among them as you wish. All moves are available. You can watch a raise and a reraise, and come over the top of both players, and still have plenty of chips left for another move later in the hand. In the Green Zone you're a fully-functional poker player, and it's worth taking some risks to stay here.

One step below the Green Zone is:

**The Yellow Zone: You have 10-20 times the pot.** As you go from the Green Zone to the Yellow Zone, you lose the ability to play conservative poker. The blinds are starting to catch you, so you have to loosen your play. You can be aggressive or super-aggressive, but you have to start making moves with hands weaker than those a conservative player would elect to play. Oddly enough, however, certain hand types (small pairs and suited connectors) become less playable in the Yellow Zone. More about that later.

Moving down further we come to:

**The Orange Zone: You have 6-10 times the pot.** In the Orange Zone, you lose the ability to make certain kinds of complex moves that require a reasonable stack size to succeed. Here's a typical example. A player in early position raises the pot two or three times the big blind. You know from past experience that he's probably trying to steal the pot. But before the betting gets to you, another player sticks in a raise. You realize that he's probably seen what you saw, and knows he doesn't need much of a hand to take the pot from the first bettor. If you have any kind of hand at all, you can come over the top of both players. The first player will probably lay his hand down, and if your raise is substantial and you have more chips to back it up, the second player will probably quit as well. But to execute this maneuver, you need a big stack relative to the pot. If you have to go all-in to make this play, the second bettor may be able to call you just based on his pot odds, since he knows you can't do any further betting.

In the Orange Zone, of course, you have to play even more aggressively than in the Yellow Zone.

Moving down another notch, we get to:

**The Red Zone: You have 1-5 times the pot.** In the Red Zone you've lost any ability to make a bet other than an all-in bet. If you make a smaller bet, it consumes so much of your stack that you're committed to the pot anyway. In that case, you might as well go all-in, since it gives you the best chance of winning the pot with your first bet. (When your M is lower than 3, however, in most cases your all-in bet will not be enough to drive other players out of the pot. The combination of your weak situation plus the attractive odds will usually result in at least one call.)

Is there a level below the Red Zone? Yes — I call it

**The Dead Zone: You have less than the pot.** In the Dead Zone you appear to be alive but you're not. You're a pokerwraith, not a player anymore but a gnat to be swatted. You have only one move left — all-in — and when you make it they'll call just to get rid of you.

You should never allow yourself to get to the Dead Zone by having your chips blinded away. Your chances of surviving from here are so small that you would have been much better off making a stand earlier. Players arrive here only by accident. You go all-in against someone with a slightly smaller stack, lose, and bang! — you're in the Dead Zone.

In the Dead Zone you're simply looking for a spot to move in with all your chips. It's essential here to be the first player into the pot, so you must make a move before the big blind arrives. By moving first, some hands that would call you because of your tiny stack will fold because of the danger of someone coming over the top behind them. The need to move first is so great that your cards really don't matter anymore.

# More About M

As your stack shrinks, you need to estimate your M before every hand, and also maintain a rough idea of the Ms of the other players at the table. As you move down through the lower Zones — Yellow, then Orange, then Red — your M becomes one of the key pieces of information about your hand, every bit as important as your cards themselves.

Another way of looking at M is to see it as a measure of just how likely you are to get a better hand in a better situation, *with a reasonable amount of money left*. There are two dangers in being too tight in the middle Zones. The first is obvious: you stack will get blinded away. The second is more subtle: you may wait for a good hand and get it at a time when it's no longer useful to you.

For example, imagine a player who drifts through the Orange Zone, passing on a couple of chances to make a stand with a marginal (for the situation) hand. When his M finally gets to 2, his dream scenario occurs. He picks up a pair of aces, someone in front of him moves all-in and he calls. He wins the hand and doubles up. Fantastic. But now his M is about 5! He's still in the Red Zone, and still needs to double up again very soon. If he'd made a riskier move when his M was something like 7, a double-up would have taken him to 14, well into the Yellow Zone, and bought him some valuable time.

# Yellow Zone Strategy

As you move from the Green Zone into the Yellow Zone, three major strategy shifts occur.

The first shift is obvious. You become somewhat more aggressive with your high pair and high card hands, both in betting at pots and in calling bets. The pre-flop play criteria that I described in Volume I should be adjusted downward a bit, so that you will raise or call with a few more hands than before. At the same time, your criteria for calling someone else's raise will also drop, reflecting the fact that your opponent may be raising with weaker hands than before.

Be aware that not all players will be adjusting their playing requirements in the Yellow Zone. In fact, there are some players on the circuit who don't change their requirements until they hit the Red Zone! (This was even more true ten years ago than it is today.) You need to watch the table closely and see if you can recognize who is adapting to circumstances and who is not. Hand showdowns are especially important. If a player whom you know to be generally conservative shows down an ace-ten unsuited in a hand where he opened the pot from second position with an M of 13, you can be pretty sure that he understands inflection point play and has modified his game. That's extremely valuable information to remember. If he shows down a hand of normal strength for his position, it doesn't really tell you anything. He might have been willing to open with a much weaker hand but picked up something really good instead.

The second shift is less obvious. Although you want to be generally more aggressive, you must be more conservative when playing small pairs. (This is true in both the Yellow Zone and the Orange Zone. In the Red Zone, another shift occurs and small pairs become very strong.) The reason for caution with small pairs lies in the absence of the implied odds required for the hand.

To illustrate, imagine that you're in second position at a full table, early in a tournament, and you pick up a pair of fours. For argument's sake, we'll postulate that you have the following mixed strategy for this situation:
1. Fold half the time.
2. Call half the time.

That's a bit more aggressive than I advocated in my basic Volume I strategy, but it's still perfectly okay for an experienced player.

Now let's look at what happens when you call with your puny pair of fours. How do you show a profit with this play? Actually, several things have to happen.

1. You must not be raised pre-flop. If you are raised, you're going to throw the fours away.

2. You'd like some limpers. Three or four would be great, but you at least want one or two besides the big blind.

3. You need to hit a four on the flop. If you don't flop a set, there are only going to be a few freak situations where you can win the hand without improvement.

4. You need to get some action after you hit the set.

That's quite a long list of requirements. What's the likelihood that all these events occur? Let's put some reasonable numbers down and see what happens.

1. Let's group the first two categories together, and say that about half the time, you won't get raised and you'll collect a limper or two. That seems a bit generous, but still plausible.

2.  The probability of hitting a set or quads on the flop when you hold a pair is well-established: approximately one in eight.

3.  You're a favorite to get some action after you make a set, although just how much action is hard to quantify. Let's say the probability here is two-thirds.

There are random other possibilities, of course. You might make a set and still lose all your chips to a straight or flush. You might not make a set, but somehow win anyway. Let's say those possibilities roughly cancel out.

So the probability that we get the sequence we're playing for — we stay in the hand, we hit our set, and we win a big pot — is about 4 percent.

$$.04 = \left(\frac{1}{2}\right)\left(\frac{1}{8}\right)\left(\frac{2}{3}\right)$$

When the sequence happens, we need to win a big pot to compensate us for all the times we just lost our initial bet. In fact, the pot needs to be about 24 times the big blind to enable us to break even. It's a rough calculation, but the conclusion is clear: Both we and our opponents need big stacks for this play to make sense.

Early in the tournament, that requirement is not a problem. When the stacks are 50 or 100 times the big blind, we're justified in sometimes coming into the pot with a small pair, in the hope of the occasional big payoff. But if we're in the Yellow Zone with an M of 12, even a double-up won't earn enough chips to compensate for all the accumulated small losses from this play. Hence, the small pairs just aren't playable in this area.

There's another closely related situation where you have to throw small pairs away. It's the case where you are still in the Green Zone, but most of your opponents at the table have drifted into the Yellow Zone. In this case, winning all their chips won't give you the payoff you need, so once again you must let small pairs go in early position.

A similar analysis applies to small suited connectors. Like the small pairs, these hands are heavily dependent on big implied odds to compensate for the many times when the hand doesn't pan out and has to be discarded. Small suited connectors are also not playable in the Yellow Zone.

Another strategy shift that occurs in the Yellow Zone affects your choice of moves. The "longball" moves that we discussed in the last chapter now become too dangerous, because a failure consumes too much of your chip stack. Instead, you have to switch to smallball moves: get in, win the pot, but get out when you encounter resistance.

# Orange Zone Strategy

In the Orange Zone, the basic strategy constraints of the Yellow Zone continue and are amplified. Small pairs in early position become even more undesirable as opening hands. Suited connectors suffer the same fate. (This restriction applies when contemplating normal-sized bets and raises; all-in moves are different. See the comment below.) Long moves are even less playable than before; effective moves must be short and to the point. Win the pot, or get out when resistance surfaces.

In the Orange Zone, however, an old idea assumes crucial importance: *first-in vigorish*. The concept is simple enough. Whoever is first to enter a pot has two ways to win:

1. **First way:** You can win because no one else contests the pot with you.

2. **Second way:** You can win a showdown against the other hand (or hands) that do contest the pot.

First-in vigorish is not unique to the lower zones of play. It's present throughout the tournament. The main reason you can raise with weaker and weaker hands before the flop as your position at the table improves is because there is less and less of a chance that someone behind you will actually call since the number of players behind you is shrinking as your position improves. The simple way of expressing this idea is that your first-in vigorish grows as your position at the table improves, hence you don't need as strong a hand to bet.

In the Orange and Red Zones, however, first-in vigorish assumes major importance, especially in association with an all-in move. In the Orange Zone, you'll often need to consider opening the pot with an all-in move. These moves put exceptional pressure on your opponents, and in the right circumstances can allow you to make perfectly rational moves at pots with very unlikely hands. (For a good example, carefully study the chapter on "Structured Hand Analysis" at the end of this section.) When contemplating an all-in move as your opening play, small pairs become playable hands once more, as can suited connectors.

In the Orange Zone, you mostly need to conserve your chips, saving them for big moves that could double your stack. Semi-speculative moves based on good pots odds, which are perfectly appropriate in the Green Zone and to a lesser extent the Yellow Zone, become costly and inappropriate in the Orange Zone. Although the ostensible pot odds may be good, you're spending a larger and larger proportion of your chips as your M shrinks.

**Example 5. Final table of a multi-table online tournament. Just six players remain. Blinds are $1,500/$3,000 with $150 antes, so the starting pot is $5,400. The table looks like this:**

|  |  |
|---|---|
| Player 1 | $11,600 |
| Player 2 | $35,200 |
| Player 3 | $73,600 |
| Player 4 | $8,200 |
| Sm Blind (You) | $33,000 |
| Big Blind | $18,500 |

**Player 1 folds, Player 2 raises to $6,000, and Players 3 and 4 fold. The pot is now $11,400. Your hand is**

*What do you do?*

**Answer:** Seen purely as a pot-odds problem, this is a reasonable call. The pot is $11,400 and it costs you $4,500 to call, so you're getting around 2.5-to-1 on your call. Even your poor position after the flop shouldn't dissuade you from calling here in an early-tournament situation.

The real problem here is your stack. Before the hand, your M was just about 6, low in the Orange Zone. Just posting the small blind and ante has sliced your stack by about 5 percent. You should be cautious about investing in marginal hands with poor position. Instead, you'd rather preserve your stack and make a decisive move when the situation warrants. I would let this hand go.

# Red Zone Strategy

By the time you reach the Red Zone, the alarm bells should be ringing loudly — "Danger, Will Robinson! Danger! Danger!" You're now in a critical situation, and you'll have to be alert and active to steer you way back to safety.

In the Red Zone, you have very little leverage in terms of bet size. A bet of two or three times the big blind will typically consume at least half your stack, effectively committing you to the pot. As a result, there's rarely any reason to make a bet other than all-in. Moving all-in gives you the maximum chance of taking down the pot without a fight, which is your main goal anyway.

"What about a super-strong hand?" some will ask. "If you're lucky enough to pick up a pair of aces with a small stack, shouldn't you just make the minimum raise, to lure others into the pot?" In general, the answer is no. If you've made a couple of all-in moves and now just make the minimum bet, even the most doltish fellow at the table will realize something is amiss. A better approach is to hope that your previous actions will be sufficient disguise, and just go all-in with a strong hand. There's no greater delight in poker than moving all-in a couple of times with weak hands, stealing the pots, then moving all-in with a pair of bullets and getting called by someone who just won't be pushed around any more. It's enough to make up for a month of bad beats.

Your hand selection itself should be very liberal. Big pairs, medium pairs, and two face cards are of course premium hands. Now, however, the small pairs and suited connectors have regained their value, and constitute very good hands as well. The truth is simply that in the Red Zone, first-in vigorish now dominates your actual cards as the determining criteria in the selection of hands to play. If your position is good enough (say because five or six players have folded to you) then you should be willing to go all-in with all but the very worst hands. If this sounds overly aggressive (if not suicidal), remember these two salient facts:

1. Your opponents don't know what hands you're playing, or why. While you know you're playing weak hands, they have to consider the possibility that you're simply on a run of good cards. If you are called, you'll mostly be an underdog, but often you will just pull down the pot. When your M is 4, just stealing the blinds increases your stack by 25 percent, a huge gain.

2. Failing to make these plays just means your stack mostly gets lower and lower. As your stack drops, your first-in vigorish shrinks. As your M gets to the lower end of the Red Zone, your first-in vigorish drops to just about zero. That's a disaster, and you must fight to avoid it.

Here's a simple example of first-in vigorish in the Red Zone that's easily remembered:

1. If your M is exactly 3,
2. No one has entered the pot yet,
3. You think there's a 50 percent chance that your remaining opponents will fold to an all-in bet,
4. You're a 2-to-1 dog to win if you are called, then
5. You can move all-in with a positive expectation.

I call this the "3-to-1 Rule," and it's very handy to remember when you're slogging through the Red Zone.

# Red Zone Strategy in Action

Now let's take a look at just what good Red Zone play looks like in practice. Here's an actual sequence of 11 hands from the ending stage of an online tournament. There are only three significant prizes, with the money trailing off rapidly from fourth place on. At the beginning of the sequence, your situation is critical. Your M is only 2, and you're at the final table of ten players, three of whom actually have smaller stacks than you. Six players, however, have larger stacks, some of which are much larger. If you play a lot of tournament poker, this should seem a familiar situation — you made the final table, but you just have a few chips left. Compare how you would handle the situation to what actually occurs in these final hands.

**Example 6-1: In this first hand you're seventh to act. The blinds are $1,000/$2,000, and the antes are $100. The initial pot is $4,000. Here are the chip counts and the Ms of the players at the final table:**

| | | |
|---|---|---|
| Player 1 | $33,400 | M = 8 |
| Player 2 | $10,400 | M = 2.5 |
| Player 3 | $4,700 | M = 1 |
| Player 4 | $26,500 | M = 6.5 |
| Player 5 | $52,200 | M = 13 |
| Player 6 | $17,300 | M = 4 |
| You | $8,000 | M = 2 |
| Player 8 | $2,500 | M = 0.5 |
| Sm blind | $20,400 | M = 5 |
| Big blind | $4,500 | M = 1 |

This is a pretty typical chip distribution at the end of a large, multi-table online tournament. The Ms are generally low; even the

142

big chip leader only has an M of 13! Three players have Ms of 1 or lower.

In live events, the situation will be slightly better. The chip leader will have an M in the 30 to 40 range, but there will still be one, two, or even three players in the Red Zone, with the other players scattered in between. If you're one of those Red Zone players, your plays should look like the plays I'm about to describe.

### In the first hand you pick up

**The six players in front of you all fold.** *What do you do?*
**Answer:** You push all-in. With a Red Zone M, your only decision is whether you move all-in or not. Whether you push all-in or not depends on the answers to two questions:

1.  *Has anyone entered the pot in front of me?* If the answer is yes, then you need a reasonably good hand to play, a little weaker but similar to the sort of hand you would require early in the tournament.

2.  *How good is my hand?* The answer to the question is much less important than the answer to Question No. 1. I'm only folding the very worst hands here. Ten-six offsuit is plenty good enough.

Notice the question I *haven't* asked: What is my position? With a low M, your position doesn't matter much any more. The reason is that the worse your position (i.e., you're first or second to act), the closer you are to the blinds, which will chop away a huge percentage of your stack. Paradoxically, when your position is bad, you're under even more pressure to be the first player into the pot and grab your first-player vigorish. When your position is good (at or near the button), you are under less pressure to jump right in as it happens.

**You move all-in, and Player 8 (the button) calls, moving in \$2,400. The blinds fold. He shows**

**and the board comes**

**You lose the hand.**

A disaster on Hand No. 1! Not because you lost the hand, but because everyone else at the table got to see the kind of hand you were willing to play all-in. An ideal (and more common) sequence is successfully stealing a couple of pots before you get called by a better hand, then get lucky and win. At that point you've won enough chips that you can pull back a bit. Now it's back to work with a smaller stack, and with your cover blown.

**Example 6-2. Next hand, same blinds and antes. You are sixth to act with 6♠2♣. The table now looks as follows:**

| | | |
|---|---|---|
| Player 1 | $10,300 | M = 2.5 |
| Player 2 | $4,600 | M = 1 |
| Player 3 | $26,400 | M = 6.5 |
| Player 4 | $52,100 | M = 13 |
| Player 5 | $17,200 | M = 4 |
| You | $5,500 | M = 1 |
| Player 7 | $8,800 | M = 2 |
| Player 8 | $19,300 | M = 5 |
| Sm blind | $2,400 | M = 0.5 |
| Big blind | $33,300 | M = 8 |

**The first player folds, but Player 2 goes all-in. Players 3, 4, and 5 all fold.** *What do you do?*

**Answer:** You fold. Without the first-in vigorish, your hand is as worthless as it looks.

**All the players behind you fold, and Player 2 collects the pot.**

Note that the big blind made a huge blunder. After Player 2 moved all-in, the pot contained $8,500 and it cost the him only another $2,500 to call. He was getting almost 3.5-to-1 odds. Since Player 2, with his M of 1, could have moved in with almost anything, I would have called in the big blind with any two cards.

**Example 6-3. Next hand, same blinds and antes. You are fifth to act with**

The table now looks as follows:

| Player 1 | $8,500 | M = 2 |
|---|---|---|
| Player 2 | $26,300 | M = 6.5 |
| Player 3 | $5,200 | M = 13 |
| Player 4 | $17,100 | M = 4 |
| You | $5,400 | M = 1 |
| Player 6 | $8,700 | M = 2 |
| Player 7 | $19,200 | M = 5 |
| Player 8 | $1,300 | M = 0.3 |
| Sm blind | $31,100 | M = 8 |
| Big blind | $10,200 | M = 2.5 |

**Player 1 goes all-in. Players 2, 3, and 4 all fold. *What do you do?***

Answer: You fold. Without the first-in vigorish, you need a real hand to play, and queen-seven offsuit isn't good enough. Notice that on the first hand I was happy to make the initial move into the pot with ten-six offsuit, but now I'm folding a much better hand, just because the first-in vigorish is lacking.

**Player 6 calls the all-in and the other players fold. Player 1 had a pair of tens, Player 6 a pair of jacks. Player 1 survives when he makes a straight on the river.**

Although no one got eliminated (Player 6 had Player 1 covered) there was some good news this hand. Look how strong the hands were that the players showed down. While this may have been a coincidence, it may also be a sign that the players at the table require much better hands than you do to get involved. If true that's a big plus going forward.

**Example 6-4. Next hand, same blinds and antes. You are fourth to act with 3♣2♥. The table now looks as follows:**

| Player 1  | $26,200 | M = 6.5  |
|-----------|---------|----------|
| Player 2  | $51,900 | M = 13   |
| Player 3  | $17,000 | M = 4    |
| You       | $5,300  | M = 1    |
| Player 5  | $200    | M = 0.05 |
| Player 6  | $19,100 | M = 5    |
| Player 7  | $1,200  | M = 0.3  |
| Player 8  | $30,000 | M = 7.5  |
| Sm blind  | $8,100  | M = 4    |
| Big blind | $20,800 | M = 5    |

**Players 1, 2, and 3 all fold.** *What do you do?*

**Answer:** I don't play every hand when I'm potentially first to act, just most of them. Fold the trey-deuce. There are too many players left to act, and the combination of the position and the hand is too bad.

**Player 5 goes all-in for his last $100 and Player 6 raises $4,000 to chase out the players behind him. The other players fold. Player 5's seven-six offsuit loses to Player 6's ace-jack.**

Note that Player 6 could have merely called to let others in to cooperate in eliminating Player 5. In this case cooperation was trumped by greed.

We've sat out three hands in a row, but that could potentially be beneficial for us. In the first hand we were forced to show down T♣6♠. Hopefully by now some of the players will have forgotten the move, or at least forgotten that we made it, and our next all-in move might get more respect as a result.

**Example 6-5. Next hand, table now nine-handed, same blinds and antes. You are third to act with**

The table now looks as follows:

| | | |
|---|---|---|
| Player 1 | $51,800 | M = 13 |
| Player 2 | $16,900 | M = 4 |
| You | $5,200 | M = 1 |
| Player 4 | $23,100 | M = 6 |
| Player 5 | $1,100 | M = 0.3 |
| Player 6 | $29,900 | M = 7.5 |
| Player 7 | $7,000 | M = 2 |
| Sm blind | $18,700 | M = 4.5 |
| Big blind | $26,100 | M = 6.5 |

**Players 1 and 2 fold.** *What do you do?*
   **Answer:** You now have first-in vigorish with a medium-strength hand, so you go all-in and take your chances.

   **You go all-in. Everyone folds down to the big blind, who calls and shows**

**The board comes**

**and your straight takes the pot.**

Good news and bad news. We won a nice pot, increasing our stack by $7,000, but again we had to shown down a weak hand, this time nine-seven. In addition, our M only increased to 3, so we must keep fighting.

**Example 6-6. Next hand, same blinds and antes. You are second to act with 8♠7♦. The table now looks as follows:**

| | | |
|---|---|---|
| Player 1 | $16,800 | M = 4 |
| You | $12,100 | M = 3 |
| Player 3 | $23,000 | M = 3 |
| Player 4 | $1,000 | M = 0.25 |
| Player 5 | $29,800 | M = 7.5 |
| Player 6 | $6,900 | M = 2 |
| Player 7 | $17,600 | M = 4 |
| Sm blind | $20,900 | M = 5 |
| Big blind | $51,700 | M = 13 |

**Player 1 folds. *What do you do?***
  **Answer:** You push all-in again. Again you have first-in vigorish, and now your stack is big enough to seriously damage anyone at the table except the big blind. In addition, you're hitting the blinds in two hands, so your situation is worse than it appears.
  Notice that as you move from the low end of the Red Zone to the high end, you're theoretically less desperate to

attack the pot, but your stack gives you much more clout when you do attack.

**Everyone folds and you take the blinds.**

Your M moves up another notch, this time to 4.

**Example 6-7. Next hand, same blinds and antes. You are first to act with**

**The table now looks as follows:**

| | | |
|---|---|---|
| **You** | **$15,900** | **M = 4** |
| **Player 2** | **$22,900** | **M = 5.5** |
| **Player 3** | **$900** | **M = 0.25** |
| **Player 4** | **$29,700** | **M = 7.5** |
| **Player 5** | **$6,800** | **M = 1.5** |
| **Player 6** | **$17,500** | **M = 4.5** |
| **Player 7** | **$19,800** | **M = 5** |
| **Sm blind** | **$49,600** | **M = 12.5** |
| **Big blind** | **$16,700** | **M = 12.5** |

*What do you do?*
    **Answer:** You fold. Your M is back up to 4, at the top of the Red Zone. If you hadn't been so active, you might even bet here, but having played (and won) the last two hands means your opponents will be getting antsy and you're now a target. Take away their target and relax for a hand. You'll be in action again soon enough.

You fold. Players 3 and 6 get all-in against each other, and Player 3 survives when his K♦9♣ triumphs against Player 6's pair of jacks.

**Example 6-8.** Next hand, same blinds and antes. You are the big blind with Q♥6♠. The table now looks as follows:

| | | |
|---|---|---|
| Player 1 | $22,800 | M = 55 |
| Player 2 | $5,500 | M = 1.5 |
| Player 3 | $29,600 | M = 7.5 |
| Player 4 | $6,700 | M = 1.5 |
| Player 5 | $16,600 | M = 4 |
| Player 6 | $19,700 | M = 5 |
| Player 7 | $48,500 | M = 12 |
| Sm blind | $14,600 | M = 3.5 |
| BB (You) | $15,800 | M = 4 |

Player 1 folds. Player 2, who just survived last hand, goes all-in for his last $5,400. Everyone else folds to you. *What do you do?*

**Answer:** This problem has very little to do with stack sizes or Ms, but everything to do with pot odds. The pot was $3,900 and Player 2 called your big blind for $2,000 and then raised you his last $3,400. The pot is now $9,300, and it costs you another $3,400 to call, so you're getting not quite 3-to-1 on your money. Player 2 had an M of only 1.5, with his blinds coming in two more hands, so he could have raised with almost anything. On average, you'll probably be a slight underdog in the showdown since queen-six offsuit is just about an average hand, and he wouldn't go all-in with his very worst hands. But you're getting huge odds, so that's fine.

**You call, and he shows A♠5♣. His hand holds up to win.**

A bad break, as that was a way-above-average hand for his situation. You can't complain, though, since you've done well in the luck department so far.

While you know that you made this call because of the pot odds, not all of your opponents will be aware of this. Many players are too lazy to calculate pot odds on the hands where they're actually involved, let alone the hands where they're sitting out. To these players, you're just the lunatic at the table who will push all his chips with a queen-six offsuit! Always stay aware of the perceptions your plays are creating. The sophisticated players at the table will understand what you just did and see you as a dangerous opponent. The fish will see you as an even bigger fish.

**Example 6-9. Next hand, same blinds and antes. You are the small blind with**

**The table now looks as follows:**

| | | |
|---|---|---|
| Player 1 | $12,700 | M = 3 |
| Player 2 | $29,500 | M = 7.5 |
| Player 3 | $6,600 | M = 4 |
| Player 4 | $16,500 | M = 4 |
| Player 5 | $19,600 | M = 5 |
| Player 6 | $48,400 | M = 12 |
| Player 7 | $13,500 | M = 3.5 |
| Sm B (You) | $10,300 | M = 2.5 |
| Big blind | $22,700 | M = 5.5 |

**Player 1 folds. Player 2 raises to $6,000. Player 3 folds. Player 4 goes all-in. Players 5, 6, and 7 all fold.** *What do you do?*

> **Answer:** Fold, of course. Someone is serious about this hand and it's sure not you.

**The big blind folds and Player 2 calls. Player 2 shows A♦T♣, and Player 4 shows a 9♥9♠. The nines hold up.**

The small stacks are winning all these confrontations, so the table is not shrinking.

**Example 6-10. Next hand, same blinds and antes. You are on the button with 6♦4♣. The table now looks as follows:**

| | | |
|---|---|---|
| Player 1 | $13,000 | M = 3 |
| Player 2 | $6,500 | M = 1.5 |
| Player 3 | $36,700 | M = 9 |
| Player 4 | $19,500 | M = 5 |
| Player 5 | $48,300 | M = 12 |
| Player 6 | $13,400 | M = 3.5 |
| You | $9,200 | M = 2.5 |
| Sm blind | $20,600 | M = 5 |
| Big blind | $12,600 | M = 3 |

**Players 1 through 6 all fold.** *What do you do?*

> **Answer:** You'd like a better hand than six-four offsuit in this spot, but that's what you got dealt. The situation, with six players already out and no callers yet, is just too good to fold. Go all-in, and see if anyone will call you. Remember that your stack is plenty big enough to hurt the players behind you, so they will be cautious.

**The blinds fold, and you take the pot.**

A quick win with no cards boosts your stack by almost 50 percent.

**Example 6-11. Next hand, same blinds and antes. You are on the cutoff seat with**

**The table now looks as follows:**

| | | |
|---|---|---|
| Player 1 | $6,400 | M = 1.5 |
| Player 2 | $36,600 | M = 9 |
| Player 3 | $19,400 | M = 5 |
| Player 4 | $48,200 | M = 12 |
| Player 5 | $13,300 | M = 3.5 |
| You | $13,000 | M = 3.5 |
| Player 7 | $19,500 | M = 5 |
| Sm blind | $10,500 | M = 2.5 |
| Big blind | $12,900 | M = 3 |

**Players 1 through 5 all fold.** *What do you do?*

    **Answer:** Finally you pick up a semi-real hand. You go all-in, of course, but now your previous play has put you in a good position, as you might actually get called by a weaker hand.

**The button and the blinds fold. You take down another $3,900 pot, and your chip stack reaches $16,800, with an M over 4.**

We'll end our little Red Zone movie at this point. You survived a difficult stretch, teetering on the brink of elimination most of the time, and pulled up to fifth place out of nine players.

The summary of the 11 hands looks like this:

1.  You folded five hands, mostly when someone entered the pot ahead of you.

2.  Three times you went all-in and were not called.

3.  Twice you went all-in and were called. Both times you were an underdog when called. You won one, and lost the other to a small stack.

4.  Once you called an all-in from the big blind with great pot odds; again you were an underdog and lost.

This was not a very unusual sequence in these situations. Your best hand was only a king-jack offsuit. You won more than half of your all-ins when no one called you. You were never a favorite when you were involved in a showdown, but your two losses were to stacks smaller and more desperate than you. Most important, you survived and moved up to the middle of the pack.

# Some Other Examples
# of Inflection Point Play

In the Yellow and Orange Zones, many tough decisions revolve around how to raise a pot. Will you make a straight raise of a few times the big blind, or push all-in instead? Here's an example of that kind of decision-making in action.

**Example 7. An hour or so into a multi-table online tournament. Blinds are currently $25/$50, but in a few hands they will rise to $50/$100. Your stack is $1,180, and you're in the big blind. Players began with $1,500, and at this point the average stack is a little over $2,000.**

Before you start a hand with a short chip stack, you want to review your M and perhaps your Q as well. With the blinds totaling $75, your M is about 15, right in the middle of the Yellow Zone. In a few hands, however, the blinds will double and your M will shrink to between 7 and 8. In addition, your Q is about ½, so on all counts you're looking to make some sort of a move.

**You're at a full table of ten players. The first five players fold. The sixth player to act, with a stack of $3,500, makes a minimum raise to $100. The button (stack of $3,300) calls, as does the small blind (stack of $1,700). The pot is now $350, and it's your turn to act. You have**

Your first reaction should be that this is a great result for you, with three other players in the pot and no one indicating great strength. This is actually one of my favorite tournament situations — you have a legitimate hand, and the potential squeeze play against multiple opponents magnifies the strength of your hand.

Calling is out of the question; your tens are probably best right now, but are unlikely to be best after taking a flop against three opponents. You need to narrow the field to a single opponent. Your only decision now is whether to make a modest raise ($500 to $600), or go all-in. With tens, I strongly advocate the all-in move. Winning a decent sized pot right here is not a bad result for you, and your stack is big enough so you still have the leverage to push out any non-premium hands. If my pair were aces, kings, or queens, a smaller bet looks right. I'll still probably chase out a couple of players, but someone might read my hesitancy to go all-in as weakness, and look me up. If my pair drops as low as jacks, however, I want to chase people away.

If I do get a call, I'm still pretty happy. I'll have at worst slightly the better of a coin-flip situation, with some dead money in the pot giving me some extra odds. Once your M drops toward the Orange Zone, *that's a great result for you*. Don't get cute and imagine that you can creep back into contention with some artful bluffs and pot-stealing. You're going to have to double up in an all-in situation, and you're going to have to do it more than once. That's what inflection point play is all about — picking the right moment for your all-in moves. You're either going to get a decent amount of money in front of you, or you're going to get knocked out. This problem shows a perfect moment.

**You move all-in, and everyone folds. You take the pot**.

If your M were high here, the best play would still be a healthy raise, to something like $600 to $800, which should narrow the field to a single opponent. If they do call, I'm willing to accept being out of position with a pair of tens.

# Playing
# Styles in the Endgame

In Volume I a lot of time was spent discussing the three main playing styles in no-limit hold 'em: conservative, aggressive, and super-aggressive. I described the kinds of starting hands that each style requires and the problems that players of different styles typically encounter after the flop.

At this point, you might well wonder how players of each style approach the problems of the endgame. The answer is surprising to many people: No matter which style you naturally play, your approach to endgame problems will be very similar. The rising blinds and your shrinking stack size will force you to play in a super-aggressive way. Players who naturally play in a super-aggressive style tend to adapt more naturally and quickly to endgame problems, which I think is the main reason their tournament results tend to be better than players whose natural style is tighter. But by and large, the problems of the endgame tend to be problems of technique, not style. Just as there are no atheists in foxholes, there are no conservative players at the tail end of tournaments. Someone who's waiting for premium starting hands with a short stack isn't playing conservatively, he's just playing badly.

When good players get together and argue about an endgame problem, it's usually an argument about degree and balance. For instance, consider this problem. You're down to the last 40 players in a tournament, spread around four tables. You have to act under the following conditions:

1.    Your hand is T♠9♠.
2.    Your M is 7.
3.    You're fourth to act, and three players have folded in front of you.

4.  The players behind you are mostly tight, with one big stack
    and one very small stack.

*Do you go all-in, or just make a normal-sized raise, or fold?*

**Answer:** Any good player would agree that you're very close
to the point where you want to take a reasonable hand and
make a move with it. The argument would be whether or not
the circumstances described make this the right time to act,
or are the conditions not quite strong enough, and you should
wait. Is ten-nine suited good enough, or do you need, say,
queen-jack? Is 7 a low enough M, or would your M need to
be 5 to move here? Does the presence of an even more
desperate small stack behind you discourage you from acting,
or would you like to move here to take him out? These are
the real questions players ask themselves.

The characteristic endgame blunder made by players
who are both tight and weak is waiting too long to pull the
trigger. There's some hidden value in moving all-in sooner
rather than later. Let's look at that value a little more closely.

# Beware the Great Overthink

A desire to be brilliantly clever has undone many a poker player. Most small-stack play is pretty obvious and straightforward once you understand the role played by M in determining your strategy. However, it's possible to overthink some situations, with tragic results. Warning: What you are about to see may be disturbing to some viewers.

**Example 8. Final table, five players remain, all very experienced. Blinds are $15,000 and $30,000. You are the small stack with $160,000 in second position. The big blind, a conservative player, has about $240,000. The other three stacks range from $200,000 to $500,000. The first player folds. You pick up T♦T♣. *What do you do?***

**Answer:** Your M is just under 4 and you have an excellent hand. The best play is to go all-in and try to pick up the blinds. The second-best play is to call, looking for action by hoping to trap someone into putting you all-in. This would be a great play with aces, kings, or queens, but tens are just a little weak for this purpose. But it's an aggressive play and can't really be criticized too much.

**You actually just call with your pair of tens. The button and the small blind fold. The big blind goes all-in. *What do you do?***

**Answer:** You call, of course. What happened is exactly what you wanted when you initially called with your pair of tens. Someone moved all their chips in the pot and you're sitting there with the fifth-best (maybe sixth behind ace-king suited) starting hand in hold 'em. If you're going to check a strong hand hoping you can trap someone, and they move all-in against you, then you have to call. If you need even more reason, you're being offered attractive pot odds. The pot now contains $235,000 ($45,000 from the blinds, $30,000 from your call, and $160,000 from the big blind) and it costs you $130,000 to call, representing odds of 1.8-to-1.

In fact, Player 2 thought for quite a while before folding. You'll sometimes see this happen when players decide, for whatever reason, that their opponent just "has" to have a high pair. In the early stages of a tournament you can occasionally make a reasonable fold like this. In the endgame, when Ms are low, you virtually never can. Consider all the possible scenarios that could account for the big blind's all-in raise:

1. The big blind has two high cards and is betting for value. He thinks your call indicates weakness and puts you on a hand like a low pair or suited connectors.

2. The big blind has a medium pair and, as before, thinks that your call represents a drawing hand.

3. The big blind has a low pair and thinks he is a favorite against your likely two high cards.

4. The big blind has ace-x and thinks his M of 6 justifies an all-in move.

5. The big blind has nothing but thinks you can be bluffed out.

6. The big blind has a high pair and is betting for value.

Note that only Scenario No. 6 justifies laying down your hand.

# Structured
# Hand Analysis (SHAL)

Most poker opinions are formulated from a combination of experience and intelligent guesswork. Consider problems like the following:

1.  "I'm at an eight-handed table, in third position with ace-jack suited. My M is down to 5. The players behind me have been tight. There's one stack even smaller than mine. He's getting desperate. Am I strong enough to push all-in here?"

2.  "I'm in the big blind at a six-handed table. I'm holding king-ten offsuit. The guy in first position went all-in. His M was 4. I think he was desperate, but I'm not sure. I've got plenty of chips. Is my hand good enough to call?"

These are tough questions. If you went to a poker tournament and posed these questions to a collection of good players, you'd get a bunch of reasonably informed opinions, based loosely on their experiences over the years. (Most would answer "no" to both questions.) But when you were done, would you really know anything?

Actually, you wouldn't. Guesswork, even informed guesswork from strong players, isn't the same as real knowledge. In poker, as in every other area of human endeavor, the considered opinions of a collection of the world's best practitioners might be right, but it might also be quite wrong. The consensus of what is considered true seems obvious and inevitable until some brave soul comes along and says "No, the truth is really like this."

In this section, I'll show you a way to get beyond opinion and guesswork and figure out some real answers to tough problems.

It's a method I call Structured Hand Analysis (SHAL for short). SHAL gives us a way of actually calculating answers to a variety of endgame problems. It's especially useful in resolving all-in problems of the sort posed at the beginning of this section, but it's useful for others as well. To give you the idea, I'm going to pose a question and work through the answer in a step-by-step fashion.

Before we get started, however, there's a caveat. SHAL isn't a method that you can use at the poker table. It's a technique for posing and solving problems at home, when you're out of the action. You'll need time, some facility with using a spreadsheet like Excel, and one of the programs that lets you input a couple of starting hands and gives you the probability that each hand triumphs in a showdown. (I like *PokerWiz*, but there are others.) If you're willing to put in the time and effort, and you enjoy noodling over numbers for an hour or two, you'll be able to figure out things that no one else knows. If that kind of work doesn't appeal to you, no harm done. Just skip this section and move on to the problems at the end of the chapter. If the thought of exploring the dark corners of poker and discovering hidden treasures is intriguing, then let's get to work.

We'll start by considering a sample problem.

**Example 9. It's the final table of a major tournament. Nine players remain. The blinds are \$3,000/\$6,000, with \$300 antes, so the pot is \$11,700 to start. You're fifth to act, with a stack of \$90,000 after posting the ante. The first four players all fold.**

**You pick up**

The four players yet to act behind you are a mixture of tight and loose. All have stacks slightly larger than yours, although none are very much larger. You briefly contemplate moving all-in with your ten-eight offsuit since you've been playing tight for awhile and no one would have any reason to suspect you'd be making a play. But your better judgment prevails and you muck your hand.

The cut-off seat, the button, and the small blind now fold, and the big blind takes the pot. Again you wonder, should I have made a play with that hand? And if not, *how good a hand did I need to make a play?*

> **Answer:** We've really posed two questions here, one specific (what happens if I go all-in with T♦8♠?) and one more general (what's the minimum hand I need to make going all-in a profitable move?). We'll start by trying to answer the specific question. It's easier, and it's also possible the answer to the specific question will contain a big clue to the answer to the general question.
>
> Our first step is to build a profile of the four players who act behind us. In our first statement of the problem, we just described them as a mixture of "tight and loose." Now we need to get more detailed, which will also necessarily involve a little guesswork and speculation. Let's say that the cut-off seat player is rather tight, as is the player in the big blind. Let's say that the button is a considerably looser player, and the small blind is the loosest of all. From now on we'll refer to these players as A, B, C, and D, in order from the cut-off seat to the big blind.
>
> To finish our profile, we're going to write down the specific hands that each player would use to call an all-in bet. Here are my guesses:
>
> - Player A (tight): Will call all-in with AA through QQ, and AK (suited or unsuited).

- Player B (looser): Will call all-in with AA through 99, AK and AQ (suited or unsuited).

- Player C (loosest): Will call all-in with any pair, AK, AQ, AJ, and KQ (suited or unsuited).

- Player D (tight): Same requirements as Player A.

Do these estimates make sense? I think so, although a reasonable person could certainly argue about the exact distribution of calling hands. Remember we specified that each player had a stack slightly larger than ours, although not enormously larger. Since our stack is $90,000, our M is about 8. These four players will have bigger Ms, let's say in the range of 8 to 11. None of them should feel particularly desperate, and since we specified that we'd been playing tight, no one has any reason to think that we're moving in with other than a good hand.

Now that we have our player profiles, the next step is to figure out how often we'll be called, and by whom. This is pretty easy. We know there are 1,326 possible poker hands (52 times 51 divided by 2). Once two cards are removed, however, (in this case our ten and eight) the remaining fifty cards form only 1,225 hands. For every pair, there are six possible ways of dealing the pair. For every non-pair, there are 16 possible ways of dealing the hand, 12 unsuited and four suited. Let's start with player A and figure out how often he will call.

**Player A's Number of Possible Hands**

| | |
|---|---|
| AA | 6 |
| KK | 6 |
| QQ | 6 |
| AKs | 4 |
| AKo | 12 |
| **Total** | **34** |

Of the 1,225 possible hands, only 34 are calling hands for Player A. So the probability that Player A calls our bet is 2.8 percent.

$$.028 = \frac{34}{1,225}$$

We can do the same calculation for Players B, C, and D. I won't list them separately, but here are the answers:
- Player B: 65 calling hands or 5.3 percent
- Player C: 136 calling hands or 11.1 percent
- Player D: Same as A or 2.8 percent

Now we'll make an assumption which is just slightly inaccurate, but which simplifies the calculations enormously. We'll assume that only one person will call us. With that assumption in place, here's how the hand will turn out:
- Player A calls: 2.8 percent
- Player B calls: 5.3 percent
- Player C calls: 11.1 percent
- Player D calls: 2.8 percent
- No one calls: 78.0 percent

So almost 80 percent of the time we pull down the pot uncontested. The rest of the time we get called by somebody.

Now we're ready for the next step of the problem, figuring out how often we win against each opponent, assuming that we're called. Let's start with Player A (the easiest case).

Our first job is to figure out how often our ten-eight offsuit actually wins in a showdown against the five possible different hands that Player A might hold. (This is where we need a program that calculates the results for two hands matched against each other in a showdown.) Again, we'll make a simplifying assumption that is slightly inaccurate, but makes our work much easier. It affects the calculation a little bit if the suits of our cards match the suits in his hand, or if just one suit matches, or none. For simplicity's sake, just assume the suits don't match. Now it turns out that our T♦8♠ wins 18 percent of the time against his aces, 17 percent against his kings, 16 percent against his queens, 34 percent against ace-king suited, and 36 percent against ace-king offsuit.

Now we construct a chart that looks like this:

| A's Hand | Hand Count | Probability of Hands | |
|---|---|---|---|
| | | Winning | Won |
| AA | 6 | 0.18 | 1.08 |
| KK | 6 | 0.17 | 1.02 |
| QQ | 6 | 0.16 | 0.98 |
| AKs | 4 | 0.34 | 1.36 |
| AKo | 12 | 0.36 | 4.32 |
| Total | 34 | | 8.74 |

The winning percentage is 25.7.

$$.257 = \frac{8.74}{34}$$

The first line of this table, for instance, shows that Player A has six ways of being dealt a pair of aces, that we are 18 percent to win if he holds aces, and the average number of hands we win out of six is just 1.08 hands. Adding up the hands won in each category gives us, on average, 8.74 hands won out of 34 total hands, for a winning percentage of 25.7 percent. On average, if Player A does call us, we win only about one hand in four.

Player D's chart looks exactly like Player A's, of course. The charts for Players B and C are more extensive, since they call with more hands. Against Player B, we end up winning 26.7 percent, and against Player C's loose calling, we actually win 34.3 percent.

Now we're ready to put together a final chart, combining the probability that each player calls us, the probability that we win if they call, and the size of our stack if they call and we win. (If they call and we lose, our stack unfortunately goes to zero since everyone has us covered.) I'll lay out the final chart, then explain what the various entries mean.

| Event | Probability | Stack After Play | Expectation |
|---|---|---|---|
| No call | 78.0% | $101,700 | $79,326 |
| A calls, I win | 0.7% | $191,700 | $1,342 |
| A calls, I lose | 2.1% | $0 | |
| B calls, I win | 1.4% | $191,700 | $2,684 |
| B calls, I lose | 3.9% | $0 | |
| C calls, I win | 3.8% | $188,700 | $7,171 |
| C calls, I lose | 7.3% | $0 | |
| D calls, I win | 0.7% | $185,700 | $1,342 |
| D calls, I lose | 2.1% | $0 | |

**Expectation if all-in: $91,865**
**Expectation if fold: $90,000**

The first column, "Event," just lists the various possible outcomes of the hand. The second column, "Probability," shows the probability of the events in the first column. The most likely outcome, as we have seen, is that all players fold and you take the pot (first line). The second and third lines show what happens when Player A calls. Note that the sum of the probability that A calls and wins (0.7 percent) and the probability that A calls and loses (2.1 percent) add to 2.8 percent, which we already calculated was the probability that A called, given his mix of calling hands. The same is true for Players B, C, and D.

The third column, "Stack After Play," shows the size of your stack if the event in the first column happens. In the case where no one calls, for instance, your new stack becomes your old stack ($90,000) plus the existing pot ($11,700), which equals $101,700. In the other cases where you are called and win, your stack more than doubles, although you win a little less from Players C and D since they were in the blinds and had already contributed some money to the pot.

The last column, "Expectation," is the key. To find the expectation for a given event, multiply the probability in column 2 by the stack size in column 3, giving the expectation in column 4. By adding all the expectations for all possible events, you get the expectation for the play itself (going all-in). At the bottom of the table, you can see that the expected value of your stack after the play is $91,865. Now compare that to your expectation if you fold instead, which is just the size of your current stack, or $90,000. The comparison shows that going all-in is a positive expectation play (meaning the play *earns* money, rather than *loses* money), with an average earn of $1,865.

That's a pretty startling result, so let's take a step back and see just what we think we have learned.

We began by trying to solve two problems: Was moving all-in with a ten-eight offsuit in fifth position a good play, and what was the minimum hand we needed to go all-in from that position? If our assumptions were correct, we answered the first question and came close to answering the second question. The ten-eight offsuit showed a small profit on average, so moving all-in was a reasonable play, and it only showed a small profit, so it's probably close to the theoretical worst hand needed.

Still, however, this is a pretty startling result, so before we jump to conclusions, let's review our assumptions and see if we really trust them.

Our key assumption is our estimate of the hands that each player would require to call an all-in bet at this point in the tournament. Once we settled on a hand distribution for each player, the rest was just straight mathematics. So let's look at those hand distributions again.

- **The tight players**. For Players A and D we specified that they would need one of the three high pairs or ace-king (suited or not) to call the all-in. Reasonable? I think so. After all, their stacks were stipulated to be eight to ten times the pot, so they weren't really desperate, and we were supposed to be a tight player, so they have no reason to believe we're making a move with other than a pretty good hand. Would you put your tournament up for grabs with a pair of tens or ace-jack after an all-in move from a solid player? I know plenty of players who would, but they're not players I'd describe as tight. In fact, Players A and D are following the strategy recommended in most poker books: don't call an all-in unless you have a really strong hand.

- **The loose player**. We characterized Player B as loose, and said that he would call an all-in with any pair down to nines, plus ace-king and ace-queen. Again, this seems reasonable for a not-so-tight player with an M of 8 to 10.

- **The loosest player**. For Player C, we specified he would call the all-in with any pair, plus the ace-jack and king-queen combinations. That's pretty loose. Would you call an all-in bet with a pair of deuces? I wouldn't unless I was way down in the Red Zone and just looking for a chance to get into an even-money situation for all my chips. With an M of eight or ten, I wouldn't consider this play. Player C qualifies as loose in anybody's book.

All in all, I'm comfortable with our description of the playing styles of our four imaginary opponents. But to get a better handle on the problem, let's look at three additional cases and see what happens. All three of these cases can be solved just as our initial problem was solved. (In fact, if you do the calculations in a spreadsheet, it becomes a trivial matter to just plug in new assumptions and get a new answer.) I'll spare you the details and just give you the final answers:

- **Case 1**: Four tight players is the best possible case. Your expectation rises to $98,524, for an expected profit of $8,524. Going all-in is now a clear play.

- **Case 2**: Four loose players is not as good as our original distribution of profiles. Your expectation is now $90,863, for a profit of just $957. All-in is still a positive expectation play, but just barely.

- **Case 3**: Four of the loosest players behind you is bad news. Your expectation dips to $85,229, for an expected loss of $4,771. Now going all-in is a bad play indeed.

Of course, these results are just what we might expect. Going all-in against loose players with a weak hand just plays into their style, since they call you with hands that aren't very strong, but are still good enough to beat you.

In short, our speculative play was able to show a profit against a mix of loose and tight players, and a big profit against tight players only. It was just the case where we faced loose players only that we were better off laying the hand down.

**Conclusions**. If this play is theoretically profitable, should we use it? The answer, as in many other plays in poker, is that we can employ the play as part of a balanced strategy, but any abuse of the move will quickly render it useless. Don't forget that we postulated in the original problem that we were both a tight player and seen as tight by the other players. The first time we use this play, they'll give us credit for making a value bet and only call with hands they regard as appropriate, given their individual styles. As we use this play more and more, their calling requirements will start to dip, and they won't need to dip very much before the play is unprofitable. However, we learned a valuable lesson and a good tactical play: From middle position with four players left to act, all with Orange Zone-type stacks, and with mixed styles, you can make a profitable first all-in move with hands down to something like ten-eight offsuit.

# The Problems

The most basic inflection point problems arise in the Red Zone. Do we go all-in or not? Problems 9-1 through 9-14 show examples of these situations.

Orange Zone play allows a little more discretion in how you play your hand. Problems 9-15 through 9-17 show a few examples.

Problems 9-18 and 9-19 show some more issues involving all-in play. Problem 9-20 discusses what to think when facing an all-in bet.

Playing small pairs and suited connectors is always a problem with small stacks. We'll look at a few examples in Problems 9-21 through 9-24. The last two problems, 9-25 and 9-26, cover some miscellaneous tactical ideas.

## Hand 9-1

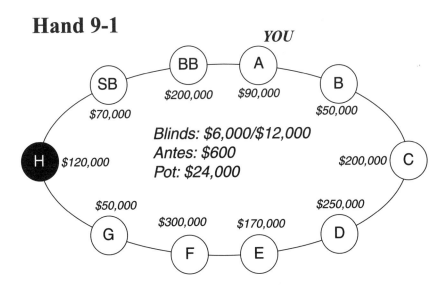

**Situation:** The final table of a major tournament. This is the first hand of the final table, and you have no information on the other players.

**Your hand:** 9♣9♠

**Action to you:** You are first to act.

**Question:** *Do you fold, call, raise $30,000, raise $50,000, or go all-in?*

**Answer:** Under normal circumstances, a pair of nines under the gun wouldn't be considered a particularly strong hand. Early in a tournament, a call or a small raise might be in order here, hoping to see a flop cheaply.

But here, the time for small bets and cheap flops is long past. You've made it to the final table, but you're not in good shape at all. Your stack of $90,000 is less than four times the size of the blinds and antes, so you'll be blinded away after only four more turns around the table. You need to make a move now, while your stack is still large enough to cause some pain even to the largest stacks at the table. I move all-in with this hand.

Am I hoping to steal the blinds, or am I rooting for a call? The quick answer is — I don't much care. I'll be satisfied if I pocket a quick $24,000 with my nines. But if I get called, I'm only an underdog against one of the five larger pairs. Against every other hand, I'm a favorite to double my stake, and get back in the running for one of the top positions. Given my smallish stack, this hand is a great situation for me, and I'm going to try to make the most of it.

Some players would play this hand quite differently. If you showed this hand to a bunch of reasonable players, you'd hear at least some advice that would go like this — "I'd make a small raise, to about $30,000. That's enough to chase out some weak hands, but if I get reraised behind me, I can still get away from the hand because I've only invested a third of my stack." A plausible argument, but quite wrong.

Suppose you try this approach. What's likely to happen? Sometimes, you will win the blinds, just as you did when you went all-in (but not as often). Sometimes, you'll only be called, and the flop will mostly not contain a nine. Now, depending on the flop, you're throwing your hand away when someone bets at you. And if someone reraises you before the flop, you're throwing your hand away as well (sometimes in situations you would have won had the hand been played to a conclusion.)

When you bet and throw your hand away, your stack is now down to $60,000. On the next two turns, you're in the big blind and small blind, which will most likely reduce your stack another $24,000, down to $36,000. That means that three hands from now, you've gone from $90,000 to $36,000. That's a disaster for you! Now any bet you make will certainly be all-in, and will be treated as an all-in bet from a very short stack — hence one that must be called. You'll have lost any ability to steal pots, which is a crucial part of your overall equity in any hand.

With that fate just three hands away, it's clear that a pair of nines in this situation is a fantastic hand for you — very likely the best hand at the table right now. You must take advantage of it, so shove in your chips.

# Hand 9-2

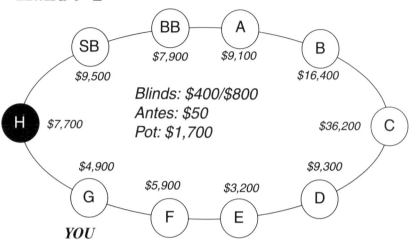

**Situation:** Middle of the second day at a major tournament.

**Your hand:** A♠7♦

**Action to You:** Players A through F all fold.

**Question:** *Do you play or fold?*

**Answer:** Here's a basic, and easy, inflection point play. With the blinds and antes totaling $1,700, your M is just under 3. Your $4,900 stack is enough to last you just three rounds of the table. You're up against only three opponents, so your ace-7 offsuit isn't even objectively a weak hand any more. You're definitely playing the hand.

How much should you bet? The minimum bet now is twice the big blind, or $1,600. That's one-third of your dwindling stack. If you made the minimum bet, then exited the hand later, you'd be even more crippled than you are now. So go all-in. Notice that the three active players behind you have Ms ranging from slightly more than 4 to slightly less than 6. Right now your stack is big enough to ruin any of these players if they call and lose, so only a strong hand rates to call you, and the odds of not finding a strong hand in three random hands are quite good.

No need to look or feel nervous when making this play. Sure, if you make it, get called, and lose, you're out of the tournament. But you're almost out of the tournament anyway, and "conservative" play won't save you.

**Resolution:** You go all-in, and the three players behind you fold.

# Hand 9-3

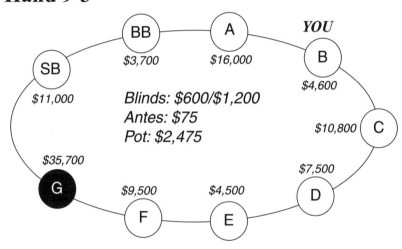

**Situation:** Late in the second day of a major tournament.

**Your hand:** Q♦6♠

**Action to you:** Player A folds.

**Question:** *Do you fold, call, or raise?*

**Answer:** Here we have $4,600 in chips and the blinds and antes now total $2,475. Our M is just under 2. In just two hands the big blind will be upon us. We have enough chips to play 13 hands, including this one.

Once you're down to an M below 2, almost anything justifies a move at the pot, provided that no one has entered the pot ahead of you. Any ace, king, or queen, or two medium cards that are either suited or connected would be enough for me to go all-in here. I'm really more interested in a situation where I am the first to enter a pot, than I am in waiting for a better hand. Two unsuited low cards are about the only hand I'll automatically throw away in this situation.

**Action:** You go all-in. Everybody folds.

# Hand 9-4

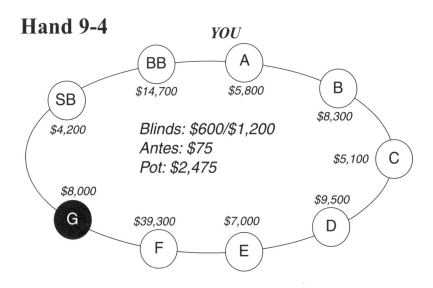

**Situation:** Middle of the second day at a major tournament.

**Your hand:** K♣9♠

**Action to you:** You are first to act.

**Question:** *What's our play?*

    **Answer:** With an M between 2 and 3, even a king is a good enough reason to go all-in. Remember that once you go all-in, you don't need to worry about position any longer — the hand becomes a simple showdown. The only disadvantage of your position is that you haven't had a chance to see anyone fold yet. Of course, this is partially compensated by the fact that no one gets to try and steal the pot before you!

**Resolution:** You go all-in and get called by Player F with a pair of tens. A king comes on the turn and you double up.

# Hand 9-5

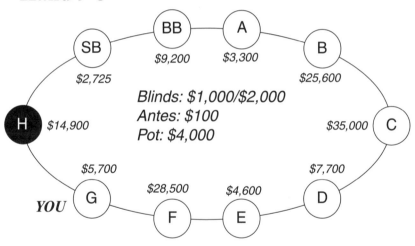

**Situation:** Major tournament, end of the second day.

**Your hand:** 8♠7♥

**Action to you:** Players A through F all fold.

**Question:** *Do you fold, call, or raise?*

    **Answer:** Here's an absolutely clear example of inflection point play. You're down to your last $5,700, and the antes and blinds now total a whopping $4,000. You've only got enough for two rounds of play, so any reasonable situation justifies an all-in move. Here we have connectors (admittedly low ones), but what's more important is that six players are already out of the hand. In addition, none of the three players left behind us have enough chips to call us with impunity. Even the button, with his $15,000, can't relish the thought of losing 40 percent of his chips, and the other two players are in even worse shape.

    Don't be fooled by the fact that you have more chips than three other players at the table. You're still desperate, and just because those players will be leaving the game in a round or two doesn't make you any less desperate.

**Resolution:** You go all-in, and lose to the big blind, who calls with a pair of kings.

    Your desperation turns out to be a lucky break for the pair of kings, who otherwise would have had the hand folded around to him.

# Hand 9-6

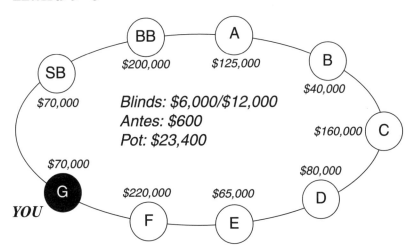

BB $200,000
A $125,000
B $40,000
SB $70,000
C $160,000
D $80,000
E $65,000
F $220,000
G $70,000 YOU

Blinds: $6,000/$12,000
Antes: $600
Pot: $23,400

**Situation:** Final three tables of a major tournament. About 28 players remain. Player C has been seen to play small pairs in early position.

**Your hand:** Q♦T♠

**Action to you:** Players A and B fold. Player C calls for $12,000. Players D, E, and F all fold. The pot is now $35,400.

**Question:** *Do you fold, call, or raise?*

    **Answer:** Your stack of $70,000 represents an M of only 3, so you're desperate. Your hand isn't great, but an unusually favorable situation has arisen. At a nine-player table, you already have five folds and one call. Player C called instead of raising, so he has a reasonable hand, but not a big pair. There are only two players still to act behind you.

    This is a position where you're looking to make a stand. Queen-ten is actually a good holding for your situation. If Player C has a small pair and elects to call, you'll just be a small underdog. There's a significant chance he'll fold to your raise — he'll need to put in another $58,000 to call — in which case your stack goes up to over $100,000 if you win the hand. If he calls and you do win, you'll be within striking distance of the leaders.

**Action:** You go all-in. The blinds fold, but Player C calls for an additional $58,000. He shows a pair of eights. The board comes T♥7♥3♦5♣A♣, and your pair of tens wins the hand. Your stack grows to $163,400.

Your M has now risen to just over 7. You still need to be aggressive, but you've bought a little breathing room.

# Hand 9-7

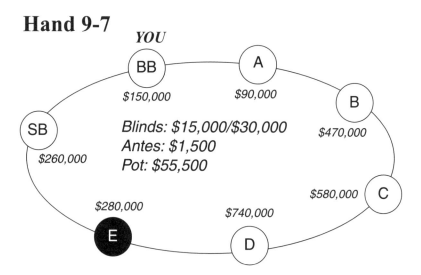

**Situation:** A major tournament. There are two tables still in play with seven players each. Player D has been on a massive rush, playing most pots for the last half hour and piling up a huge number of chips with bets that have not been called.

**Your hand:** A♣J♣

**Action to you:** Player A folds. Player B folds. Player C folds. Player D calls. Player E calls. The small blind calls for an additional $15,000. The pot is now $130,500.

**Question:** *Do you call or raise?*
    **Answer:** You move all-in here. Your hand, ace-jack suited, is reasonably strong. Your position is not a problem since going all-in eliminates any positional considerations. You almost certainly have Player D beaten, and it's unlikely he'll call your bet. Player E called knowing that Player D has been bullying the table, so his hand may be weaker than usual. The small blind was being offered 8-to-1 on his call, so he could have justifiably called with almost anything. And your M is only 3, so you have to make a move very quickly. This is an ideal situation for you and you could reasonably have gone all-in with a weaker hand than what you have. You have an excellent chance of winning a substantial pot right here, large enough to put you back in the hunt, and you'll have good chances even if you're called, as there is no indication that a big hand is out against you.

**Action:** You move all-in. Players D and E fold. The small blind calls and shows you a pair of fours. The fours hold up.

    Although you went out in fourteenth place, there is no need to second-guess your play. Players D and E laid down their hands as you expected. The small blind made a reasonable call with his fours, which were very much an above-average hand for him, given the pot odds he had been offered to call originally. Had you won, your chip stack would have more than doubled to $370,000, and you would have been very much in the tournament, contending for a high place.

# Hand 9-8

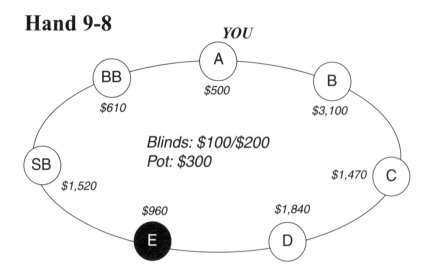

**Situation:** Toward the end of a one-table satellite. The big blind and Player B are very aggressive.

**Your hand:** A♥8♥

**Action to you:** You are first to act.

**Question:** *Do you fold, call, raise, or raise all-in?*

    **Answer:** No question here. You shove all your chips in and see what happens.

    You have $500 left and the blinds total $300, so your M is between 1 and 2, but your situation is actually much worse than that. In the next two hands you'll be the big blind and then the small blind, which will gobble up $300 of your $500. Then you'll have five hands where you won't put any money in the pot. In the hand after that, you'll be back in the big blind with your last $200. So you really only have enough chips for this hand and eight more.

    Ace-eight suited is actually a fantastic hand for your desperate situation. Since this is really the last hand where your bet can put any kind of pressure on anyone at your table, you must make your move now.

**Resolution:** Player D and the big blind call you. The flop is K♥T♠3♠, with the 9♣ on fourth street and the T♣ on fifth street. Player D and the big blind both check the hand down. Player D's pair of fives hold up against the big blind's ace-four.

Hands where two active players check the hand down after the betting in the main pot is closed are not uncommon. Since there is no money to be won in the secondary pot, there's minimal incentive for either player to put in an additional bet without a very strong hand. When both players stay in the hand to the end, they maximize their chances of eliminating you, which is almost as important a goal as picking up your chips. We call this the cooperation play, and we'll see more examples in Part Eleven.

# Hand 9-9

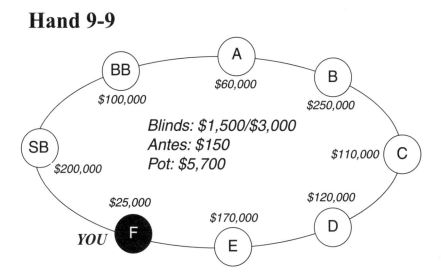

**Situation:** Late in the second day of a major tournament. Player B has been very aggressive throughout the day and has dominated the table.

**Your hand: J♥T♥**

**Action to you:** Player A folds. Player B calls. Players C, D, and E all fold. The pot is now $8,700 and it costs you $3,000 to call.

**Question:** *Do you fold, call, or raise?*
    **Answer:** Your hand is good enough for a call, especially given the almost 3-to-1 odds you're being offered by the pot. However, your chip total argues strongly for a raise, in fact for an all-in raise.
    With a chip count of $25,000, you have less than half the chips of anyone else at the table, and with the blinds and antes at $5,700, your M is just slightly over 4, so you can survive about 30 more hands. Right now your chips are enough to cause a little pain to someone if you double through them, but in a couple of rounds you'll be down to $15,000, and at that level no one will care if you get in a pot or not.
    The primary reason to move now is not the great strength of your hand but the strength of your position. Four players are already out of the pot. If you go all-in, the blinds will need very big hands to get involved, since Player B will still be able to act behind them. And Player B is known to be very aggressive, so you may have caught him without much of a hand. If worse comes to worse and you get called, jack-ten suited is still a favorite against an average hand, so you'll have some reasonable chances.

**Action:** You go all-in. The blinds fold. Player B folds. You take the pot.

# Hand 9-10

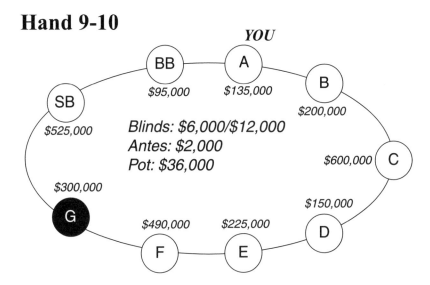

*YOU*

BB $95,000

A $135,000

SB $525,000

B $200,000

Blinds: $6,000/$12,000
Antes: $2,000
Pot: $36,000

$600,000 C

$300,000

G

$150,000

$490,000

$225,000

D

F

E

**Situation:** Down to the final three tables of a major tournament.

**Your hand:** K♥Q♠

**Action to you:** You are first to act.

**Question:** *Do you fold, call, or raise?*

> **Answer:** This is a very easy problem. At the beginning of a tournament, with an M of 50 or 100, entering the pot here in first position with king-queen offsuit would be a slightly loose play. (In Volume I it was recommended to call with this hand 50 percent of the time and to fold 50 percent.) Here, with an M of just over 3.5, it's mandatory to move all-in.
>
> Moving all-in, as opposed to calling or raising twice the big blind, gives you the best chance of winning the pot without a fight, which is what you want. Your stack is still large enough to do some damage to most of the other stacks at the table, but another pass through the blinds will eliminate more than one-quarter of your chips, after which you'll be

increasingly toothless. Besides, you may not see a hand as good as this for quite awhile.

**Action:** You move all-in. Player C calls. Everyone else folds. He shows K♣K♦. The board comes Q♥9♦7♣K♠3♣, and your two pair lose to his three kings.

This hand occurred at the end (for me) of the Commerce Club tournament in February of 2005. My opponent was Ted Forrest, one of the very best players around. I was unlucky that a pair of kings was at the table, but lucky to have had a hand as good as king-queen when I made my move with a low M.

# Hand 9-11

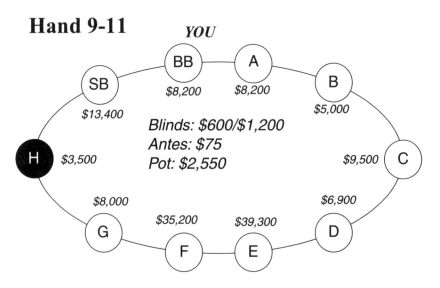

*YOU*

BB — A
$8,200 — $8,200

SB
$13,400

B
$5,000

Blinds: $600/$1,200
Antes: $75
Pot: $2,550

H $3,500

$9,500 C

$8,000

$6,900

G
$35,200 $39,300
F — E

D

**Situation:** Major tournament, late on the second day.

**Your hand:** Q♣6♦

**Action to you:** Players A through D fold. Player E raises to $2,400. Players F, G, and H all fold. The small blind calls for a further $1,800. The pot is $6,750.

**Question:** *What's your play?*

    **Answer:** Call. Your hand is weak, and the pot has been contested. (The big stack is in, and the third biggest stack has called him.) Those are both good arguments for letting the hand go. On the other side, however, there are a couple of good arguments for sticking around. All the Ms at the table are low, so you shouldn't expect raising and calling hands to be as strong, in general, as hands you would see early in the tournament. Most important, you have fantastic pot odds of more than 5-to-1. Those odds are so good (given only two opponents) that they swamp all other considerations.

    Call, and bet if your hand hits.

**Action:** You actually fold.

# Hand 9-12

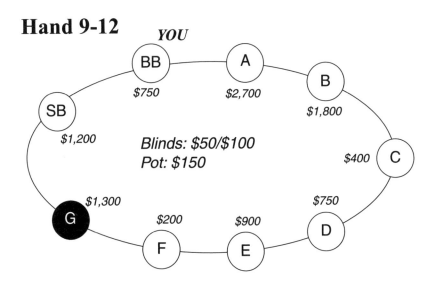

**Situation:** Nearing the midpoint of a one-table satellite.

**Your hand:** A♠2♣

**Action to you:** Players A through F all fold. Player G on the button raises to $350. The small blind folds. The pot is now $500.

**Question:** *Do you fold, call, or raise?*

**Answer:** This is a tough one. After putting in the big blind, you have just $650 left. With the blinds at $150, that gives you between four and five rounds left to play. So you're certainly eager to make a move. You have the advantage of acting last, so you see exactly what you're up against — a single opponent who acted on the button, after six folds. There's a reasonably good chance that he's on a steal.

But there are two problems. The first is that you don't have quite enough chips to put real pressure on him. If you go all-in, he'll have the option of calling for $400 into a pot that has $1,150 in it. Those are 3-to-1 odds, so unless he's sure that you're raising with a high pair, he has a trivial call with any two cards.

The second problem is that your hand, ace-deuce, is a hand you shouldn't like to play. Way too often, the deuce plays no role in the hand, so it's not that much different from just calling with a single ace. If your hand were just a little better, say ace-seven or ace-eight, you could eagerly put all your chips in the center and be confident that you were making a good move. But here you should fold and wait for a better opportunity.

**Action:** You fold. Player G takes the pot.

# Hand 9-13

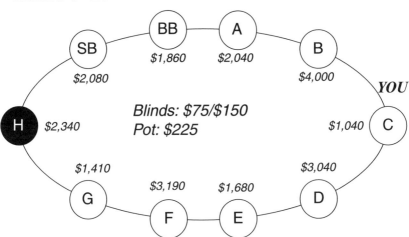

Blinds: $75/$150
Pot: $225

**Situation:** Four rounds into a multi-table online tournament. The table has been very aggressive with several players contesting each pot. Most all-in bets have been called. Your cards have been mediocre and you've played very few hands. Player A seems to be one of the few solid players at the table.

**Your hand:** T♠2♠

**Action to you:** Player A calls. Player B folds. The pot is now $375.

**Question:** *Do you fold, call, or raise?*

    **Answer:** This is a tough problem, typical of many online multi-table tournaments, particularly those with low entry fees. Your M is now just 4.5, so you're interested in making a move at the pot provided the situation is right. An active table with a lot of action, however, may not offer many good entry points. Here your hand is very weak, but Player A's call creates a couple of opportunities. An all-in raise after a call from a solid player creates more of an impression of strength than a simple all-in move from a short stack after several folds. That might be enough to quiet down some of the rabble at an active table. At the same time, a solid player is a little more likely to be chased away by an all-in move than a loose player, especially if he called with what he considered was a marginal holding.

Balanced against those positives are a few glaring negatives:

1. Your hand is really very weak.
2. Seven players are still to act.
3. All-in bets have been getting called.

On balance, I would lay this hand down. It's just too weak, and your position is bad as well. You need to pull the trigger on a hand fairly soon, but I don't think this situation is quite good enough.

**Action:** You fold.

# Hand 9-14

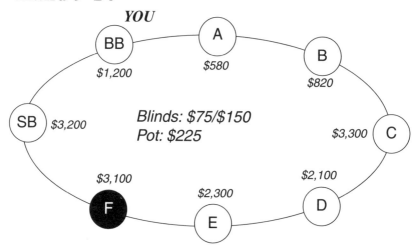

**Situation:** Two hours into a multi-table online tournament. The table has been generally tight. Player B has played quietly and been unlucky. Player E has been solid and shrewd. Most of the stacks at the table are below average for the tournament.

**Your hand:** A♦4♠

**Action to you:** Players A folds. Player B goes all-in for $820. Players C and D fold. Player E calls. The button and the small blind fold. The pot is now $1,865.

**Question:** *Do you fold, call, or raise?*

**Answer:** Your M is just 5, and you're flirting with the Red Zone. A short stack whose M was just under 4 has gone all-in. A bigger stack whose M was just over 10 has elected to call. Should you take your ace and make a stand here?

No. There are three problems with the hand:

1. Someone has already gone all-in.
2. Someone else, who was under no pressure to call, has called.
3. You're calling instead of raising.

Even though Player B had a short stack, he didn't have to make a move right now. He has something. The real problem is Player E, who certainly has something, since he's willing to play the hand down to the end. Even if he thinks Player B is making a desperation move, he still must have some cards to get in the pot.

Ideally, you want to be the first one in the pot with a short stack. That gives you the vigorish that everyone else may fold and you'll take an uncontested pot. That's big vigorish, and without it you need a hand of pretty much normal strength to play. I'd call here with ace-king or perhaps ace-queen, but not much less. With ace-four it's an easy fold.

**Action:** You fold. Player B turns over J♣J♥ and Player E shows K♠K♣. A jack comes on the flop and Player B survives.

# Hand 9-15

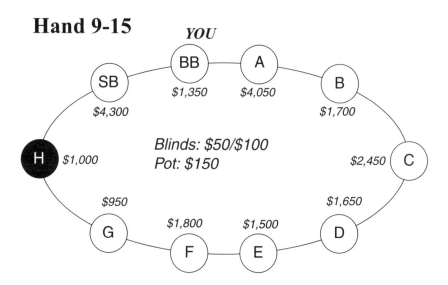

*YOU*

BB $1,350

A $4,050

SB $4,300

B $1,700

H $1,000

C $2,450

Blinds: $50/$100
Pot: $150

G $950

D $1,650

F $1,800

E $1,500

**Situation:** About 30 hands into a multi-table online tournament. The table is very active, with three to six players in every pot, mostly with calls. Many players seem to be slow-playing. There have been a few all-in bets so far, some of which have been called and some not. Players have gone all-in with not much and called with not much. You've been playing tight but not getting any cards.

**Your hand: 9♦7♥**

**Action to you:** Players A and B fold. Player C calls. Player D folds. Player E calls. Player F folds. Player G calls. The button folds. The small blind calls. The pot is now $500.

**Question:** *Do you check, raise, or go all-in?*
   **Answer:** The action here is typical of a loose, weak, small-stakes online tournament. Lots of players limping in to see

flops with two suited cards or other random hands, coupled with some explosive all-in action with small provocation.

Your M of 8 (after you post the big blind) puts you squarely in the middle of the orange zone. You have a little leverage beyond a simple all-in move, but not very much. You could put in a raise of $300, throw your hand away if you were reraised, and still have $950 left with an M of 6. That might be an option at a very tight table, where your raise could actually win the pot. At a table like this, that raise will get called by three or four of your opponents. Realistically, if you don't want to just check, you should go all-in.

Let's list the pros and cons of the all-in play.

**Position**. Very favorable. In the big blind, you've seen the entire table act and no one has shown strength. There are probably no big pairs or ace-king type hands out there, although with some slow-players at the table you can't be sure.

**Your hand**. Unfavorable. Nine-seven offsuit is weaker than an average hand, so if you do get called, you'll be an underdog to anything, even a low pair.

**Your opponents**. The players who called have the following chip stacks after making their bet — Player C, $2,350; Player E, $1,400; Player G, $850; the small blind, $4,200. Players C and E have the kind of stacks you'd like to see in a situation like this — medium-sized stacks that could be crippled if they call and lose. But Player G and the small blind have the kind of stacks you definitely don't want to see. Player G's M is under 6, so he might well take a shot at you with a hand that's just a little better than yours, while the small blind has you easily covered and may just decide to swat you. Of course, the fact that you're facing four opponents rather than one or two is also very bad news; there's simply more of a chance that someone out there has a hand and wants to play.

**The Pot Odds**. If you go all-in, you'll be raising $1,250 into a $500 pot. Anyone who wants to call you will have to call $1,250 into a $1,750 pot, so he'll be getting 7-to-5 pot odds. Your most likely holding (as far as your opponents can tell) is a medium to low pair, so anyone with two high cards would be getting almost the right pot odds to call.

**The Table**. What you've seen so far, a combination of loose, weak play, coupled with slow-playing, is the worst combination possible for making your move. Ideally you would like a nice, tight table full of people betting for value.

**Conclusion?** Only your position — acting last after a series of limpers — is favorable for making an all-in move. Every other consideration is moderately to severely unfavorable. As the old-time poker writers used to say, keep your pants hitched and your powder dry.

**Action:** You check.

**Flop: J♠9♥3♠**

**Action:** The small blind checks. *What should you do now?*
    **Answer:** That's a reasonably good flop for you. You've hit middle pair, the flop is pretty nondescript, and only one higher card has appeared.
    Should you go all-in now? Against one or two opponents, that's not an unreasonable move. Against four opponents, I wouldn't recommend it. There's too great a chance that someone is out there with a jack, or a nine that's better than yours.
    If your M were lower, say down in the Red Zone at 4 or 5, an all-in move has a lot more merit. But if necessary you can fold this hand and still have an M of 8, and that seems a

better choice than making your move right now. Just check the hand and see what happens when someone bets.

**Action:** You check. Player C checks. Player E bets $100. Player G calls $100. The small blind folds. The pot is now $700 and it costs you $100 to call. *What do you do?*
    **Answer:** With middle pair, 7-to-1 odds are very compelling. Call.

**Action:** You call and Player C folds. The pot is now $800.

**Fourth Street:** K♣

**Question:** *What do you do?*
    **Answer:** Definitely bad news as more potential calling hands now have you beaten. Just check again.

**Action:** You check. Player E checks. Player G bets $300. *What now?*
    **Answer:** It now costs you $300 to see an $1,100 pot, so your odds are 3.6-to-1. If you need to improve, you only have five outs with one card to come, not nearly good enough to justify the pot odds. Player G, with the short stack, might be bluffing, but Player E is still alive in the hand and may have you beaten as well. Fold.

**Action:** You fold, but Player E calls. The river is a 7♠, and Player E wins with a spade flush, beating Player G's pair of kings.

# Hand 9-16

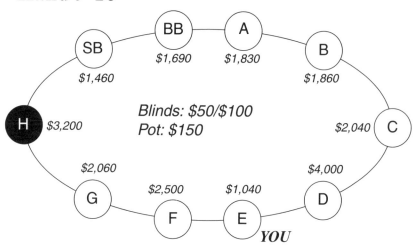

SB $1,460
BB $1,690
A $1,830
B $1,860
H $3,200
Blinds: $50/$100
Pot: $150
C $2,040
G $2,060
F $2,500
E $1,040
D $4,000
YOU

**Situation:** An hour into a multi-table online tournament. The table has been generally tight. Player A has been playing solid values. The button has been the most aggressive player. In two or three hands the blinds increase to $75/$150.

**Your hand:** T♣7♣

**Action to you:** Players A calls for $100. Players B, C, and D fold. The pot is now $250.

**Question:** *Do you fold or make a move?*
   **Answer:** Your M is currently 7, but in a couple of hands it will drop to 4.5. You're certainly looking for a situation where you can make a move. *Does this qualify?*
   In my judgment, no. Here all the relevant factors come up just a little short.

**Position:** You'd like to have everyone in front of you fold, so that at least you can be sure that some number of players are out of the pot. Here you have three folders but a caller, and the caller seems to be a player that plays real hands. Calling is weaker than raising, so he may go away if you raise or raise all-in, but you can't be sure. Right now you only know for sure that three of your nine opponents are uninterested in the hand.

**Your M**: An M of 7 is low but not yet desperately low. You're in the Orange Zone, not the Red Zone. You need to make a move, but you don't yet need to grab the first opportunity that comes along. A couple of hands from now, when your M really is 4.5, you can evaluate things differently, but not yet.

**Your hand**. Ten-seven suited is very weak. Something like queen-ten suited or king-jack suited might be a reasonable holding for this situation.

On balance, the situation just doesn't offer much. Fold.

**Action:** You fold.

# Hand 9-17

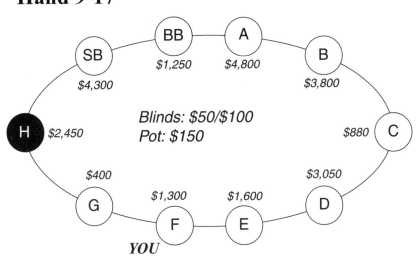

**Situation:** An hour into a multi-table online tournament. The table has been generally tight. The small blind has been a solid player.

**Your hand:** A♥8♥

**Action to you:** Players A through E all fold.

**Question:** *Do you fold, call, or raise?*

**Answer:** Your first decision this hand is not really an inflection point decision. Your M is between 8 and 9, so you're squarely in the middle of the Orange Zone, but your ace-eight suited is a good enough hand for raising at a full table with high Ms from sixth position. (In Volume I it was recommended to start raising with this hand from fifth position given that everyone had folded in front of you.)

How much should you raise? A little more than three times the big blind is a good amount. You want to make a slightly higher-than-normal raise because you're quite happy if everyone goes away.

The alert reader will note that the overall situation here is somewhat similar to our SHAL example at the end of the chapter. Here five players have already folded, and just four remain to act. Since we showed in that example that all-in with a ten-eight offsuit was a profitable move, why not go all-in here?

The answer is that there are two key differences between this hand and that example. Our ace-eight suited is a much stronger hand, so we don't have such a need to end the hand quickly. In addition, there are now extreme stack sizes behind us. Player G has a very small stack and may go all-in with almost anything, while the small blind has a huge stack and might not be frightened by an all-in move. On balance, we should just play the hand normally.

**Action:** You raise to $360. Players G and H fold. The small blind calls, putting in another $310. The big blind folds. The pot is now $820.

**Flop: T♥9♣7♥**

**Action:** The small blind checks. *What do you do?*

**Answer:** That's a very good flop for you. You now have both a flush draw and an open-ended straight draw. There are nine flush cards and six other cards to complete the straight (don't double-count the J♥ and the 6♥), for a total of 15 outs. Your aces may also be outs, but that's less clear, as your opponent could certainly have called with an ace and a higher kicker than yours.

If we give you 15 outs, then you're a favorite in the hand. David Solomon, an excellent player from Boston, invented a nice formula for calculating winning chances from a moderate number of outs: multiply the outs by four, then subtract the excess of the outs above eight to get an approximate winning percentage. Using Solomon's formula, we get 53 percent.

$$53 = (15)(4) - (15 - 8)$$

So we're slightly better than 50 percent to win, and a little more if the aces help us.

*How much should we bet?* The pot is $820, but our stack is only $940. Any reasonable bet is going to leave us pot-committed, so we might as well get full leverage for our stack and go all-in.

**Action:** You go all-in, and the small blind calls, showing 8♦8♠. The turn and river come 6♦ and A♦ respectively, and your straight splits the pot.

You were unlucky to make the straight, as the ace on the river would have won outright for you. You should note for the future that your opponent played the hand well.

# Hand 9-18

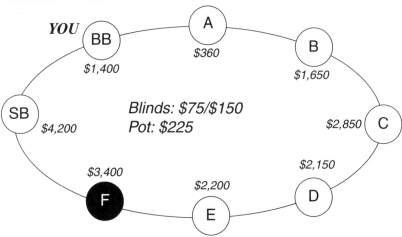

**Situation:** Several hours into a multi-table online tournament. The table is a mixture of loose and tight players. The small blind has been the table bully.

**Your Hand:** 6♥6♦

**Action to you:** Players A through F all fold. The small blind puts in $225, raising you $150.

**Question:** *Do you fold, call, or raise?*
    **Answer:** Move all your chips in.
      With an M of 6, you're not required to move all-in. You could just raise the pot to something like $600. But a pair of sixes is low enough that you don't want any action in the hand. You should be quite happy to take the pot down right

here. If you are called, you'll probably be a 6-to-5 favorite in a coin flip hand, which is a fine result for an M of 6.

With a higher pair, say nines or tens or better, you're happy with action. And you could consider a smaller raise, which then might be interpreted as weakness and result in getting your opponent all the way in the pot. But sixes is just too small a pair to fool around. You'd really like this opponent to go away.

Weaker players in no-limit hold 'em tend to get too involved with too many pots. They flounder around, calling with weaker hands, putting smaller raises, building pots where they don't know if they're a favorite or an underdog. Remember that the pot is a dangerous place in no-limit. Every hand where you get involved is another chance to leave the tournament. There's a lot to be said for ending pots quickly when you have a medium-strength hand.

**Action:** You go all-in, and the small blind folds.

# Hand 9-19

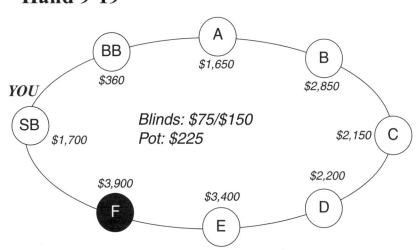

**Situation:** Several hours into a multi-table online tournament. This hand immediately follows the previous hand, and you have moved into the small blind. The table is a mixture of loose and tight players. Player F has been the table bully. Player C is moderately loose.

**Your hand:** K♥K♣

**Action to you:** Players A and B fold. Player C raises to $400. Players D, E, and F all fold.

**Question:** *Do you call or raise?*

    **Answer:** The temptation here is to call or make a small raise, trying to gently lure Player C into battling your monster hand. Resist this temptation!

    Your action last hand (an all-in raise which was not called) provides you with the perfect cover to go all-in again this hand. Players don't like to be pushed around, and if Player C has any kind of hand at all (which presumably he does since he raised with several players yet to act) *he will call you.*

    You must be alert to these situations late in a tournament. Once you make an all-in move or two with hands that don't get called, you become a prime target for everyone else at the table. If you then pick up a great hand and you act after a raiser, you will be called.

**Action:** You go all-in, and Player C calls. He shows K♠Q♣, and your kings hold up.

# Hand 9-20

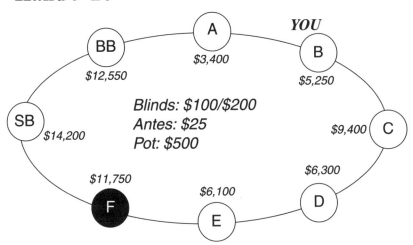

**Situation:** Several hours into a multi-table online tournament. The small blind has seemed moderately tight.

**Your hand:** T♣T♦

**Action to you:** Player A folds.

**Question:** *Do you call or raise?*
> **Answer:** With $500 in each pot, your M is just over 10. You're at the bottom of the Yellow Zone. You've just picked up a great hand, and you have to play it. Still, a pair of tens is vulnerable to overcards, as we saw several times in Volume I, so you're looking to discourage rather than encourage action. You should raise about four to five times the big blind.

**Action:** You raise $700. Players C through F all fold. The small blind goes all-in. The big blind folds. The pot is now $6,450. It costs you the rest of your stack, $4,550 to call. *What do you do?*

**Answer:** You raised just a little less than I would recommend, but it probably didn't matter, as it appears that the small blind would have put you all-in anyway.

This is a tough decision given our M. If we were down in the Red Zone I would call without any thought. Here we'll be squarely in the Orange Zone if we fold, which is not a spot I really like. But it's not hopeless to play from the Orange Zone, so we need to do a little math to see just how the odds look.

The pot odds are fairly attractive. The pot has $6,450 and we need to put in $4,550 to call, so our pot odds are about 7-to-5, or 1.4-to-1. If we can win 42 percent of the time after we call, we're on the right side of the odds. Now, what hands could we be facing and what are our winning chances against those hands?

1.  Obviously we could be up against a higher pair. Those are the hands we fear, and if we're facing a higher pair, we're only 20 percent to win. The argument for a higher pair is the all-in bet itself. But that bet is also an argument against the higher pair. If you had aces in the big blind, would you push all-in or just raise, say $2,000? You shouldn't mind encouraging action from a single opponent, but the big blind instead made a bet that maximized the chance we would go away.

2.  The second possibility is a couple of high cards. If we're up against ace-king or ace-queen, the all-in bet makes more sense. Those hands would really like to win the pot without a fight. If we're up against one of those hands, we're a 55-to-45 favorite.

3.  The third possibility is a lower pair or a bluff. A lower pair might easily believe *we* had two high cards, and think that an all-in move was the easiest way to push us

out of the hand. The same is true of an all-out bluff. In either case we're about an 80-to-20 favorite, so these two cases collapse together.

If we're up against some mixture of these three possibilities, what is a good guess as to our winning chances? Let's start with a moderately pessimistic view: There's a 50 percemt chance that he's holding a high pair, a 30 percent chance that he has two high cards, and just a 20 percent chance that he has a lower pair or a bluff. In that case, we can estimate our winning chances as follows:

- High pair = 50% times 20%, or 10% chances
- Two high cards = 30% times 55%, or 17% winning chances
- Low pair/bluff = 20% times 80%, or 16% winning chances
- **Total winning chances** = 10% + 17% + 16% = 43%

We need 42 percent to call, based on our pot odds, so this mix leaves us right on the margin.

If his chances of holding a high pair are something less than 50 percent, we slide into clear calling territory pretty quickly. We could do some more math, but it's not really necessary. We've got a borderline situation, which means we need to ask some other questions to tip our decision one way or the other. The most basic questions to ask are:

- Do I feel comfortable at this table?
- Do I want to keep playing here with a small stake, or would I rather take a chance to double up?
- Do the players seem soft or tough?
- Am I energetic and alert tonight, or tired and cranky?

Depending on how these other factors line up, I'll make my decision. Of course, I'm only asking these questions because the pot odds look like a tossup. If the odds clearly pointed one way or the other, I'd go with the odds.

**Action:** You call, and the big blind turns over J♣J♥. The board comes A♣6♦5♦7♦3♦, and your flush wins.

Piece of cake.

# Hand 9-21

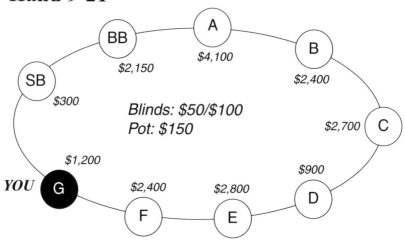

Blinds: $50/$100
Pot: $150

**Situation:** Two hours into a multi-table online tournament. The table has been generally tight. Player C has been tight. Player D has been loose.

**Your hand:** 5♦4♦

**Action to you:** Players A and B fold. Players C and D call. Players E and F fold. The pot is now $350.

**Question:** *Do you fold, call, or raise?*
　　**Answer:** Early in a tournament, with everyone having high Ms, this would be a reasonable call. (Folding would also be

reasonable). With small suited connectors, you're looking to limp into a pot cheaply and possibly flopping a well-concealed monster or a draw to a well-concealed monster.

You need great implied odds to play low suited connectors, because so much can go wrong with the hand. For example:

- A raise behind you will chase you off the hand and force you to throw away your initial bet, never seeing the flop.

- You get to see the flop, but you miss it completely and throw away your hand to the first bet.

- You get a draw, pay to see a card or two, and still don't hit your hand.

- You partially hit your hand, get involved, and lose a pot to a better hand.

- You hit your hand but lose a huge pot to a bigger monster.

That's a lot that can go wrong, so when you hit your hand and win a pot, you need to make a lot of money to make up for all the small losses.

In the Yellow Zone or the Orange Zone these hands aren't normally playable. You're limited to making M times the initial pot, and if M is small, that just isn't enough money. Here your M is 8, and you're squarely in the Orange Zone, so just fold.

**Action:** You fold.

# Hand 9-22

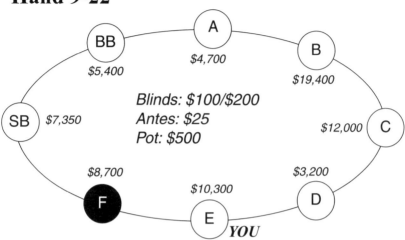

Blinds: $100/$200
Antes: $25
Pot: $500

**Situation:** Several hours into a multi-table online tournament. The table is playing a little tight, but Player B, the big stack, has been aggressive. The big blind is a solid player. You've had to sit out a long stretch of hands with garbage.

**Your hand:** 8♦7♦

**Action to you:** Player A folds. Player B calls. Players C and D fold.

**Question:** *Do you fold, call, or raise?*

> **Answer:** Your M is a bit over 20, so you're still in the Green Zone, although just barely. In the Yellow and Orange Zones I throw away low to medium suited connectors, for the reason discussed earlier. I just can't be sure of winning enough money when I hit the hand to compensate for all the small bets I'll lose when the hand doesn't come through.
>
> It's perfectly acceptable to throw the hand away here as well, but calling is all right too. Notice that in addition to being in the Green Zone yourself, the only other player in the

pot has you covered, so if you do make a big hand you will have a chance to double your stack. And the fact that you've sat out a long stretch of hands might lend some credibility to a later bluff.

**Action:** You call. Player F and the small blind fold. The big blind checks. The pot is now $900.

**Flop:** A♦T♥6♣

**Action:** The big blind and Player B check. *What do you do?*
  **Answer:** This is a bad flop for your hand. The ace is a dangerous card obviously, and as I previously explained, the ten is a dangerous card as well since it feeds into so many straights. The only bright spots are that a third diamond appeared, giving you an outside chance at a flush, and you now need a nine to hit an inside straight.

  Both players checked to you, however. Should you try to steal the pot?

  Absolutely not. There are two important reasons:

1.  You should be very suspicious that neither player bet at this flop. While it's possible they were both calling with low pairs, this flop should have helped someone at the table. After a dangerous flop and two checks, your immediate reaction should be that someone's slowplaying.

2.  You don't want to take yourself off the hand. A nine on the turn will give you a monster hand, while some other cards could set you up for a big draw on the river. If you bet now and get reraised, you will have to fold, and that's a disaster when you have a free shot at a big hand. If the flop were A-J-6 instead of A-T-6, you could justify betting half the pot. Mostly you would be chased off the

hand, but that wouldn't matter much since you were very unlikely to win anyway, and you'd probably steal the pot just often enough to average a small profit.

**Action:** You check. The pot remains $900.

**Fourth Street: 9♣**

**Action:** The big blind bets $500. Player B calls. The pot is now $1,900. *What do you do?*

**Answer:** Ecstasy! You hit your miracle card and the table woke up and started betting. Doesn't get any better than this!

Now calm down and consider your next move. You have the nuts right now, and you have to get as much money as you can in the pot. With two players betting, you can afford to stick in a nice raise, as someone is likely to come along for the ride. Player B has you covered, so you hope it's him, but you'll settle for the big blind.

I'd raise $2,000 here, a pot-sized raise. That's an easy call for Player B if he has something. If the big blind wants to call he's committing himself to the pot, so if he sticks around he'll probably go all-in. That could chase away Player B as a result, but you have no control there. (The ideal arrangement for you is to have the big stack act before the smaller stack. Then the big stack could call and the small stack could go all-in.)

**Action:** You raise $2,000. The big blind goes all-in for his last $4,700. Player B folds. You call. The big blind shows A♥6♠ for top and bottom pair. You dodge an ace or a six on fifth street and win the pot.

The big blind was trapping with two pair after the flop. Had you tried to steal at that point, his likely reraise would have chased you off the hand and cost you a huge pot.

# Hand 9-23

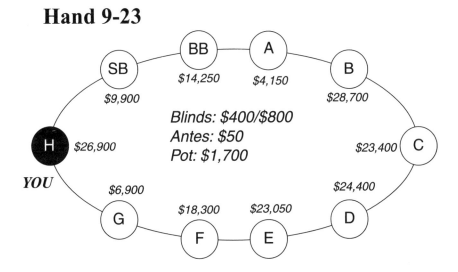

SB $9,900
BB $14,250
A $4,150
B $28,700
H $26,900 YOU
C $23,400
G $6,900
F $18,300
E $23,050
D $24,400

Blinds: $400/$800
Antes: $50
Pot: $1,700

**Situation:** Approaching the end of a multi-table online tournament. Two tables remain in action.

**Your hand:** 9♣8♠

**Action to you:** Players A through E fold. Player F calls. Player G folds. The pot is now $2,500.

**Question:** *Do you fold, call, or raise?*

**Answer:** Your M is about 16, so you're in the middle of the Yellow Zone. Suited or unsuited connectors are a hand you're reluctant, in general, to play in this Zone. Here, however, there are two big reasons for venturing a call with the hand:

1.  You're on the button, so you will have position after the flop.

2.  It costs you $800 to see a $2,500 pot, so you're getting better than 3-to-1 odds. Those are compelling odds, and

you really want to take advantage of those situations when they arise.

Note the role played by the antes in this decision. If there were no antes, the pot would only be $2,000, and you'd be getting only 2.5-to-1 to call. With nine-eight offsuit, that would make the difference in my mind between calling and folding. By improving pot odds to all players, the antes loosen playing requirements in later rounds.

**Action:** You call. The small blind folds. The big blind checks. The pot is now $3,300.

**Flop:** 7♥4♠2♦

**Action:** The big blind and Player F both check. *What do you do?*
**Answer:** You should make a probe bet, about half the pot, in the hope of stealing it. Unlike the last hand, here you have two compelling reasons for betting:

1. You have absolutely nothing — no pair and no draw. If you are raised and have to throw your hand away, you haven't been made to sacrifice any long-run equity.

2. The flop, 7-4-2, three different suits, isn't dangerous, so it probably missed your opponents. The flop in the last hand was very dangerous, and it was suspicious that neither of your opponents was betting.

**Action:** You bet $1,500. The big blind folds but Player F calls. The pot is now $6,300.

**Fourth Street:** 2♠

**Action:** Player F checks. *What do you do?*

Answer: You tried to steal the pot but Player F wouldn't go away. Whatever he has, it beats what you have (nothing). Just take your free card.

**Action:** You continue to try to steal, betting $4,000. Player F raises you to $10,000. *What do you do?*

Answer: He's not kidding, although you should have known that before. You threw away $4,000, but be glad you still have a sizeable stack left. Fold.

**Action:** You fold.

# Hand 9-24

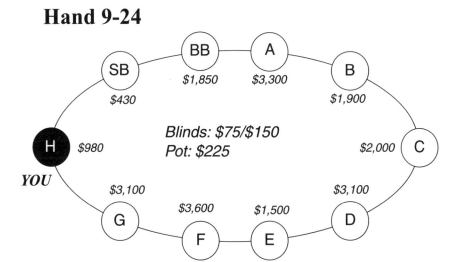

**Situation:** Two hours into a multi-table online tournament. Several new players have just joined the table, which has been playing tight. Player E has been in a lot of pots.

**Your hand:** 4♥4♠

**Action to you:** Players A through D all fold. Player E calls. Players F and G fold. The pot is now $375.

**Question:** *Do you fold, call, or raise?*

**Answer:** Your M is between 4 and 5, so you've drifted into the Red Zone. Although small pairs are a mostly unplayable hand in the Yellow and Orange Zones, they become an excellent all-in hand for the Red Zone. Note that there's no need to make less than an all-in bet here. If you try to make a normal raise of three times the big blind (normal for an early-tournament situation), you'll have bet half your stack and be committed to the pot. Just be happy with whatever leverage your all-in move earns you, and shove in your chips.

You would, of course, be happier if Player E hadn't entered the pot at all. But in the Red Zone you can't be too choosy. Player E didn't raise, and pairs can be hard to come by, so don't think too long about folding. Make your move.

**Action:** You go all-in. The blinds and Player E fold, and you take the pot.

# Hand 9-25

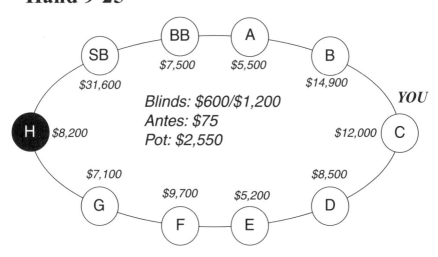

**Situation:** Major tournament, middle of the second day. This is your first major tournament, and you've arrived at this table a short time ago.

**Your hand:** K♦Q♥

**Action to you:** Players A and B fold.

**Question:** *What's your play?*
> **Answer:** With the blinds and antes now totaling $2,550 per pot, our M is 5. Most players don't feel any great need for urgency at this point, but I do. This is when I like to start moving and accumulating some chips. The players behind me are a collection of smallish but not too small stacks, so I can expect them to still be a little conservative but not yet desperate. My king-queen offsuit is a reasonable hand, although early in the tournament, I'd only be looking to call with this hand. So I'm going to make a move at the pot, and the only question is how much to bet.
>
> An all-in bet is perfectly reasonable here. It threatens to knock out anyone who calls me and loses, except for the small blind. But I'm just going to bet $6,000. To a shrewd and experienced player, this bet is even more menacing than a simple all-in bet. It signals that I'm looking to get called and I'm not really trying to chase people away. Of course, to a weak player it doesn't signal anything, but that's all right. I don't really have a top hand, so it's the good players I'd like to chase away.

**Action:** You bet $6,000. Everyone folds except the small blind, who puts in $5,400 to call. The pot is now $13,950.

**Flop:** 7♠6♠6♣

**Action:** The small blind bets $3,500.

**Question:** *What's your play?*

    **Answer:** Our own clever strategy is being thrown back at us! The small blind could easily have put us all-in, but he didn't. His bet gives us 5-to-1 pot odds, making a call almost irresistible.

    This is a standard strategy for sucking more money out of weak players. (In fact, in the trade it's also known as a "suck bet.") With a lock hand, just make a small bet, pulling a little more money into the pot, or ideally, inducing your opponent to try and chase you out with an over the top raise. But when one good player faces another, this can be the most sophisticated of bluffs. Make a small bet with nothing, hoping that your savvy opponent will interpret this as a trap and go away.

    So now we need to ask, how does he see us? Does he think we're cannon fodder, or a formidable opponent? In the introduction to the problem I specified that this was our first tournament, and we're new to this table. So he doesn't know us from Job, and therefore the answer is clear — we're cannon fodder. He's got a big hand (I'd guess a small pair to go with the sixes on board, but trip sixes is a possibility) and we're probably huge underdogs to win this hand.

    What about the fact that we'll have only $6,000 if we fold this? Doesn't that argue for an all-in move, no matter what? No, it doesn't. If you know you're beaten, you have to get out. We're probably better off taking any two cards and going all in on the next hand than playing this one out.

**Resolution:** We fold.

# Hand 9-26

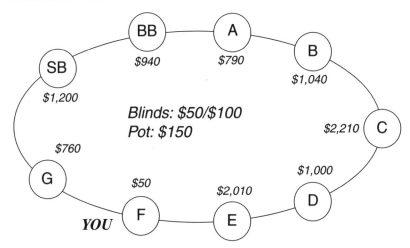

**Situation:** An hour into a single-table satellite tournament.

**Your hand:** 4♠3♠

**Action to you:** Player A folds. Player B calls. Player C raises to $350. Player D calls. Player E folds. The pot is now $950.

**Question:** *Do you fold or go all-in?*

**Answer:** You're in the Dead Zone now, down to just $50. The only question is when you move all-in. You have five more hands before you'll be in the big blind and the decision will be made for you.

What's appealing about this hand is that you have a chance to quintuple your money if you call. You'll be all-in for the main pot against the $50 from the blinds as well as Players B, C, and D. That pot will have $300 in it. The rest of the money will go into a much larger side pot that will continue to be contested.

The chance of quintupling up looks enticing, but your hand is incredibly weak. Against five random hands, your winning chances are only about 10 percent. While the pot is giving you 5-to-1 odds, your hand is about a 9-to-1 underdog. You've still got five hands left before you're forced to put up all your chips in the big blind. Let this one go, and wait for a better chance.

*What does a better chance look like?* Any ace or king is certainly enough to make your move. You could also go in with most queens, jack-ten or jack-nine, or suited connectors. The main idea is to have at least one high card, which gives you the best chance of pulling out a win.

**Action:** You fold.

# Part Ten

# Multiple Inflection Points

# Multiple Inflection Points

# Introduction

In the last section we introduced the idea of zones and inflection points, and showed how your M affects the decisions you make toward the end of a tournament. Now we have to consider another layer of complexity. Your opponents at the table will all have their own Ms and their own set of problems. As you play the hands, you have to be aware of the different Ms around the table, and how the other players are reacting to their own changing circumstances.

The picture gets even murkier, however, when we note that not everyone at the table understands what is happening. There are plenty of players on the poker circuit who don't adjust their hand selection until their stack has almost evaporated. While you're looking across the table at an early position raiser and thinking "His M was 4, so he could have made this move with almost anything," he may be thinking "Good thing I picked up this pair of kings — finally a hand strong enough to play!"

Although the reasoning can get complex, the real game remains the same: position, pot odds, and careful analysis. Let's look at some of the problems you'll encounter as the stacks shrink.

# Assessing Position

Be aware that as the number of players with low Ms at the table increases, the positional advantage of being last to act decreases. The reason is simply that more and more hands result in an all-in situation pre-flop. Once betting is concluded, all positional advantage disappears.

This doesn't mean that you're not happy being on the button, only that your position won't turn as much of a profit as it did in the earlier stages of the tournament. The next example shows how complex the decision-making becomes when hands with widely different Ms get involved in the pot.

**Example 1: A single-table online tournament, with eight of the original ten players remaining. The blinds are $50/$100. The remaining players are arranged as follows:**

| Player | Amount |
|---|---|
| Sm Blind | $400 |
| Big Blind | $550 |
| Player 1(You) | $1,500 |
| Player 2 | $1,300 |
| Player 3 | $2,300 |
| Player 4 | $1,500 |
| Player 5 | $1,200 |
| Player 6 | $1,250 |

**Your M is 10, and the average number of chips at the table is $1,250, so your Q is a favorable 1.2. The Ms at the table range from 3-to-4 for the two short stacks in the blinds**

to just over 15 for the big stack. You're in first position and pick up

*What do you do?*

**Answer:** A pair of eights is a tough hand for first position at this table. You'd be delighted to play this hand against the small stacks in either the small blind or the big blind. Imagine that you could switch position with the big blind, so that he was first to act with his $550 stack, and you were last to act in the big blind. If he raised all-in and everyone folded to you, your pair of eights would be a great hand for calling, since you'd be a favorite against most of the hands he might be playing, and you'd be getting pot odds besides.

But in your current position, you've got some real problems. Eights isn't really good enough so that you're happy about facing an all-in move from the other medium to large stacks at the table. Since none of them have Ms lower than 8, none are under desperate pressure to play the hand. Let's run through your possible options and see which play makes the most sense:

**Raise $400.** A big raise gives you the best chance of chasing out the players in positions 2 through 6 and isolating on the blinds. But the raise consumes more than a quarter of your stack, and leaves you with compelling odds for calling an all-in bet from one of the bigger stacks. For instance, suppose players two through four all fold, Player 5 goes all-in with his $1,200, and the other players fold to you. In that case, the pot becomes $1,750 and it costs you just $800 to call, so you're getting almost 2.2-to-1 on your money. Those are big odds; if you believe he's a very tight player, and there's a 70 percent chance that he's making this raise with a higher pair, and just a 30 percent chance that he's moving with two overcards (and no chance that he's bluffing), then you're *still* getting the right odds to call. If you think he's not that tight, then you have an easy mathematical call, but you'll only be left with $300 in your stack if you lose, and you're not delighted about putting your tournament up for grabs on a pair of eights. Notice as well a paradox that's characteristic of these late-tournament betting situations: *The bigger your initial bet, the more favorable are your calling odds on a subsequent all-in raise.*

**Raise $300.** A more normal raise still gives you a good chance of eliminating the players with weak hands, but now you have more choice when confronted by an all-in reraise. In the scenario we just examined, where Player 5 goes all-in for $1,200 and the others all fold, the pot is now $1,650 and it costs you $900 to call. The combination of a smaller pot and a larger call has reduced your calling odds to about 1.8-to-1. Whether you call at this point depends on your read of your opponent. A mixture of 60 percent high pairs and 40 percent overcards now makes this a barely proper call. A tight player is more likely to be making his move with a high pair, and you can throw the hand away. A loose player will be raising more often, and to do that he'll have to be raising with more unpaired high cards, so you can call. If you have no read, you can toss a coin with your 1.8-to-1 odds.

Note that if it's the big stack that goes all-in, rather than the $1,200 stack, your calling odds change. Now you're being raised the last $1,200 in your stack, so the pot is $1,950 and it costs you $1,200 to call, with odds of 1.6-to-1. These represent fair odds if his mix of raising hands includes 60 percent higher pairs, 30 percent overcards, and 10 percent bluffs. Now I would fold my eights against all but the very loosest players.

**Raise $250**. This is the smallest raise that's more than the minimum. In the scenario that we've been watching against an all-in from Player 5, you'd now have to put in $950 to see a pot of $1,600, with odds of about 1.7-to-1. Now you call only the looser players.

**Call**. This looks passive, but considering the vulnerability of your hand to some of the previous scenarios, it's a reasonable play. You've only invested a small piece of your stack and you can throw your hand away after an all-in from one of the big stacks. With some luck, the hand might get folded around to the blinds, one of whom might make an all-in move. The most dangerous scenario now is a call from one of the big stacks, followed by an all-in move from one of the blinds. Now you'll have to call the all-in without knowing what the other caller is going to do. He might fold, but he might elect to put you all-in anyway.

**Fold.** Not an absurd choice under these rather unusual circumstances. I'd certainly be folding smaller pairs under these circumstances. (Remember our discussion in the previous chapter about the weakness of small pairs in the Yellow and Orange Zones.) When every other choice has some significant drawbacks, folding is always a cheap option.

So what's the right play? It's by no means an easy problem. If the hand were a pair of tens or higher, I'd be very comfortable raising $400 and then calling any all-in raise. If the hand were a pair of sixes or lower, I'd just throw it away here. Holding a pair of eights makes the play very difficult because I'm mostly getting marginal calling odds when I end up facing an all-in bet from one of the larger stacks. On balance, I would raise $400 and wait to see what happens. If I steal the pot or end up all-in against one of the blinds, I'm happy. If I get reraised all-in, I've made my future decision-making easier by getting the biggest possible pot odds. If I make one of the smaller raises ($300 or even $250), I've complicated my subsequent decision-making. With my style, that's a no-no. Keep it simple.

# Isolation Play

The isolation play is a combination of a value bet and a bluff that's common at tables with widely varying stack sizes. The basic idea is a simple one. A player in front of you with a small stack and a low M goes all-in. You have a hand with some strength, but not a monster. Considering the number of hands your opponent might be playing, you think your hand is good enough for a call. However, you don't really want to face other players with large stacks in a showdown. Instead of just calling and leaving yourself vulnerable to the players acting behind you, you raise instead. Hopefully, the players behind you see his all-in move and your raise and decide to stay out of the pot. In that case, you take back your extra chips and your raise has enabled you to isolate on the original raiser — hence the name "isolation play."

Isolation plays can be tricky, and there are several ideas you need to consider.

1. **Does the raiser know what's going on?** If the raiser has both a low M and a low Q (so that his stack is not just small but small in relation to the table) and he seems to be a knowledgeable player, then his all-in raise could indicate anything from a high pair down to low suited connectors or hands like queen-nine. But if he doesn't know what's happening, then his raise probably means a premium hand. The isolation play works best in response to a strong player, and less well in response to a weak player.

2. **Is a raise necessary?** If the original raiser has a stack that was 30 to 35 percent the size of the average stack at the table, piling in with another raise may not be necessary. A simple call will indicate strength, while saving your chips in case

someone behind you has a big hand and will come in no matter what you do.

3. **How many players are yet to act behind you?** The need for a raise is greatest when both the original raiser and you are in early position, with lots of players still to act. If he raises from middle position and you are on the button with just the blinds to act behind you, a simple call is a better percentage play.

Now let's look at a situation from real life and see if we agree with the moves that were made.

**Example 2. End of the first day at a major tournament. Ten players at a full table, with blinds of $200/$400 and antes of $25. The starting pot is $850. The average number of chips at the table is about $12,000. You have $10,000 and are third to act. The player in second position, a well-known top player, has just $2,000.**

**Player 1, a world-class player with a $15,000 stack, calls. Player 2 goes all-in for $2,000. You pick up 7♥7♦ in third position and decide to make an isolation move, going all-in for $10,000. The table folds back around to Player 1, who after long thought decides to fold his ace-king offsuit. You take back your extra $8,000, leaving the pot at $5,650. Player 2 turns up king-queen, and your sevens hold up.**

Your play worked, but was it a sensible move? I don't think so. Here's why.

Your first problem was the presence of Player 1, who had called in first position at a full table. This indicated that there was at least one hand as strong as yours (and probably stronger) at the table, adding an extra level of risk to your bet.

You were right to think that merely calling would not enable you to isolate on Player 2. A call on your part would create a pot of $5,650. In the best case, where all the players behind you plus the blinds fold, the action would get around to Player 1 who would be getting 4.5-to-1 odds to call. Any hand that could have initially called would make that call as well. But a smaller raise on your part might have done the job. A raise to $4,000 or $5,000 would have surely chased out any weak holdings behind you, while giving you a chance to escape with part of your stack if Player 1 chooses to put you all-in. (If you reraise $4,000 and Player A moves all-in, the pot will contain $16,850 and you'll need to put in $6,000 to call. You'll be getting 2.8-to-1 odds, not enough since his bet very likely represents a higher pair.)

The final problem was your hand itself. Even knowing that Player 2 had an M of 2.5, the only hands he could reasonably hold that make you a big favorite are the pairs below your sevens. It's much more likely that he went in with two high cards, where you're just a small favorite. And in order to become that small favorite, you had to jeopardize all your chips.

Your move makes a lot of sense if you hold a pair like jacks or tens. Now he's much more likely to hold a pair below you than above you, and you're still a favorite against all the non-pairs. In that circumstance, an isolation play is a good move. In the actual hand, you were better off just folding. Calling is too weak, and all-in is too risky.

As we saw in the previous hand, an isolation move, even an all-in isolation move, may indicate some strength but not overpowering strength. You need to be aware of this if you're one of the players on the other side of the move. In the next example, we'll see an isolation move in conjunction with a multiple-inflection-point situation.

**Example 3. Single-table online tournament. Eight players remain from the original ten. Your stack is $1,800, the largest at the table. The blinds are $15/$30. You are third to act. You pick up**

**Player 1 folds. Player 2, with $1,300, raises to $75, a small raise of just two and one-half times the big blind.** *What do you do with your pair of queens?*

**Answer:** You have no reason to believe your queens aren't good, so the normal play is just to raise to something like $200 or $250. That would be my play almost all the time. In fact, Player 3 elected to just call.

Calling here can't be labeled a mistake. It's a somewhat unusual deception move, which will probably be interpreted by the other players at the table as indicating a low pair of some sort. The advantage of the play is that you may win a very big pot when a queen flops and no one suspects you might have queens in your hand. The disadvantage is that you're allowing some drawing hands in behind you, which could be costly if an ace or a king flops.

The call here is a very useful balancing play in a couple of situations:

1.  In cash games where you play with the same crowd night after night. In that case you have to adopt these randomizing plays a certain percentage of the time to confuse your opponents, whether you think they're optimal or not. With a pair of queens against an early, weak raiser, a combination of 80 percent raises and 20 percent calls is a good mix.

2.  In high-stakes live tournaments when you're at a table with a bunch of good, experienced players who've

played with you many times before. It's not quite as necessary as in the first case, but it's still a good idea.

In online play, especially in small-stakes events, this kind of randomizing deception isn't necessary. You just won't run into the same players often enough and they won't be skilled enough to warrant departing from the play you think is optimal.

**You call. The pot is $195. Players 4, 5, 6, and the small blind all fold. The big blind goes all-in for $500. Player 2 goes all-in for his remaining $1,225.** *What do you do?*
**Answer:** After a slow start, an explosion of activity. Let's look at the hand through the lens of the other two players' eyes and see what they see before we decide what to do.

**The big blind.** His stack is $500, so his M is 11, just at the bottom of the Yellow Zone. He's not desperate yet, but he's certainly interested in making a move under favorable circumstances. He's seen a smallish raise from Player 2, and only a call from Player 3. Someone could be sandbagging, but there's a good possibility there's no real strength out there. With a very strong hand, the big blind could consider a raise to about $225, hoping for some action. With a weaker hand that still has some real value, all-in is a good move. I'd certainly go all-in here with a hand like tens, nines, or perhaps even eights. Below that it's a matter of taste, although I can't see many good players playing the real low pairs like fours or below. With unpaired hands, I have to respect the fact that two players already entered. I'd raise here with ace-king or ace-queen, but nothing weaker than that. Remember, the big blind doesn't have to pick this hand to make a stand, so getting involved with a holding like king-jack is just foolish.

**Player 2**. Player 2 raised and was just called, so he probably doesn't think you have great strength. From his point of view, a medium-to-small pair is your most likely holding. If he did a similar analysis to what we just did, he thinks the big blind has something, but again not necessarily a great hand. So he doesn't need a super hand to make an all-in play here, which looks like he wants to isolate on the big blind. He could be making his move with a pair as low as jacks or tens, or some high-card hands like ace-king or ace-queen. (ace-king is much more likely as we have two of the queens.)

The only hands we really fear in this situation are aces and kings. It's likely that the big blind doesn't have either of these hands (since he raised all-in instead of making a more easily callable raise.) Player 2 might have one of these hands, but there are plenty of other hands he could have as well. On balance, the queens should call.

**Player 3 actually folded his queens, and the other players showed their hands: The big blind had a pair of nines, and Player 2 had ace-king suited. After the board played out, Player 2 made a flush, although Player 3 would have made queens full.**

Excessive conservatism proved costly as Player 3 missed a chance to double up and eliminate two opponents at the same time. It happens to the best of us (although not as often as it happens to the worst of us.)

# Calculating Pot
# Odds in All-In Situations

In Volume I we spent some time calculating pot odds in situations where your opponent had put you all-in early in the tournament. Now let's look at a situation common towards the end of tournaments. You get involved in a pot with a player whose M is much lower than yours. He makes a bet large enough to commit himself to the pot, so if you continue to play, all his money will go to the center. You need to evaluate the pot odds you're getting *before the all-in actually happens*. Let's see how it's done.

**Example 4. Middle stages of a major tournament. Sixty players remain and 30 will get paid. Nine players at your table, and you are second to act with a stack of $37,000 and an M of 41. From the TV monitors, you appear to be in the top-10 in chip standings. Blinds are $150/$300 and antes are $50, so the pot to start is $900. You pick up A♠K♥ and raise to $1,200, four times the big blind. Everyone folds to the player in the cutoff seat, who has $11,200 and an M of 12.5. He raises to $5,000, leaving him with $6,200 in his stack. The last three players fold around to you. *What do you do?***

**Answer:** You have three plays to consider:
1. Fold
2. Call
3. Reraise all-in.

Calling is the worst option here. With ace-king, you'd usually prefer to make an all-or-nothing decision, since that enables you to see all five cards and thus get the most value for your two high cards. That's especially true when you're out of position and your opponent is on a short stack and mostly committed to the pot already. He will usually put you all-in after the flop, and since you know that, you need to make your decision now whether or not to play the hand for his full stack.

Before you decide to put him all-in, you need to give a little though to just what he might be holding. Considering his relatively low M (bottom of the Yellow Zone) and his eagerness to get involved with someone who showed strength in early position, it's very likely that he has a pair lower than your cards. You can't dismiss the possibility that he has a pair of aces or kings, but there are several reasons why you're not overly worried:

1.  As stacks get low, any pair is a strong inducement to make a move.

2.  Most pairs are lower than kings.

3.  You hold an ace and a king, reducing the chances still further. (There are six possible ways to be dealt a pair of aces. But holding an ace yourself reduces that number to three. The same argument holds for the kings.)

4.  Pairs of aces and kings are so strong given his low M that he might have made more of an effort to keep you in the pot by just calling.

These arguments don't eliminate the chance that you are up against aces or kings, they just show that the likelihood is less. There's also some possibility that you're not even facing a pair. I actually think that's more likely than the chance that you're up against the high pair, but let's simplify things and just say that those two possibilities cancel out. For our purposes, you're up against a pair lower than kings, and you want to know the mathematics of putting him all-in or not.

Right now the numbers look as follows:
1. $900: In the pot to start
2. $1,200: Your raise
3. $1,200: He called your raise, and
4. $3,800: Put in a raise of his own.
5. $6,200: The money he has left in his stack.

So now you can fold, or put him all-in by moving another $10,000 into the pot. (True, he might fold this bet, but if he has some medium pair, he's going to call rather than try to play with $6,200 and an M of 7. After your all-in raise, he'll be looking at a pot of $17,100 and he'll need just his last $6,200 to call, and those 3-to-1 odds will just be too good.)

If you put him all-in, you'll be risking $10,000 to win $10,000 (his raise plus his stack) plus $3,300 (the amount in the pot after your last raise was called). Your bet is getting you $13,300-to-$10,000 odds, or 1.33-to-1.

Is that a good deal for you? To answer that question we have to look at a bunch of factors: your real odds of winning the hand, the difference that winning or losing will make to your stack and your standing in the tournament, and the importance of eliminating this particular opponent. Let's take a look at these issues one by one.

1. **Your real odds.** If you hold ace-king against a smaller pair, you're somewhere between a 12-to-10 and a 13-to-10 underdog, depending on exactly what pair you're facing. This means the odds you're receiving make for a fair bet, but no more. Whether you want to make a fair bet for about 30 percent of your stack depends on other circumstances.

2. **Your standing in the tournament.** You're in very good shape right now, toward the top of the leader board and with a very healthy M. A fair bet increases the volatility

of your position *without increasing your equity*. Most good players wouldn't be interested and would pass here. If you thought you were one of the weaker players left in the tournament, or if the table seemed particularly tough, so good bets were hard to find, then this might be a great time to try to score some extra chips. (But then, if you could reason that out, you wouldn't be a weak player.) In general, however, you shouldn't be interested in a high-stakes even-money bet here.

3.   **Need to eliminate the opponent**. Later in the tournament, where each player eliminated means another step up the ladder, you like to take advantage of these situations to try to knock out another player. But here, there's not much difference in having 60 players in or just 59. Again, no strong reason to get involved.

The weight of the evidence here argues for throwing your hand away. You're getting a fair price on the bet but no more, and your chip situation is very comfortable. Fold, and wait for a genuinely favorable situation later.

**Example 5. All conditions are the same as the last hand, but this time your opponent had a stack of $16,200 when he made his $5,000 bet.**
    **Discussion:** Giving your opponent a bigger stack changes the position considerably. First, let's look at the pot-odds calculation if you decide to move him all-in. He now has $11,200 left in his stack after his raise, so to put him all-in you have to move $15,000 into the pot. ($3,800 to call his raise plus $11,200 more, a total of $15,000). As before, there's $3,300 in the pot to win. So your pot odds are now

$$(\$15,000 + \$3,300)/\$15,000$$

which are about 1.22-to-1. Now you're definitely taking the worst of it if your ace-king is up against a pair, so the all-in move is out. At this point it's call or fold. If you call, you're getting a little less than 2-to-1 odds on your bet (the pot is $7,100 and you need to put in $3,800 to call) and the odds of hitting an ace or a king on the flop are a little better than 30 percent, so your chances of hitting are a little less than 2-to-1.

Do your implied odds if you hit your hand compensate? Probably. Your opponent might decide he's done with the hand if an ace or King flops, but then again he might not. I'd call here against anyone but a super-tight player.

**Example 6. All conditions are the same, but this time your opponent had a stack of $8,200 when he made his $5,000 bet.**
**Discussion:** Giving the opponent a smaller stack again changes the problem, this time making the all-in move mandatory. Now his remaining stack is just $3,200 after he makes his raise, so when you put him all-in you just have to move $7,000 into the pot. Your pot odds are now

$$(\$7,000 + \$3,300)/\$7,000$$

Which are about 1.47-to-1. When I see odds approaching 1.5-to-1, I'm very comfortable going all the way with my ace-king. Compared to the original problem, my stack is also in better shape if I call and lose, yet another reason for playing.

Study these three examples carefully. You will find situations where you're trying to decide whether to put your opponent all-in or just fold your hand. In poker, the pot odds will be the first thing you need to consider, so make sure you're very comfortable with these calculations.

# The Problems

Problems 10-1 through 10-4 show how to handle the situation where a small stack at the table goes all-in. Problem 10-5 shows a variation on the same theme: How to get all the chips of a small-stacked player into the center.

Problems 10-6 and 10-7 cover the analogous situation: playing against (or avoiding) a bigger stack. Problems 10-8 and 10-9 involve situations where you face multiple opponents with both larger and smaller stacks.

Problems 10-10 and 10-11 merit careful study. The issue is picking the proper bet size when facing multiple opponents with widely different Ms.

The remaining problems focus on various issues. Problem 10-12 shows how to evaluate a flop in the light of pre-flop action. Problem 10-13 is a pot-odds dilemma. Problem 10-14 deals with the always-difficult problem of playing low pairs in low-M confrontations. Finally, Problem 10-15 shows what to do when your M and Q numbers offer conflicting advice.

# Hand 10-1

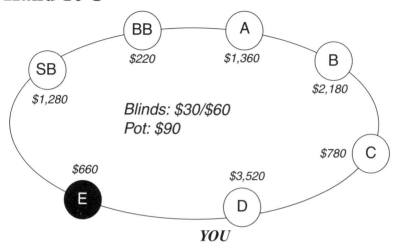

**Situation:** In the middle of a single-table online tournament. The small blind and Player B have been very aggressive.

**Your hand:** A♦9♦

**Action to you:** Player A folds. Player B calls. Player C folds. The pot is now $150.

**Question:** *Do you fold, call, or raise?*

> **Answer:** The short-handed table and your relatively good position means you can loosen up your raising and calling requirements somewhat. If no one had entered the pot when the betting got to you, your ace-nine suited would certainly be strong enough for an opening raise. With an opener in front of you who is known to be aggressive, the ace-nine suited is good enough to call in this position, but it's not strong enough for a raise. Just call.

**Action:** You actually raise to $120. The button folds, but both blinds call your bet, and Player B puts in another $60 to call. The pot is now $480. You will act last, but both aggressive players are in the pot, along with the big blind, who has only $100 left.

**Flop: 6♦6♣4♠**

**Action:** The small blind checks, the big blind goes all-in for his last $100 chips, and Player B folds. *What do you do?*

> **Answer:** The bad news is you've missed the flop and your flush is now a long shot. But the good news is that the pot is offering almost 6-to-1 odds, you still have an ace-high hand, and you have a cheap chance to knock out a player who moved in with an M of just 1. Take it and call. There's an excellent chance that your ace is good here. If the small blind makes a move, you'll have another decision to make, but he has to be more afraid of your stack than you are of his, so he'll probably just go away quietly.

**Resolution:** You call and the small blind folds. The big blind shows K♣Q♣. Fourth and fifth street are the 7♥ and the 9♠, and your pair of nines win the hand.

The big blind didn't make an error, since there was some chance his hand was good at that point.

# Hand 10-2

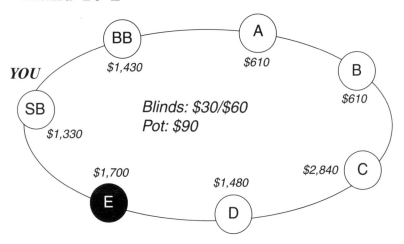

**Situation:** Toward the end of a one-table satellite. Players B and E are aggressive. Player C is super-aggressive.

**Your hand:** A♥T♦

**Action to you:** Player A folds. Player B raises to $120. Players C, D, and E all fold. The pot is now $210.

**Question:** *Do you fold, call, or raise?*

> **Answer:** At a full table, facing a raise from a player in second position, you would normally fold ace-ten offsuit in the small blind. Not only are you out of position, but the Gap Concept applies directly here. He needed a better hand than you have now to make his raise, and you need an even better hand than that to call. So your default play should be to fold.
>
> Here the situation is quite a bit different. The table has seven players rather than ten, Player B is on a short stack with an M of just over 6, and he's known to be aggressive. All these facts mean that you need much less of a hand to call. Ace-ten unsuited, combined with your 2.3-to-1 pot odds,

is probably good enough. There's no need to raise however. You can wait until the flop to decide how aggressively you want to pursue the hand.

**Action:** You call for an additional $90. The big blind folds. The pot is now $300.

**Flop:** J♣6♠5♥

**Question:** You're first to act. *What do you do?*
**Answer:** This should be a safe flop You may have the best hand now, so you should lead out with a probe bet of about half the flop. It gives your opponent a way to let the hand go now. If the bet is called or raised, you know it's likely that your opponent is going all the way with this hand.

If you don't bet, your opponent will find the opportunity to try and steal the pot irresistible, so he'll probably move in with a big bet. Ask yourself a simple question: If you check and he goes all-in, do you intend to call that bet? If your answer is yes, *and you don't have a really strong hand*, then you're almost certainly better off making the first bet yourself. Many times leading off will lead to exactly the same place as checking, but sometimes you'll win a hand that you would have lost if played down to the end.

**Action:** You in fact check, and he goes all-in for his last $490. *Do you call?*
**Answer:** By not leading off with a bet, you now face a pretty tough problem. If your opponent has any hand at all, then you don't have the right odds to call. The pot now has $790, and it costs you $490 to call, so you're getting about 8-to-5 pot odds. But if he has, say, a low pair, you're about a 3-to-1 underdog in the hand right now. (That's a good number to commit to memory right now, by the way. Most players know that before the flop, two overcards are about a 13-to-10

underdog to a lower pair. Few players know that after the flop, the odds increase to 3-to-1.)

To call, you have to believe that there's a substantial chance that he's on a bluff. Even if you can't tell anything from his mannerisms, I think that's a reasonable assumption here. He's an aggressive player, he's down to his last $490, and by checking you almost forced him to bluff. So you should call.

If you had led off with a bet of say, $150, he might just have folded. But if he then came back over the top with an all-in bet, notice how easy your decision-making gets. Now the pot is $940 and it costs you $340 to call, Those are 2.7-to-1 odds, and you have to call, unless you're sure he's playing with a high pair (and you never are). Train yourself to look for the plays that make future decisions easy.

**Resolution:** You call. He shows 7♣7♠. The river and turn come T♠ and 9♥, and your pair of tens win the pot.

# Hand 10-3

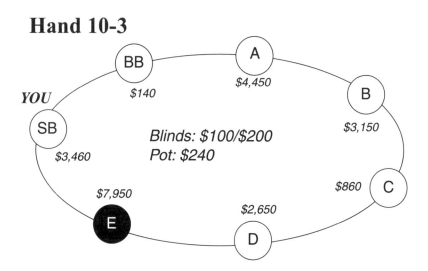

**Situation:** In the middle of a multi-table online tournament.

**Your hand:** T♠3♣

**Action to you:** Players A through E fold. The pot is $240, since the big blind is all-in.

**Question:** *Do you fold or call?*

>    **Answer:** This is an easy problem but it's worth mentioning because it's so often misplayed, especially by beginners and especially in online events. The big blind is all-in and everyone else has folded, so the only question is whether or not you should put in another $40 to see a pot of $240. The answer is yes, and has nothing to do with the strength of your hand. The 6-to-1 pot odds justify playing with any two cards; holding a ten is actually a bonus, since you may be a favorite right now. (Ten-three offsuit is actually 42 percent against a random hand — that's mighty nice when you're getting 6-to-1 odds.)

**Action:** You call, and the big blind shows 7♦6♠. The board comes K♣J♦T♦T♥6♥, and your trip tens win the pot.

# Hand 10-4

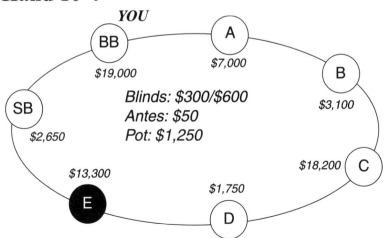

YOU

BB
$19,000

A
$7,000

B
$3,100

SB
$2,650

Blinds: $300/$600
Antes: $50
Pot: $1,250

C
$18,200

E
$13,300

D
$1,750

**Situation:** Late into a multi-table online tournament.

**Your hand:** T♥4♦

**Action to you:** Players A, B, and C fold. Player D goes all-in for $1,750. Player E and the small blind fold. The pot is now $3,000.

**Question:** *Do you fold or call?*

**Answer:** This is a straight pot-odds play. The pot is $3,000 and, since you were the big blind, it costs you only another $1,150 to call. Those are odds of almost 3-to-1, so you're getting the price you need to play, even with your pathetic hand, unless your opponent has one of the top five pairs. Since his M was only 1.5 before the hand, he could have gone in with almost anything. He might well have decided to play with nine-eight suited or even six-five suited, in which case you're actually a favorite.

**Action:** You call. He turns over 9♦9♠.

One of his best hands, but notice that if you had known what he had, you still would have called! Your single overcard makes you about a 2.5-to-1 underdog to the nines, and the pot was giving you better odds than that.

**Action:** The board comes 6♠6♣2♣7♥T♦, and your pair of tens win the pot.

# Hand 10-5

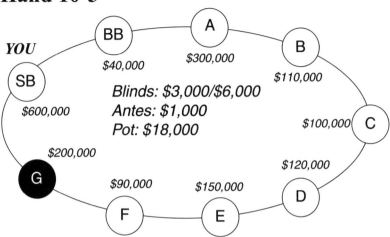

**Situation:** Final table of a major tournament. Player B is a very experienced, conservative player.

**Your hand:** 8♥8♦

**Action to you:** Player A folds. Player B raises to $18,000. Players C through G all fold. The pot is now $36,000. It costs you $15,000 to call.

**Question:** *Do you fold, call, or raise?*

> **Answer:** A pair of eights is a good enough hand to call. Your opponent opened with something, but if it was two high cards, you have the best hand right now. The pot is also offering you good odds (2.4-to-1) which make up in part for your bad position.

**Action:** You call. The pot is now $51,000. The big blind folds.

**Flop:** K♦8♠7♦

**Action:** *What's your move?*

**Answer:** Trip eights is a huge hand heads-up, so your job is just to extract the most money from the situation. Your conservative opponent must have some value in his hand to make the opening bet, so you should just check, and allow him to bet.

**Action:** You check. Player B bets $20,000. The pot is now $71,000. *What do you do?*

**Answer:** Now you have a tough decision. Your opponent now has about $70,000 left in his stack, and you'd like to get as much of it as possible. There are three ways to go with the hand. Let's look at all three plays.

1. **Raise all-in.** Uncool. If you like this play, you're probably the sort of fellow that trips over himself trying to get to the front of the buffet line. The all-in bet is likely to chase your opponent out of the pot, and your hand is too good for that.

2. **Make a small reraise, perhaps $20,000** Your opponent will be very suspicious of this reraise, because he'll be looking at irresistible pot odds. He'll need to put in $20,000 to call a $111,000 pot. Of course, he knows that you deliberately gave him those odds, and therefore you must want him to call. But he'll probably call anyway, because the odds are just too tempting.

3. **Just flat call.** This is almost as suspicious as the small reraise. You're trying to sell the idea that you're drawing to a diamond flush. It's unlikely, but you might get away with it. The problem is that you haven't drawn any more money into the pot.

On balance, I like the small raise here. It's your best shot at getting some more money in the pot right now. It might be the only extra money you make on the hand, and that's worth something.

**Action:** You raise $20,000. After a long think, your opponent calls. The pot is now $131,000.

**Fourth Street:** 3♥

**Action:** *What do you do?*

> **Answer:** That card certainly didn't help your opponent. (He raised before the flop in early position, remember, and he's a conservative player, so there aren't any treys in his hand.) But his stack is down to about $50,000, which presents you with a problem. If you make even a modest bet, he can't call it without reducing his chip stack to the point where he's better off just shoving all his chips in and hoping to catch a bluff. In light of that, your choices are really down to three:
> 1. Put him all-in now and see if he calls.
> 2. Bet $20,000 or so, to deny him a free card.
> 3. Put him all-in on the end and see if he calls.

There's a possibility that he might interpret an all-in move on the end as some sort of pot-stealing play, and if so, he might lose all his chips. But he might not. The big bet on the end is actually part of a different play, one where you bet a strong hand pre-flop, continue bet after the flop, check on the turn (feigning weakness), and then go all-in on the river (pretending to desperately steal the pot.) It's not quite as convincing a move in this hand.

Should you worry about giving him a free card? Not really. Look at the hands he might have.

1.  AA, QQ, JJ, TT, 99. Any of these hands would have justified an opening raise in early position, followed by a bet after the flop, followed by a call of your small reraise. With one card to come, he has to fill his trips to beat you, and he's a 22-to-1 underdog.

2.  AK, KQ. He's drawing dead since a king gives him trips but you a full house.

3.  AQ. He's drawing dead unless he has precisely A♦Q♦.

4.  KK. He's going to double up no matter how you play the hand.

On the hands that matter, he's either a 22-to-1 underdog or drawing dead, so you don't have to worry about a free card.

The strongest argument for the small bet, however, is simply that it gets more money into the pot with a bet that's hard to fold because of the great pot odds. And if he calls that bet, then putting him all-in on the end will also be hard to fold. That's the surest way to get his whole stack.

**Action:** You actually go all-in and he folds, laying down Q♠Q♥. You take the pot.

A top player who was laying down a pair of queens would be pretty certain you had trip eights. What else could you have that would beat him and still match your plays? If you have ace-king, you would have reraised before the flop. You probably didn't have king-queen because he had two of the queens. And you wouldn't have called with king-x when 'x' is a jack or less. Hence, trip eights.

# Hand 10-6

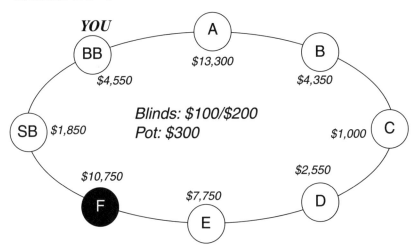

**Situation:** In the middle of a multi-table online tournament. Several new players have just joined the table, including Player A.

**Your hand:** 9♥8♣

**Action to you:** Player A raises to $400. Players B through F fold. The small blind folds. The pot is $700, and it costs you $200 to call.

**Question:** *Do you fold, call, or raise?*

   **Answer:** The minimum raise from the player in first position should arouse some suspicion. That's usually a play someone makes to lure others into the pot, which in turns indicates a very strong hand. But online the bet has another interpretation. There are players who play a sort of dumbed-down smallball, just taking stabs at pots with minimum bets in the hope of picking up blinds and antes cheaply. The bigger their own stack, the more they like this strategy.

   Right now you don't have any information on Player A, so you can't say for sure what he's doing. Keep both possibilities open in your mind, and turn your attention to the pot odds, which at 3.5-to-1 are very favorable. Even if Player A is trapping with a big pair, the implied odds if you hit your hand big make a call worthwhile.

One last consideration is the discrepancy in stack sizes. You have $4,350 left and an M of 14. Player A has $12,900 and an M of 43! He has you covered easily, so the pot is potentially much more dangerous for you than for him. Call, but proceed with caution thereafter.

**Action:** You call. The pot is now $900.

**Flop:** 8♥6♥4♠

**Quetion:** *What do you do?*
   **Answer:** That's a pretty good flop for you. You have top pair plus some vague straight and flush possibilities.

   If he started with a high pair, you're still second-best. If he just started with a couple of high cards, you're now a solid favorite. But you don't know which, and your small M requires you to be cautious. Just check and see what he does.

**Action:** You check and he checks behind you.

That's good news, although a strong player with a high pair would most likely check also. But a weak player would probably have bet with a high pair, so the evidence is mounting that you have the best hand right now.

**Fourth Street:** 7♥

**Action:** *What do you do now?*
   **Answer:** Wow. That's a really great card. You now have top pair plus an open-ended straight flush draw. You may be best right now and have 15 outs to a monster hand. Now you're

trapped into the hand. Lead out with a bet of about two-thirds of the pot and see if he wants to play with you. Why two-thirds of the pot instead of one-half? Because the bet is partially a value bet (you may have the best hand right now) and you need to draw more money in the pot when you might have the best hand.

**Action:** You bet $600 and he folds.

You won the pot and you learned something about Player A. He didn't have a high pair when he made that minimum raise from first position. He probably just had a couple of high cards, and saw a minimum bet as just a cheap blind-stealer. He also didn't make a continuation bet when he could have, so when he does bet, he's more likely to have a hand. File that away under "valuable information."

# Hand 10-7

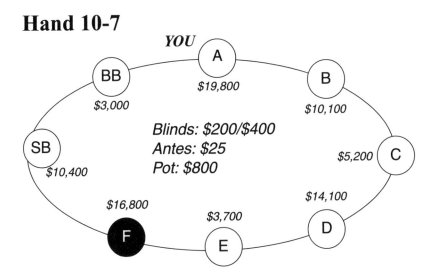

**Situation:** In the middle of a multi-table online tournament. Player F has been aggressive lately and has built up his stack by pulling in several pots.

**Your hand:** A♥J♥

**Action to you:** You act first.

**Question:** *Do you fold, call, or raise?*
    **Answer:** Ace-jack suited is not a premium opening hand in first position at a full table. Here, however, the table is eight players rather than nine or ten, and you're the big stack with an M of 24, which is worth something since the other players will be less inclined to go against you. You should open here for about three times the big blind.

**Action:** You raise to $1,200. Players B, C, D, and E all fold. Player F, on the button, calls. The blinds fold. The pot is now $3,200.

**Flop:** 9♥7♠3♠

**Question:** *What do you do?*
    **Answer:** You weren't happy to see the second-biggest stack come in against you. Now you've missed the flop. Should you make a continuation bet, or just check?

    When I have nothing against another big stack, I like to keep the pots small. It's more likely than not that he didn't have a medium or large pair, since he didn't reraise. If I had to put him on a hand, he probably has a couple of face cards. It's possible you can take the pot away from him with a continuation bet, but it's also possible you'll get embroiled in a big pot with nothing. Much earlier in the tournament, I might go that way and see what happens, but here, even though I'm still in the Green Zone, I like to be cautious against another big stack. I would just check.

    Note that if Player B or C had made the call, I'd be much more likely to make a move here. I can threaten them with the loss of their whole stack, while they can't make a corresponding threat against me. That gives me more leverage to help win the hand.

**Action:** You check and Player F checks.

**Fourth Street: K♠**

**Question:** *What do you do?*
  **Answer:** The turn missed you and may have helped him. Now you should definitely check.

**Action:** You check. He bets $1,000.

Nothing to do here but fold.

**Action:** You fold.

This looks like a passively-played hand (and it was), but an aggressive player could have lost nearly his whole stack here trying to bully the pot. Remember that you may have been beaten all along.

# Hand 10-8

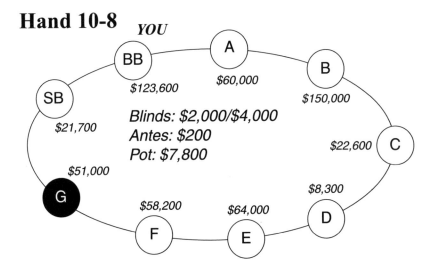

YOU

BB
$123,600

A
$60,000

B
$150,000

SB
$21,700

Blinds: $2,000/$4,000
Antes: $200
Pot: $7,800

$22,600 C

G
$51,000

$8,300

F
$58,200

E
$64,000

D

**Situation:** Final two tables of a multi-table online tournament. Player G is loose and aggressive.

**Your hand:** 8♠4♥

**Action to you:** Players A, B, C, and D fold. Player E calls $4,000. Player F folds. Player G calls $4,000. The small blind calls $2,000. The pot is now $17,800.

**Question:** *Do you check or raise?*
   **Answer:** Check. You're delighted to see a free flop with your mediocre hand. Right now you're in very good shape, with an M of 16. Although you're in the Yellow Zone, you're doing very well.

**Action:** You check. The pot remains at $17,800.

**Flop:** J♦8♣4♦

**Action:** The small blind checks. *What do you do?*
   **Answer:** You've flopped bottom two pair, which is a great result. You should now slow-play and check. Remember we said that the more players there were in the pot, the less you wanted to bluff. The flip side of that insight is that the more players there are in the pot, the more you want to slow-play, since someone is likely to have some sort of a hand.
   Your goal here is to get someone to bet so you can check-raise them out of the pot. With trips you might check and call, but bottom two pair isn't quite good enough for that. You're happy here to pick up an extra bet. The small blind, however, has only $17,500 left, so if he shows any interest, he's liable to commit himself to the hand.

**Action:** You check. Player E checks. Player G bet $16,000. The small blind goes all-in for his last $17,500. *What do you do?*

> **Answer:** Player G, last to act, made a move at the pot, which you expected. The small blind checked and raised, which you didn't expect. His most likely holding is a pair of jacks with some sort of kicker. (If so, he'll have five outs against you on fourth street and eight on fifth street, assuming no eight or four comes.)
>
> Your best play now is an isolation move. Player E has $59,800 left, and Player G has $31,000. Bet enough to put Player E all-in, and hope they both go away. You don't want several players drawing to beat your low two pair.

**Action:** You raise to $60,000. Players E and G both fold. The small blind turns over 7♦5♦.

The small blind check-raised with a low flush draw which didn't make much sense. Remember the small blind's M was just under 3! He should have just pushed all-in.

**Fourth Street:** 5♣

**Fifth Street:** 9♦

The small blind makes his flush and wins the pot.

# Hand 10-9

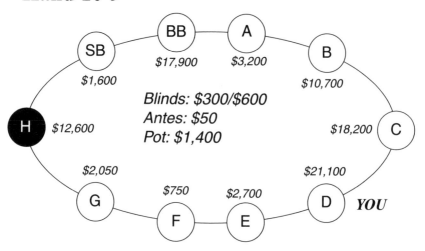

**Situation:** Late into a multi-table online tournament. Only two tables remain. This table has been playing tight for awhile.

**Your hand:** K♣J♦

**Action to you:** Players A, B, and C fold. The pot is still $1,400.

**Question:** *Do you fold, call, or raise?*

> **Answer:** In fourth position at a full table, king-jack offsuit would normally be a very marginal opening hand, to say the least. Early in the tournament, I would almost always just toss the hand. Here, a combination of three factors tip the balance towards playing:
>
> 1. The table has been tight. You take advantage of that by leading out with slightly marginal hands. If you are called or reraised by someone with chips, you can be sure you're beaten.

2. You are the chip leader. Players are more likely to fold marginal hands against you. As before, to exploit this you must be willing to play marginal hands.

3. Of the six players to act behind you, four have micro-stacks, with Ms between 0.5 and 2. You're not afraid of a call by them, and they will be calling with weaker than usual hands.

Put all the factors together, and raising with the king-jack looks pretty reasonable here.

**Action:** You raise to $1,200. Player E folds. Player F goes all-in for $700. Players G and H fold. The small blind goes all-in, putting his last $1,250 in the pot. The big blind folds. It's $350 to you to call the small blind.

You call, of course, given the gigantic pot odds. This has been a great result, giving you a chance to eliminate two small stacks on a single hand.

**Action:** You call. Player F turns over Q♥T♥, and the small blind shows K♥T♦. The board comes J♠J♥8♣3♠6♠, and you scoop the pot.

The play of the small stacks could not be faulted, as these were pretty good all-in hands given their Red Zone status.

# Hand 10-10

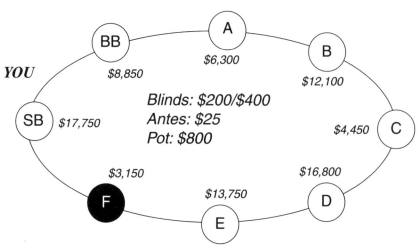

**Situation:** In the middle of a multi-table online tournament. The table has been playing tight recently.

**Your hand:** Q♦Q♠

**Action to you:** Player A calls. Players B and C fold. Player D calls. Players E and F fold. The pot is now $1,600.

**Question:** *Do you call or raise?*

> **Answer:** Your hand is certainly good enough to raise, and it's certainly not good enough to slow-play out of position, so the only question is exactly how much to raise.
>
> You have a comfortable stack, with an M of 22. Player A has $5,900 left after his bet, so his M is between 7 and 8. Player D has an M of just over 20. You have several goals here, and you need to pick a bet amount that best meets all your goals. In no particular order, here they are:
>
> 1. You have a good enough hand to encourage some action, but not a lot of action.

2.   You would like to narrow the field to one opponent.

3.   You're eager to play against the smaller stack who can't really hurt you, and who will be inclined to play weaker hands.

4.   You're not eager for action against the big stack, who could hurt you if he has a hand.

   The key player here is the small stack. In order to thin the field, you want to make at least a pot-sized bet, or perhaps a little larger. But in order to keep Player A around, you don't want to bet more than half his stack. Players tend to go away when you bet more than half their stack, but stick around when you bet less. There's a subtle notion that if they can keep more than half their stack, they can still play.
   With all that in mind, I'd bet about $2,000. It's enough to chase somebody away, but perhaps not enough to chase both players away, and if the small stack has some sort of hand, he may feel he can afford to see a flop. If the big stack comes in, so be it.
   If my hand were stronger (aces or kings) I'd bet a little less, to encourage more action. If I had jacks or tens, I'd certainly bet more, making people pay for the privilege of hitting their draw.

**Action:** You bet $2,000. The big blind folds, and Players A and D fold.

# Hand 10-11

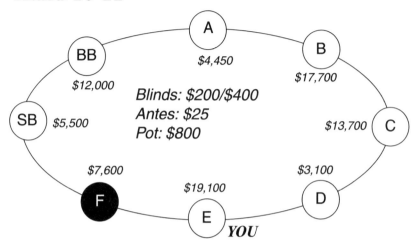

Blinds: $200/$400
Antes: $25
Pot: $800

A $4,450
BB $12,000
B $17,700
SB $5,500
C $13,700
F $7,600
E $19,100 *YOU*
D $3,100

**Situation:** In the middle of a multi-table online tournament. The table has been playing very tight recently, with most pots won by the opener with a minimum bet.

**Your hand:** Q♣J♠

**Action to you:** Players A through D fold. The pot is still $800.

**Question:** *Do you fold, call, or raise?*

> **Answer:** The advantage of being the big stack in a long tournament is that you get to steal a lot of pots cheaply. Other players realize that you're the stack that can knock them out with impunity, and they'd rather stay away from pots where you've already gotten involved.
>
> When you're thinking of playing a pot with minimal values, look at the players yet to act behind you. The ideal situation is to be followed by a bunch of Orange Zone players. They're not so short as to be desperate, but they'll be wary, and once you're in a pot they will throw away marginal calling hands.

Here the three players behind you are:

1. Player F, M = 9
2. The small blind, M between 6 and 7
3. The big blind, M just under 15.

That's two Orange Zone players out of three, which are good odds. Although queen-jack would be a pretty marginal opening hand normally, here I would play it with confidence.

How much to bet? Bet whatever amount had been winning pots without opposition. Here it's been the minimum bet, so you should just raise to $800. If three times the big blind had been winning the pots, bet $1,200. The idea is not to do anything that seems out of the ordinary.

If your bet gets called or reraised, you can be certain you need to improve to win.

**Action:** You raise $800, and take the pot.

# Hand 10-12

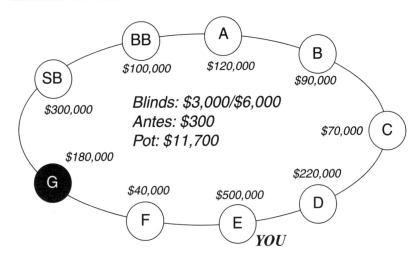

**Situation:** Final table of a major tournament. The small blind has been extremely aggressive throughout the tournament, willing to open with any two cards.

**Your hand:** T♥T♦

**Action to you:** Players A through D all fold.

**Question:** *Do you call or raise?*
> **Answer:** The medium pairs are hands you need to raise strongly before the flop to cut down on the number of hands that can outdraw you. You should raise in the neighborhood of three to five times the big blind, remembering to vary your bet size so players can't easily read you.

**Action:** You actually raise to $16,000. Players F and G fold. The small blind calls, putting in another $13,000. The big blind folds. The pot is now $40,700.

**Flop:** K♥7♠2♣

**Action:** The small blind checks. *What should you do?*
> **Answer:** Your first problem is to evaluate the flop. This flop is actually very safe for your hand. The small blind has called despite being out of position. Empirically, such a call is mostly made with one of two hands:
> 1. A small to medium pair, or
> 2. Ace-x.
>
> A higher pair would reraise, while hands like king-x are usually judged too weak for the situation. So this flop was unlikely to hit most of the common calling hands. Also remember that just because an aggressive player is willing to open a pot with any two cards, he won't therefore call a solid

bet with any two cards. His calls are more likely to reflect traditional value considerations.

The standard play here is just to bet about half the pot, around $20,000. You're representing a pair of kings, and that bet will either win the pot, or reveal that your opponent has a hand as well. Although your actual hand isn't a pair of kings, it's still quite strong. If your opponent calls that bet, he must have at least a small pair, since there are no flush or straight draws out there. If he raises, then he's representing a better hand than yours, and you'll have to decide if he's bluffing or not.

The other way to play the hand is both more interesting and more dangerous. You're up against a very aggressive player, and you have both a good hand and position on him. You could just check as well. With this play, you're trying to induce a bluff on fourth street, which you'll pick off.

If your opponent has nothing much, you probably won't make any money from him this hand with the straightforward play. But the check (which is actually a much more aggressive way of playing) might net you an extra bet on fourth or fifth street.

There are, of course, some extra risks associated with this way of playing. The primary risk is that you're giving your opponent a free card to beat you. The secondary risk is that by forgoing an opportunity to define your hand, you'll be less sure of what any subsequent bet actually means. If a jack falls on fourth street and the small blind makes a bet, is he bluffing or did he just make his hand? You'll have to guess. The last risk is that your play may not, in fact, make any extra money. Your opponent might be willing to just check the hand down.

Is either way of playing the hand actually "correct?" In most situations, the straightforward bet will win a small pot with minimal risk and fluctuation. But against an opponent that you know is capable of trying to steal, the call will probably earn you more money in the long run, but with bigger wins and bigger losses. This approach, however, is how super-aggressive players build their chip stacks. They court volatility, secure in the knowledge that they're capable of playing difficult hands better than their opponents.

**Action:** You actually check.

**Fourth Street: 9♠**

**Action:** The small blind bets $35,000. *What do you do?*
**Answer:** Any card below your tens is a good card for you. The bet was exactly what you were expecting when you checked last turn, so there's no reason to be afraid of it. You should just call.

**Action:** You call. The pot is now $110,700.

**Fifth Street: Q♣**

**Action:** The small blind checks. *What do you do?*
**Answer:** The queen was a scary card for you, but it's also a scary card for your opponent if he doesn't have a king or a queen. At this point, the prudent move is just to check the hand down. You probably have the best hand right now, but a bet here is unlikely to make you any money, and it could lose you a lot of money. Just check.

**Resolution:** You check. The small blind turns over 6♠6♣, and you take the pot.

# Hand 10-13

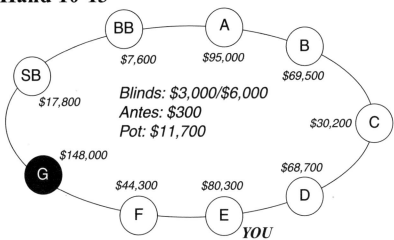

**Situation:** Final two tables of a multi-table online tournament. Player F is a very strong player who has had great success at the online tournaments at your site.

**Your hand:** A♠4♣

**Action to you:** Players A, B, C, and D fold. The pot is still $11,700.

**Question:** *Do you fold, call, or raise?*

> **Answer:** You can raise here as part of an unusual type of isolation play. Note that after posting the blinds and antes, the big blind has only $1,300 left, so he's essentially all-in. Your ace-four offsuit is a perfect hand to take against a random hand in a heads-up showdown. The small blind only has $14,500, so his stack isn't threatening either. Your only real concern are the two other players behind you, and ace-four is a good enough hand (barely) for raising them.

A very conservative player might elect to fold here, and that's not a bad play. But super-aggressive players build their stacks by moving in situations like this.

**Action:** You raise to $12,000. Player F raises to $27,000. Player G and the small blind fold. The big blind goes all-in for his last $1,300 The pot is now $52,000. *What do you do?*

**Answer:** This was a bad result for you. Not only did Player F raise you, but he didn't raise you all-in. Instead he just raised $27,000, leaving himself a mere $17,000 in his stack. Since his M was only 4 (while yours was 7), and he was certainly justified in shoving in all his chips if he wanted to play, the only reason for his move was to give you the best possible pot odds for calling, while still forcing you to commit some more chips. That means he has a very strong hand, probably a high pair, although possibly something like ace-king or ace-queen.

Although that's the bad news, there is some good news. You still have an ace, so if he made his play with a high pair other than aces, your ace would give you about a 30 percet chance of winning the hand. If he made the play with ace-x, your winning chances are down to about 25 percent. If the pot odds are right, it might be worthwhile playing.

Now we have to start doing some math. Since this is a key hand, it's worth spending a little extra time to make sure we get the decision right.

We'll start by figuring out just what we have to put in the pot to play. Right now it looks like we have to put in $15,000 to call a pot of $52,000, which would represent 3.5-to-1 odds. But there are two problems with that reasoning. Player F started with $44,000 and just put in $27,000, leaving him with only $17,000. If we just call now, he's going to be putting that last $17,000 (representing an M of just 1.5) into the pot after the flop, and the pot odds will almost certainly compel us to call. In effect, we're both pot-committed at this point. So we should do our calculations assuming that his last $17,000 has gone into the pot and we have matched it. Only if that scenario justifies a call are we going to stay in.

The second problem is that we have not one pot but two. The betting in the main pot was closed when the big blind went all-in, so that pot has the $11,700 from the blinds and antes plus $1,300 from each of the three players, for a total of $15,600. The side pot will have $43,000 from Player F (representing his whole stack, less the $1,300 he contributed to the main pot) and a matching $43,000 from me, for a total of $86,000. The money I'm trying to win is his $43,000 plus the $10,700 I've already contributed (the other $1,300 went in the main pot), or $53,700. To win that, I have to bet a total of $32,000 ($15,000 to call the current bet, and then we are assuming that I will eventually put in another $17,000 to get the rest of his chips, one way or another.)

If you have reason to believe that the odds of winning the two pots are very different (based on the action you've seen around the table), then you might want to consider each pot separately, make a rough guess at your chances of winning it, and then lump the two answers together. If your chances of winning the two pots are about the same, then the easiest solution is to lump all the money together and see if the pot odds work out. That's the case here. We think that Player F has a high pair and the big blind has a random hand, so mostly when we improve to beat Player F, we will be good enough to win the main pot as well. That's not 100 percent accurate, but this stuff is tough enough as it is!

So we're almost done. We'll have to put in $32,000 more to play the hand to the end. In return, we can win this amount:

- $11,700: blinds and antes
- $1,300: rest of the big blind's stack
- $12,000: our first bet
- $44,000: rest of Player F's stack

That's a total of $69,000. $32,000 to win $69,000 means we're getting about 2.1-to-1 on our money.

So what are our real winning chances against Player F? If we think he has a high pair like queens, we're about a 70-to-30 underdog, or about 2.3-to-1. If he has us dominated with something like ace-king or ace-queen, we're about 3-to-1 underdogs. It's just possible he's pulling a post-oak bluff, pretending that his small bet represents strength when it's really weak, but that's a very, very rare play in online tournaments. (They're just not sophisticated enough to pick up on what you're doing.) Conclusion: We just don't have the odds we need here. Let the hand go.

**Action:** You call, and the flop comes J♣J♠7♠. You put Player F all-in and he calls. He shows K♠K♥, and his hand holds up to win.

# Hand 10-14

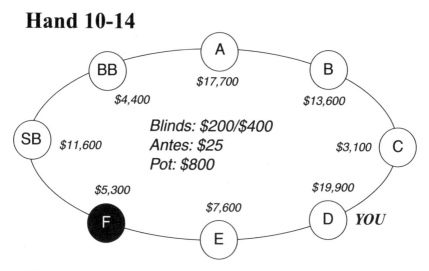

**Situation:** In the middle of a multi-table online tournament. The table has been playing very tight recently.

**Your hand:** 6♣6♦

**Action to you:** Player A folds. Player B raises $2,000. Player C folds. The pot is now $2,800.

**Question:** *Do you fold, call, or raise?*

**Answer:** As I explained in Part Nine, small pairs are problematic hands when your M is small. They may be equally problematic when your M is reasonable but other Ms at the table are small. In this situation your M is about 24, and you're holding a pair of sixes. Can you call?

The answer is actually a pretty clear no. There are two key reasons:

1. **Pot odds.** You're 7½-to-1 against improving to trips on the flop. Player B raised you $2,000 from his stack of $13,600. He only has $11,600 left. On the occasions you do improve to trips, you won't be able to win enough to justify your call on that basis alone. You'll need to win some times when you don't improve. But if you don't improve and some high cards come on the flop, you'll be hard-pressed to call a good-sized bet.

2. **Players behind you.** There are four players still to act behind you, and they all have stacks smaller than Player B. Suppose you call, Player E (whose stack is $7,600) goes all-in, and Player B folds. You'll be able to justify calling if you think there's a good chance he's not holding a pair. But if you think he likely has a pair, you must throw your hand away. The possibility of being raised by players behind you further increases the amount you need to be able to win when your hand takes the pot. Often you may feel that you understand what the player in front of you is doing, but then the death blow comes from behind.

**Action:** You fold. The small blind calls. The flop comes Q♦9♣4♦, and the small blind goes all-in and wins the pot.

# Hand 10-15

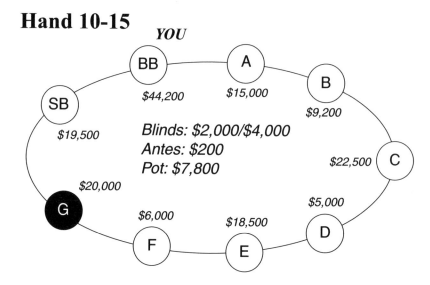

YOU

BB $44,200
A $15,000
B $9,200
SB $19,500
C $22,500
G $20,000
F $6,000
E $18,500
D $5,000

Blinds: $2,000/$4,000
Antes: $200
Pot: $7,800

**Situation:** A multi-table online tournament which has been reduced to the last 54 players at 6 tables. The tournament began with 400 players, each with $1,000 in chips. A total of 40 places will be paid. You are currently in second place in the tournament.

**Your hand:** 9♥6♠

**Action to you:** Player A folds. Player B goes all-in for his last $9,000. Everyone folds around to you. The pot is now $16,800. It costs you $5,000 to call.

**Question:** *Do you call or fold?*

> **Answer:** This is not an uncommon situation for many of the small-stakes multi-table online tournaments. Many players get confused in these positions because there are arguments for calling and arguments for folding. Let's work through the problem carefully and see which arguments win out.

1. Your pot odds are very good, which is an argument for calling, but

2. Your hand is weak, which is an argument for folding, but

3. Player B could have gone all-in with almost anything, which is an argument for calling, but

4. You're in second place in the tournament and near the money, which is an argument for folding.

So what's right?

Your pot odds are indeed very good. You have to put in $5,000 to see a pot of $16,800, so your odds are about 3.3-to-1. That's the most important consideration and it's very favorable. Only if he holds a pair of nines or higher will you not get the odds you need to call. Given Player B's desperate situation, you can assume that's unlikely, and your odds are good enough despite the weakness of your hand.

Should your standing in the tournament deter you from calling? That's the real question in this hand, and the answer is no. Your good standing is something of an illusion. The 400 starting players all began with a stake of $1,000. Only 54 players remain, about one-eight of the field. That means the average chip stack is now about $8,000. Since your stack is $40,000, your Q is more than 5. That sounds good, until you notice that your M is just over 5 as well! These low-M high-Q situations are typical of the small-stakes online tournaments with big fields and short rounds. The blinds increase so quickly that even the chip leaders are getting desperate toward the end of the event.

Your apparent chip lead here isn't just an illusion; it's a trap. If you try to protect your lead with conservative play, the blinds will simply gobble you up. The real strength of your position is that you can enter some of these very favorable all-in situations and survive a beat, whereas your opponents will get knocked out when they lose. So you must take the odds and play. It's your M that governs your strategy, not your Q.

**Action:** You call. Your opponent shows A♦J♠. His hand holds up to win.

# Part Eleven
# Short Tables

# Short Tables
# Introduction

In a large tournament, one of the tournament director's jobs is to keep the tables full as much as possible. Eight or nine players is considered an ideal number. (Ten players is considered too many, as it promotes excessively tight play.) When a table shrinks to six or seven players, the directors try to break up the table as soon as possible, distributing the players across other short tables.

When the total number of players shrinks below 30, players will find themselves spending more and more time at relatively short tables. Once the survivors reach the final table and a couple of players get eliminated, the remainder will play under short conditions for the rest of the tournament.

Short-table play is poker on steroids. The action speeds up, and all-in bets become more frequent. You must keep a careful eye on your stack and the blinds, and be prepared to make moves whenever favorable conditions appear. You may know quite a bit about some of your opponents, having played with them at different tables over the past few days. Pressure and tension are high; really big money, life-changing money for some, is just a few hands away.

For newcomers, this part of the tournament is a real test of character. Some thrive, discovering (perhaps to their surprise) that matching wits against the world's best under pressure-cooker conditions is something they were born to do. Others discover something quite different.

While the character part of the game can't be taught, the technical part can. In this section I'll explain some of the key strategies of short-table play. But first let's revisit our old friend M, who undergoes a few revisions at short tables.

# Effective M
# Adjusting for Short Tables

In Part Nine, I defined M as the ratio of your chip stack to the total of the blinds and antes, and then showed how shrinking Ms caused your strategy to change as well. That discussion, however, was in the context of full-table play, with eight, nine, or ten players sitting down at a table. When we move to short tables, we have to make an adjustment to M, creating what I call the "effective M."

Remember: What M is designed to tell you is just how long your stack will last until it's blinded away. Say you have $60,000 in your stack and the blinds and antes now total $12,000. Your M is 5, so you can survive five rounds of the table before your stack disappears. At a full table of nine or ten players, that means you can survive about 45 to 50 hands. But suppose you're at a table of just four players? Now your M of 5 only represents about 20 hands. In reality, your situation is more analogous to that of having an M of about 2 at a full table.

Clearly you need to make an adjustment to M as the table size shrinks. I call this creating an "effective M," and it's a pretty simple modification. Just calculate your M as before, and then multiple M by the percentage of a full table that remains. Here's a quick formula:

Effective M = (Basic M) times (Players Left/10)

I used 10 instead of 9 in the denominator because it makes the calculations easier. We're looking for a quick guide, not mathematical exactitude.

**Example 1: Your stack is $100,000, the blinds and antes total $12,000, and there are four players left at the table. *What's your effective M?***

**Answer:** Your basic M is 100,000/12,000, which is a little more than 8. With four players left we'll multiply 8 by 0.4 to get an effective M of 3.2.

At short tables, you want to calibrate your strategy using your effective M. Otherwise you'll be assuming you have more hands left than you really have, and your play will be too tight.

**Example 2: Final table of a major tournament. Five players remain. The blinds are $15,000/$30,000 with antes of $5,000 each. The chip stacks of the five players are as follows:**

| | |
|---|---|
| Player A | $600,000 |
| Player B | $100,000 |
| Player C | $1,200,000 |
| Player D | $450,000 |
| Player E | $220,000 |

*What are the effective Ms for each of the five players?*
**Answer:** If you do the math properly, you should get the following answers:

| | |
|---|---|
| Player A | Just over 4 |
| Player B | Under 1 |
| Player C | Between 8 and 9 |
| Player D | Just over 3 |
| Player E | Between 1 and 2 |

Notice that although Player C has a big lead and a comfortable stack, his effective M is already in the Orange Zone. He can't be tight and sit back. If he tries to be conservative, what will happen is that whoever survives the looming battle between A, B, D, and E will quickly be in a threatening or commanding position vis-à-vis C. Being tight may assure Player C of finishing in the top three, but it won't help his chances of finishing first.

# The Tactics
# of Short-Table Play

Short tables are tactical battlegrounds. With time running out on all the participants the line between bluffing and value betting quickly gets blurred. Regardless of what actually constitutes a value bet when two players have already folded at a six-player table, players will be moving at the pot with some fairly random collections of cards.

With players so eager to get involved with weaker cards, slow-playing becomes an even more powerful and dangerous option, both before and after the flop. Let's consider each case separately.

## Slow-Playing Before the Flop

When the table gets very small, the issue of slow-playing before the flop becomes more difficult. With only three or four players at the table, hands obviously rise in value, and hands that couldn't be considered as slow-play candidates at a full table now have some allure. What are reasonable standards for checking and trapping at these tables?

In my experience, most players get much too clever at short tables, giving their opponents plenty of free cards with only marginally strong hands, and frequently knocking themselves out in the process. When the tables get small, the blinds are usually getting large. Large blinds act as a powerful counterweight, giving you a strong incentive to take down the pot as soon as possible.

I have a simple set of rules for slow-playing at short tables, designed to keep me out of trouble as much as possible. Here they are.

1.   **AA, KK, QQ**. These are genuinely powerful hands under any circumstances, and I will cheerfully slow-play them, with only an occasional raise as part of a balanced strategy.

2.   **JJ, TT, 99**. Tempting but dangerous. I'll sometimes slow-play jacks, and even tens occasionally, but never nines. Even against a single opponent, you may have to throw your hand away if overcards come on the flop.

3.   **Smaller pairs**. Always bet out for value.

4.   **Unpaired cards**. Always bet out for value. I've seen many players over the years slow-play an ace-king, then look sick when three random cards come and their opponent throws in a big bet. Unpaired cards are just unpaired cards, and picking up the blinds with an ace-high hand is a good result.

# Slow-Playing After the Flop

Slow-playing after the flop is a powerful weapon at short tables. Because players have smaller Ms, they are more susceptible to the lure of apparent weakness than they were at full tables earlier in the tournament. Not only are they more eager to bet after you've shown weakness, but a bet and a call can build the pot to a size where they feel justified in committing the rest of their chips with a moderately strong hand.

**Example 3. It's the final table of a major tournament. Six players remain. The blinds are $600 and $1,200, with $200 antes, and the initial pot is $3,000. You're currently the tournament leader with $180,000, and this hand you're second to act at the table. Your reputation is that of a very smart, experienced, and aggressive player, and that's how you've been playing throughout the tournament. The player directly behind in third position is also very experienced, and known**

for his tricky and trappy play. He has $80,000. The other four players at the table are tournament veterans with chip counts between $50,000 and $160,000.

Player 1 folds. Your hand is

*What do you do?*

**Answer:** Ace-seven offsuit is a reasonable, if somewhat minimal, opening hand from second position at a six-handed table. The structure here is a bit unusual, with much smaller blinds and antes than you'll typically see at this point. The smallest stack has an M of 17 and an effective M of about 10, while your M is a whopping 60, and even your effective M is about 36. Large Ms mean no one is feeling too desperate, so you don't have to worry so much about throwing your hand away after a random all-in from a small stack. Any all-in from this table will probably indicate great strength and you'll easily be able to let go of your ace-seven.

With your big chip stack you should be happy to just make reasonable bets with promising hands at pots that haven't been opened, looking to slowly build up your lead. Your hand here is good enough for that purpose.

You raise to $4,000. The player in third position calls. The last player and the blinds fold. The pot is now $11,000.

The flop comes

**You're first to act.** *What do you do?*

**Answer:** Obviously that's a fantastically good flop for you. Your only problem is that it's a flop that's highly unlikely to have hit your opponent in any way. You now have two choices, neither of which is a perfect solution:

1.  You can check, and hope that your opponent either tries to steal the pot from you with a bet, or catches a card on fourth street that will let him put more money in the hand.

2.  You can make a continuation-sized bet, on the theory that a check from a known aggressive player like yourself will elicit more suspicion than an apparent continuation bet. If your opponent has a couple of high cards and thinks the flop missed you (a reasonable assumption), then you may get some action.

This is a typical judgment call of the sort you'll have to make many times during a tournament. My choice would be to check. Your hand is so good, and the flop so unlikely to have helped your opponent, that letting another card hit before betting looks like the most profitable approach.

At this point, some alert readers will be raising their hands with a question: "In Volume I you said that the worst mistake you can make is to give your opponent a free card to beat you. There are two diamonds on board, so why are you giving someone with two diamonds a free shot at a flush? Shouldn't you make him pay to draw at you?"

It's a good point, and here's the answer. First, you're up against just one opponent, not two or three, which cuts down on the chance that you're up against a flush draw. Second, you're at a final table against strong players, who are looking to play high cards, not flush draws. You just won't see the hands like queen-trey suited or jack-four suited, which you frequently encounter in small-stakes online tournaments, against players who think any two suited or connected cards are worth a call. That severely limits the kinds of suited holdings you might be facing. Third, your opponent will probably bet a flush draw at this point (the no-limit semi-bluff) thus eliminating the chance of his getting a free card. Finally, your hand is so good and it's so much more likely you're facing something other than a diamond draw that you simply have to go with the probabilities and play as though you're facing the more likely hands. Remember also that you have outs even against a flush draw that completes his hand on a later street. On fourth street there are three aces and three deuces left that give you a full house, plus one remaining seven to give you quads. On fifth street you'll have three more outs to fill up. Thus, you have a significant chance (over 30 percent) of beating a made flush.

**You check. Your opponent checks behind you. Fourth street is the 5♠.** *What do you do now?*
**Answer:** The check was a bad sign, indicating that either your opponent has nothing, or he was suspicious of your failure to bet. The arrival of the 5♠ was another bad sign. That's a card that almost certainly didn't help your opponent. Still, there's no reason to bet yet. There's always the possibility of making some money on the river, so just check again and hope the river card pairs him.

**You actually bet $4,500, and your opponent folds.**

Your opponent, in fact, held the 10♥9♠. He made a marginal call before the flop, based partly on your reputation — you're supposed to be a very aggressive player, so you might be playing cards even weaker than his — and partly on the reasonably good pot odds being offered. (There was $7,000 in the pot, and it cost him only $4,000 to call.) I would have weighed these considerations against the threat of the three live players yet to act and let the hand go, but it's a close call and his play was defensible.

# The Cooperation Play

As the field shrinks and the difference between each place and its associated prize grows, a new play arises known as the cooperation play. The idea of the cooperation play is to maximize the chance of eliminating the short stack by refusing to bet against other players who are also in the pot. The more players that remain in the pot, the better the chance of eliminating the short stack at the showdown. (The "cooperation" here is non-verbal, of course. It's a severe breach of the rules and poker etiquette to discuss this at the table.) Cooperation is more certain the smaller the small stack really is. If the small stack is just marginally smaller than the other stacks at the table, collecting his chips might become a higher goal than knocking him out, in which case cooperation could break down.

Here's a simple example of the cooperation play in action.

**Example 4: Final table of a major event. Six players remain. Blinds are $3,000/$6,000, with $500 antes. The starting pot is $12,000. You are on the big blind. The stacks, after posting the blinds and antes, are as follows:**

| Sm Blind | $350,000 |
|---|---|
| Big Blind (You) | $400,000 |
| Player 1 | $950,000 |
| Player 2 | $30,000 |
| Player 3 | $500,000 |
| Player 4 (Button) | $600,000 |

**Player 1 folds. Player 2 goes all-in. Player 3 calls. Player 4 and the small blind fold. You hold 9♠7♥.** *What do you do?*

**Answer:** Call, and plan on checking the hand down. You and Player 3 are like two linebackers in football trying to plug the gaps and make sure Player 2 doesn't escape. Your nine-seven offsuit is a useful holding, covering a lot of middle cards that might appear. Hopefully Player 3 has some high cards covered, and together you can throw the short stack for a loss.

Under what circumstances would you break the cooperation and bet? There's a simple answer: Whenever you flop a hand so good that you don't think beating Player 2 is an issue any more, and your goal becomes to make as much money from Player 3 as possible. This requires a great hand. Exactly how good your great hand must be is a judgment call given the particular circumstances.

The order in which the stacks enter the pot matters very much. In the previous example, the short stack went in first, and was then called by Player 3 and then by you. In this case there is no side pot and no need to start one. If a large stack enters with a bet, and then is called by a short stack, the situation is very different. Now when you call, you're involved in a tiny main pot with both opponents, but a larger side pot with your live opponent. In this case winning the side pot may be much more important to your tournament chances than the main pot, so cooperation would not play much of a role here. You will make the plays necessary to maximize your chance of winning the side pot.

# Flyswatting: The 10-to-1 Rule

As you get close to the end of the tournament, eliminating players becomes more and more important, as each player eliminated guarantees you a larger minimum prize. A quick rule of thumb for these cases is what I call the "10-to-1 Rule." If I have at least 10 times as many chips as another player, I will cheerfully put them all-in with any two cards. The combined probability that they will fold to my bet or that I will win the hand if they call is always great enough to risk the chance of at most a 10 percent hit to my stack.

**Example 5. Five players remain at a major tournament. You are the small blind, in second place with $760,000. The blinds are $5,000/$10,000, with $1,000 antes. The big blind is the short stack with $60,000. The first three players fold to you. You look at your cards and see**

*What do you do?*

**Answer:** Move all-in on the big blind. His stack at the beginning of the hand was less than one-twelfth of yours. The advantage of eliminating a player is so great that the small risk to your stack is well worth it. Your actual hand is irrelevant.

The situation is slightly different if the small stack has moved all-in first. Now you've lost the first-in vigorish, and his hand is probably somewhat better than an average hand. In this case I would require cards with some value to go along with my larger stack.

In 1995, I made a play at the final table of the World Series that was entirely governed by the 10-to-1 Rule. The blinds were $15,000/$30,000 with $2,000 antes, and I was in the big blind with close to $1,000,000. The button was Hamid Dastmalchi, an excellent player who had won the World Series a few years before. His stack was down to $110,000. The hand was folded to the button, and Dastmalchi pushed all-in. The small blind folded, and it was an $80,000 raise to me. Knowing about the 10-to-1 Rule, I took my feeble

and called.

Dastmalchi turned over

and I showed my J♣3♠. The table seemed to give an audible gasp, and I heard at least one spectator whisper "Harrington's lost his mind!" My mind was actually intact, but I did lose the hand.

Losing the hand, however, had an entirely unexpected bonus. For several rounds, no one contested my big blind! The table had decided that Action Dan had been replaced by Maniac Dan, and no one wanted to mess with my blind unless they had a real hand. Within a few rounds I had made my $80,000 back with a bit of interest. Remember this anecdote the next time you're caught playing a weak hand in some low-M situation. Unless your opponents are sophisticated about tournament tactics, they won't necessarily draw the right conclusions about what you're doing.

# When in Doubt, Let the Pot Odds Decide

At very short tables, your actual hand shrinks in importance and your pot odds rise in importance. Get in the habit of calculating the pot and your odds *before every decision*. Your mental conversation shouldn't be "I only have jack-five" but "I have jack-five and the pot odds are 2.2-to-1." By thinking of your cards and your odds as a pair of facts, you'll keep your thinking in order. Good short-table play consists of keeping the cards and the odds balanced properly.

Weak cards plus good odds = playable situation

After all, most of your cards will be weak compared to the cards you usually play, but by moving with the odds, you'll keep yourself in the game. Always remember that your opponents have to wrestle with the same bad cards you're seeing.

**Example 6. A big tournament, three players remain. Blinds are $3,000/$6,000, with $300 antes. Chips and stacks are as follows:**

| | |
|---|---|
| Button | $71,900 |
| Sm Blind (You) | $35,500 |
| Big Blind | $72,500 |

**You have K♥3♥. The button calls, putting in $6,000.** *What do you do?*

**Answer:** The pot now contains $15,900. It costs you another $3,000 to call. You're getting better than 5-to-1 on your money. Under those circumstances, king-trey suited is a monster hand, and you can certainly call. Having the short stack or being out of position after the flop are minor considerations compared to the monstrous odds.

You also have a second option, which is to raise all-in. The mere call from the button more likely means weakness than a trap, and the big blind is a random hand as far as you know. If my hand were as strong as king-seven suited, I would definitely go all-in here. (Remember that your stack is large enough so that someone who calls and loses moves into last place.) The trey kicker is weak enough so that I would lean slightly to calling.

**Example 7. Same tournament and blinds, a few hands later. Now the stacks are as follows:**

| | |
|---|---|
| **Button** | **$62,900** |
| **Sm Blind** | **$85,100** |
| **Big Blind (You)** | **$31,900** |

**You hold**

**The button goes all-in and the small blind folds. The raise to you is the amount of your remaining stack, $25,600.** *What do you do?*

**Answer:** The pot contains $31,900 (he's put you all-in) from the button, plus $3,300 from the small blind, plus your initial $6,300, for a total of $41,800. It costs you $25,600 to call. Pot odds are about 40-to-25, or 8-to-5, or about 1.6-to-1. Those are big odds when you're holding jack-ten. You're getting close to the right price if he's holding two higher cards, and better than the right price if he's holding a higher and lower card or an underpair. Only if he holds one of the top five pairs are you in serious trouble. One of the other holdings is far more likely, so you call.

# Controlling Pot Odds

If pot odds are so important, it follows that you should make an effort to control the odds your opponents see, either to force them out of the pot or to induce mistakes. With so few players in the hand, this is often more easily done than at larger tables.

A good technique for approaching these kinds of problems is to imagine the types of hands your opponent might hold, and see if there are bet sizes which would make a call incorrect for certain categories of hands. It may be the case that you can make a call incorrect for some category of hands but not for others. Here's a good example.

**Example 8. Big tournament, final table, last three players. Blinds and antes are $3,000/$6,000 with $300 antes. Initial pot is $9,900. You pick up T♥T♣. The stack sizes are as follows:**

|  |  |
|---|---|
| **Button** | **$68,900** |
| **Sm Blind (You)** | **$57,800** |
| **Big Blind** | **$53,200** |

**The button folds.** *What's the right amount to raise?*

**Answer:** A pair of tens is obviously a great hand heads-up. Of course, you can't give someone who has a random high card a free shot to beat you, but you don't want to chase them away with an all-in raise either. You need to charge something to play, encourage some action, and simultaneously give your opponent a chance to make a mistake. Is there a bet size that accomplishes all this?

Let's start by considering the kinds of hands the big blind might hold, assuming he's thinking of calling some sort of raise from us.

1.  **Two undercards**. We can ignore this. He'll almost certainly throw away two cards lower than a ten in the face of any meaningful raise. If he does play, he'll need at least 4-to-1 odds, which he won't get.

2.  **A higher pair**. If he has a premium pair, he'll probably win all our money no matter how we bet, so we'll ignore this case as well.

3.  **A lower pair**. This is the best situation, but one we can also ignore because it will take care of itself. He will need 4-to-1 odds, he won't get them, and he'll play anyway. Case closed.

4.  **Two overcards**. This case is more interesting, partly because many calls will fall in this category. We will be about a 13-to-10 favorite against two overcards. If we put in the standard raise of triple the big blind, then we'll have to bet a total of $21,000 ($3,000 to call the big blind, and another $18,000 for the raise.) If that's our action, then the big blind will need to put in $18,000 to call, with a pot of $30,900. The pot will be offering him 1.6-to-1, so his call will easily be correct. But what can we do? If we want to raise him four times the big blind, we'll have to put in a total of $27,000. Then he'll have to put in $24,000 to call a pot of $36,900. We'll have reduced his pot odds to 1.5-to-1, but that's still plenty good enough to call. If we raise much more than this, we can keep reducing his odds, but we're also committing ourselves to the pot, in which case we may as well go all-in to start. In this particular case, there just isn't much we can do to deny our opponent the odds he needs to call.

5. **One overcard**. Aha! Here's the most interesting case. A hand like ace-eight is a little more than a 2-to-1 underdog to our pair of tens. This is just what we're looking for — a hand that's definitely a potential calling hand, and a hand where we can deny the odds. Now our triple-the-big-blind bet, giving 1.6-to-1 calling odds, will force him to make a mistake to call. Since this is the *only* category of hand where we can pick a bet size that makes a difference, it's the only category we need to consider.

**Conclusion:** We raise three times the big blind, pushing in $21,000.

# Blending Strategy, Stack Size, and the Prize Fund

Now it's time to look at another factor that affects decision-making at short tables: the prize structure itself. Before you start playing at a final table, you need to commit to memory the exact prize structure for the last nine or ten places. *You need to do this even if the prize structure doesn't affect you personally.* You may be a retired gazillionaire who only cares about finishing first. If true, that's great. But the money *will* matter to most of your motley crew of opponents, and it will affect them in predictable ways. Making some intelligent, common-sense assumptions about what each player is really hoping to do and what he's playing for can enable you to make some spectacular moves.

Let's look at a few poker types and make some observations about how the money will affect them and how you should play.

**The Internet Qualifier.** He's a young kid, he paid $50 or so to get in an online qualifying tournament, he won a free shot to the big show, and now he's at the final table, staring at more money than he's ever seen before. Most of these players are just trying to move up the ladder, and every step on that ladder might represent several years' worth of income. A player who's thinking that way can be pushed around pretty easily. But some of these kids turn out to be real tigers who see their lucky break as the springboard to a real poker career. Keep an eye on them and let somebody else be the first guy to try to push them out of a pot. Watch what happens and act accordingly in the future.

**The High-Tech Millionaire.** He made money during the boom of the nineties, retired with his fortune intact, and now needs something to fill his time. He's not playing poker for money; he's playing to show you how clever he is. He will bluff liberally, and he will show you his cards when his bluffs work, so you'll know how much smarter than you he is. Whether he folds to your bluff or not depends on what sort of bluff you make. If you just shove all your money in the pot before the flop, he'll call you. (*Can't push me around.*) But if you make some sort of long, intricate play and then bet on the river, he'll go away. (*Your move was brilliant, but I figured it all out, ha ha.*) As the table gets short, he will attack more frequently, knowing that the money means more to you than to him. You won't be able to wear him down; instead you'll need to pick your spots and make a stand. The all-in check-raise is a particularly good weapon.

**The Down-on-his-Luck Pro.** He might have been a millionaire a few weeks ago, but now he's broke. Such is life in the fast lane. The money will certainly matter to him, but in unpredictable ways. He may simply want to get a bankroll back, in which case each step on the prize ladder will matter very much. A good clue is his willingness to offer deals and splits during breaks in the action. But he may have colossal debts, in which case only one of the top prizes can get him back to even. In that case, he'll be going for broke. (A story that became legend on the backgammon circuit concerned a semi-pro player in a London club many years ago. He got in over his head in a high-stakes game against seven wealthy opponents. The team eventually doubled their seven cubes to 128 apiece. As he accepted the cubes, he remarked, "I might as well take, since I can't afford to pay if I drop." He lost, walked into the night, and was never seen again.)

**The Retired Businessman.** He ran a business for a long time, had a successful career, and has taken up poker as a hobby. He's spent a lifetime making business decisions and negotiating, an ideal training ground for a poker player. He doesn't need the money, but he respects money, and you can expect his decisions to be rational and shrewd. He knows that the pros will see him as a neophyte and try to push him around, and he'll be ready for that. If he opens a pot and you have a good hand, just put him all-in. He'll call more often than not.

**The Wealthy Seasoned Pro.** This guy is one tough hombre. He's seen it all, done it all, and kept the money, so you can forget about outplaying him, and the idea of putting money pressure on him is a joke. Recommended strategy: If you can't outplay him, you need another approach. When he gets in a pot, raise him all-in with any two reasonable cards. The other players will get out of the way, and the first couple of times you do this he'll lay his hand down unless he has a big pair. Eventually he'll know what you're doing and at some point he'll pick a hand and call you, and then you'll actually have to win the hand. But maybe you'll have a good hand that time, or perhaps you'll just draw out on him. It's your best shot.

As you get involved in the poker circuit and start traveling around, hanging out with players while moving from tournament to tournament, you'll hear snippets of news, stories, rumors, and gossip. Some will be first-hand, some second-hand, some from good sources, some from bad sources. Pay attention to all of it. Try to piece it together into some recognizable mosaic. Knowing what financial or emotional state your opponents are in when you play them can be just as valuable as knowing that they like to check when they hit a flop and move in on fourth street.

Now let's look at a practical application of all this palaver.

**Example 9. A major tournament, and just three players remain besides yourself. You are an experienced pro with several recent successes under your belt. You're widely respected for being tough, shrewd, and hard to read. You're sitting on the big stack of $4,000,000. Here are your opponents:**

Opponent No. 1: A top player of many years' standing, with several big wins under his belt. Quite wealthy, totally unreadable and unflappable. His stack at this point is $1,500,000.

Opponent No. 2. An Internet qualifier, playing in his first major tournament. A polite kid, looks pretty intelligent and seems to play well. Likes to make small aggressive moves at a lot of pots. His stack: $1,200,000.

Opponent No. 3: A restaurant owner from London, probably fairly wealthy and here on a lark. His luck ran out a couple of hours ago and he's been nursing a small stack which is getting smaller. He hasn't made an aggressive move even when given a chance, so perhaps he's resigned himself to a fourth-place finish. His stack: $120,000.

The blinds right now are $10,000/$20,000, with $2,000 antes. There's $38,000 in the pot each hand. Everyone has a comfortable M except Opponent No. 3, whose effective M is now about 1.2.

The remaining prize structure looks like this:

| | |
|---|---|
| First | $1,200,000 |
| Second | $600,000 |
| Third | $400,000 |
| Fourth | $150,000 |

It's not an unusual prize structure for big tournaments these days, with a heavy weighting for first prize, but very respectable prizes for second and third. There is a sharp dropoff from third to fourth, however.

In the next hand you are first to act. The Internet qualifier is on the button, with the restaurant owner in the small blind and the old pro in the big blind.

**You pick up**

**and lead out for $60,000, triple the big blind. The Internet Qualifier raises, making it $130,000. The blinds fold.** *What do you do?*

> **Answer:** Call. You know the kid likes to make small moves, and this bet certainly qualifies. He may have nothing much but feel that by taking the lead in the betting, and by acting after you next round, he can take the pot away. You have a big stack and a playable hand under the circumstances, so call.

**You call. The pot is now $298,000. The flop comes**

*What do you do?*

> **Answer:** That's a good flop for your hand — no high cards, all low cards, and now you have an open-ended straight draw plus two running cards for a flush. You could bet, but I would be inclined to check for a reason which will soon be apparent.

**You check. The Internet qualifier bets $130,000.** *What do you do?*

**Answer:** You go all-in.

For a good player, this is almost a no-brainer, and has nothing to do with potential holdings, pot odds, or hand analysis. It has everything to do with your opponent and the prize fund.

Up until a few seconds ago, everyone at the table had mentally assigned fourth prize to the Restaurant Owner, who was just a couple of blinds away from being eliminated. In particular, the Internet Qualifier, playing in his first tournament on a free ride, was thinking "I've got $400,000 in the bag, and I'm shooting for more." Your all-in move has changed the equation. Now the kid is thinking "If I lose this hand, I'm going to lose $250,000." $250,000 looks like a lot of money to someone in their twenties playing in their first tournament, especially after thinking the money was theirs.

Your bet represents trips. Your opponent will fold this hand unless he has trips himself. He might even fold bottom trips, but he'll certainly fold a high pair rather than risk $250,000.

**You go all-in, and your opponent folds**.

The hand hinged on the presence of the restaurant owner, who was what we call a "cripple" — a player whose stack had been so low for so long that everyone else at the table had pegged themselves for one of the top three places. The existence of a cripple subtly changes the dynamic among the remaining players, like some invisible planet exerting a gravitational tug on everything in its vicinity. It enhances the position of the big stack (you in this case) who can threaten the medium-stacked players with an all-in move that they can't call without risking money they thought was already in their pocket. Once the cripple is eliminated, the threat goes away and the game returns to normal.

# Win the Hand
# or Play for the Prize Money?

Here's a key question that puzzles many tournament players. "Should you play to maximize your chance of winning the tournament, or play to preserve your chips and move up the prize ladder?" My quick answer is — play to win. In practice this means to make the "best" play with the idea of maximizing your equity in the hand, and let your final placing in the tournament take care of itself. There are three good reasons for playing this way.

Playing to maximize your equity in the hand will mostly be the right play anyway. The exceptions are rare, and usually have to do with laying down a good hand when a larger stack is in a position to go out. In most tournaments, the prize structure is heavily skewed towards the very high places, so playing to win will in most cases make you more money in the long run, if not in this particular tournament.

Most of your opponents will be playing to move up spots in the standings and bag a larger prize. As always in poker, doing the opposite of what the other players are doing is the most profitable approach.

Poker is now big business, and the perks go to the players who actually win tournaments, not to the runners-up. Winning a tournament looks much better in your resume than cashing a few times.

# Managing Bet Sizes: Carrots and Sticks

One of the most attractive features of no-limit hold 'em as a game is the ability to control bet sizes for your own purpose. In Volume I we looked at situations where you could use your bets to chase an opponent out of the pot by denying him the pot odds needed to call. In short table and low-M situations, you might have the opposite desire: offering your opponent irresistible odds to stick around and lose all his chips.

Even at a short table, of course, you need a strong hand to want your opponent to stay in rather than go away. Pre-flop, I'd want to be holding aces, kings, or queens before I'd think about trapping my opponent into the hand. Smaller pairs are just too likely to be outdrawn, and a hand like ace-king is, after all, just an ace-high hand. But if you have the right hand and the right situation, using bet sizes to trap needs to be part of your repertoire. Let's see how it's done.

**Example 10: Only five players remain from a multi-table tournament. The blinds are $2,000/$4,000, with $200 antes. The initial pot is $7,000. The table is arranged as follows:**

| | |
|---|---|
| Player 1 | $21,500 |
| Player 2 | $27,100 |
| Player 3 | $83,200 |
| Sm Blind (You) | $20,700 |
| Big blind | $37,500 |

**You pick up a pair of aces. Player 1 makes the minimum raise, $8,000. Players 2 and 3 fold.**

**Discussion:** You can hit your opponent with a stick and go all-in, of course, but that contains the risk of chasing him out of the pot. With your Red Zone M of 3.5, and an effective M of just 1.7, you really want to get all his chips and double up. A better way is to make the minimum reraise of another $6,000. Now he's put in $8,000 and you've put in $14,000, so the pot contains $29,000 and it costs him $6,000 to call. He'll be suspicious because you've given him 5-to-1 pot odds, but he will call.

After the flop, the pot will be $35,000, you'll have $4,500 left and he'll have $7,300. When you bet the rest of your money, he'll have better than 5-to-1 odds to call you. Again, he'll be suspicious, but the carrot will be too tempting. The pot odds will force him to call. Now you'll have all his money in the pot, which is all you could want with your pair of bullets. After that, you just have to win the hand!

# Tracking the Big Stack

Being aware of the location of a big stack is important at all stages of a tournament. But as the table shrinks, the blinds rise, and the Ms fall, knowing where the big stack is at all times is especially crucial. Remember that the big stack is the player who can eliminate you at minimum risk to himself. Because he can eliminate you so easily, his status directly effects your willingness to be aggressive or tight.

1. If he's out of the hand, you can be maximally aggressive.

2. If he's potentially in the hand (but has not acted yet), you need to be more cautious.

3. If he's definitely in the hand, you need solid values to play.

All this advice is true to an even larger degree when the big stack is in the big blind. Because he's already posted the blind, he gets more favorable odds than other players to enter the pot, so again you need to raise the caution flag another notch.

When the table shrinks after someone is eliminated, I like to orient myself by asking "What position am I in when the big stack is in the big blind?" Keeping the answer to that question in the foreground helps me avoid errors later in the hand. If the big stack is on my right, for instance, I know that when he's in the big blind, I'll be first to act. Even though the table might have only five or six players, I know that my first position playing criteria will more closely resemble full-table play than short-table play.

# The Problems

In short tables, all the normal aspects of poker come into play, but with slight variations of emphasis because the table is smaller, the action is faster, and the stakes are higher.

In Problems 11-1 through 11-3, we look at the starting requirements for playing in short table situations. Problems 11-4 and 11-5 show a couple of examples of betting to learn information. Some of the finer points of positional play are illustrated in Problems 11-6 through 11-8.

Problem 11-9 shows how the Gap Concept and the Sandwich Effect apply with particular force to short tables. In Problems 11-10 and 11-12 we look at examples of probe and continuation bets.

Stealing, bluffing, and slow-playing at short tables are covered in Problems 11-12 through 11-26.

For pot odds calculations in critical endgame situations, see Problems 11-18 through 11-22. Analyzing all-in moves is particularly critical. For that topic see Problems 11-23 through 11-25.

Problem 11-26 gives an example of deciding whether or not to cooperate. Problem 11-27 shows the 10-to-1 rule in action.

# Hand 11-1

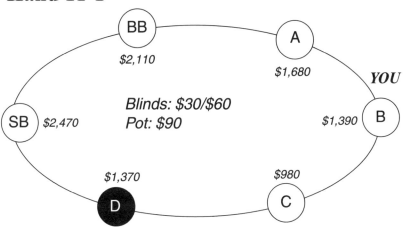

**Situation:** Single table satellite. The small blind is a very aggressive player, others are tighter.

**Your hand:** A♥8♥

**Action to you:** Player A folds.

**Question:** *Do you fold, call, or raise?*

    **Answer:** As the table shrinks, so do your requirements for starting hands. At a full table, you shouldn't be excited about making a move in early position with a hand like ace-eight suited. But with only six players at the table and one player having folded in front of you, there are only four players left to act. You're actually in the equivalent of late middle position at a full table. Now ace-eight suited is a reasonably strong hand, good enough to make a move at the pot. Put in a good-sized bet here of between two and three times the big blind, and see what happens.

**Action:** You bet $160. All the players behind you fold.

That's a great result, although you still had a hand even if you were called.

# Hand 11-2

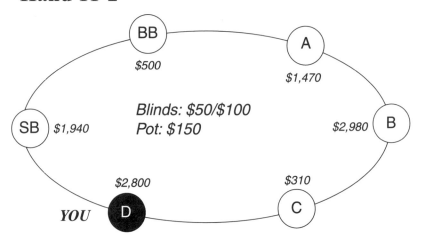

**Situation:** Late in a single-table online tournament. Player B and the small blind are very aggressive.

**Your hand:** Q♠9♣

**Action to you:** Player A folds. Player B calls. Player C folds.

**Question:** *Do you fold, call, or raise?*
   **Answer:** Fold. There are three problems with your hand:

1.  It's not really that strong. With king-queen or queen-jack you'd have a much better argument for calling.

2.  You have two players still to act behind you, one of whom is known to be very active. You don't know what either one is going to do.

3. The caller was the big stack, who can break you.

   You need to be cautious about marginal hands at active tables, even when the tables start to shrink. If there had been three folds in front of you, this hand is easily strong enough to make a move at the pot. But in a contested pot, with two players yet to act, you should want a more solid hand than this.

**Action:** You fold.

# Hand 11-3

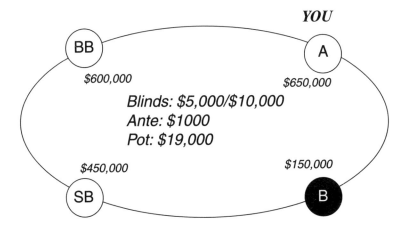

*YOU*

BB — $600,000

A — $650,000

Blinds: $5,000/$10,000
Ante: $1000
Pot: $19,000

SB — $450,000

B — $150,000

**Situation:** Final table of a major tournament. Player B has been aggressive throughout the tournament.

**Your hand:** K♦9♠

**Action to you:** You are first to act.

**Question:** *Do you fold, call, or raise?*

**Answer:** Your king-nine is not a great hand at a four-handed table, but it's reasonable enough to make a move. Raise about $35,000, and see if you take the pot.

**Action:** You raise to $35,000. Player B goes all-in for $150,000. The blinds fold. The pot is now $204,000. *Do you call or fold?*

**Answer:** This is a question that hinges on two factors: pot odds and table image. Let's look at the pot odds first.

To call the bet, you have to put in another $115,000 for a chance to win a pot of $204,000. You're getting odds of 1.77-to-1, or about 9-to-5. Those are excellent odds if you're against a pair lower than your nine, where you're only about an 11-to-10 underdog. Against the various combinations of unpaired cards that you could be facing, you're mostly getting at least the minimum odds you need to call. For instance:

1. Against a low card and an in-between card, like queen-seven, you're an 8-to-5 favorite.

2. Against two in-between cards, like jack-ten, you're a 12-to-10 favorite.

3. Against a high card and a low card, like ace-six, you're a 6-to-5 underdog.

4. Against a high card and an in-between card, like ace-ten, you're a 8-to-5 underdog.

5. Against king-x, where x is higher than your nine, you're in big trouble. Now you're between a 2.5-to-1 and a 3-to-1 underdog.

Only against the last combination, a king coupled with an ace, queen, jack, or ten, are you not getting the odds you need.

Of course, if you're up against one of the high pairs you're in serious trouble, and you'll wish you had folded. But on balance, it looks like the pot odds easily justify a call.

The other key factor is table image, and again this argues strongly for a call. When the table gets down to three, four, or five players and the blinds are relatively large, everyone will be making plays for the pot. Only the biggest stacks even have a choice in the matter, but they need to get involved just to prevent their stacks from steadily drifting downwards. Since there aren't enough strong hands to go around, good players know that a lot of these moves are based on weak hands, and the way you exploit that situation is to pick some spots and come over the top at the initial raiser. They're trying to win the pot, of course, but they're also trying to get an answer to an absolutely key question: *Will this player defend his raise, or will he throw his cards away if he doesn't have a really strong hand?*

Once you become known as a player who won't defend his raises, your raises have no clout. Everyone at the table will notice that you're the weak sister, and they'll keep attacking you. If you want to have a chance of stealing any pots in the future, you have to call this bet. After all, your bet was not a complete steal, and your hand is reasonable.

**Action:** You call, and your opponent shows A♣J♦. The flop comes K-7-4 of mixed suits, and your kings hold on to win.

# Hand 11-4

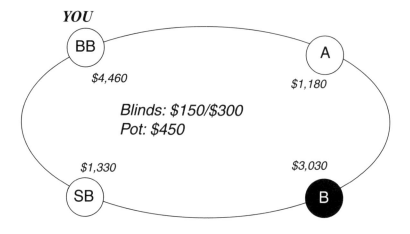

*YOU*

BB
$4,460

A
$1,180

Blinds: $150/$300
Pot: $450

$1,330

$3,030

SB

B

**Situation:** Late in a single-table online tournament. Player B is very aggressive, entering and raising a lot of pots.

**Your hand:** A♠T♣

**Action to you:** Player A folds. Player B raises to $750. The small blind folds. The pot is now $1,200.

**Question:** *Do you fold, call, or raise?*
    **Answer:** You have a reasonable hand at a four-handed table, but your position is poor. Let's look at your choices one by one.

1.  **Fold.** Can't be right. A very aggressive player at a four-handed table has raised. That's no excuse for laying down a reasonable hand. Right now it costs you $450 to see a $1,200 pot, and those 2.6-to-1 odds mean that folding is not an option.

2.  **Call**. This keeps you in the hand, but at the cost of being out of position, with absolutely no information about Player B's hand. Still, you don't jeopardize many chips, and if you decide to let the hand go, you'll still be in very good chip position.

3.  **Raise to $1,500**. In a four-handed game, ace-ten is very likely the best hand at the table right now. Your opponent might have a good hand but he also might be making a routine move from the button to take the blinds. By coming over the top, you'll find out where you stand. The fact that he's an aggressive player means it's a little more likely he has a weak hand, but I wouldn't put too much importance in that right here. In a short-handed game, everybody has to be actively involved in stealing pots. Besides, even an aggressive player can pick up a good hand now and then.

    There's yet another reason for raising right here. You're out of position against this opponent on future rounds. That's bad, and you don't want to put yourself in these positions in the late stages of a tournament. If you raise and he folds, that's great. If you raise and he goes all-in, you're probably beaten, but at least you know that now and can hold your loss at just $1,500. If he calls, you remain under pressure, but at least you know some more about his hand. (It's pretty good.)

4.  **Raise all-in**. Since your opponent is very aggressive, it's reasonable to think that a lot of his hands, perhaps as many as 70 percent, are hands that he won't want to risk an all-in confrontation. If that's true, it's not hard to see that moving all-in will be a profitable play. Let's say that Player B will fold 70 percent of his hands, but if he calls he'll be a 2-to-1 favorite over your ace-ten. In that case, the possible results break down as follows:

- 70%: He folds and your stack grows to $5,360.
- 20%: He calls and wins. Your stack shrinks to $1,430.
- 10%: He calls and you win. Your stack grows to $7,640.

If we roll these calculations together, then on average you'll have $4,802 in your stack when the hand ends, for a profit of $342 after the all-in play.

So what's the right move? Since the all-in bet shows a profit, we know that folding must be wrong. We don't know, however, whether the call or the small raise are more profitable than all-in. My intuition is that the small raise, trying to negate the positional disadvantage, is the best choice.

A very tough decision.

**Action:** You just call for another $450. The pot is now $1,650.

**Flop:** 4♦3♥2♣

**Question:** *What now?*

**Answer:** Good question. The flop missed you, but it probably missed your opponent too, unless he was trying to steal with nothing, in which case it may have hit him. Because you didn't raise last round, you still don't know anything about his hand.

I'd lead out here with a bet of $600 to $700. My ace-high may be the best hand right now, and that bet might win the pot. If that bet meets with a call or raise, my opponent has something, and I'm most likely done with the hand. As before, it's only by betting that I can gain any information about his hand.

**Action:** You check. Player B bets $300. The pot is now $1,950. *What do you do?*

**Answer:** You're being offered 6.5-to-1 money odds, so it's impossible to lay the hand down. But when you checked, a bet on his part was irresistible, so you still don't know anything about his hand.

**Action:** You call. The pot is now $2,250.

**Fourth Street: J♦**

**Question:** *What's your play now?*

**Answer:** The jack looks like a scary card, but actually it's not. The most likely hand that Player B is playing is ace-x. But if "x" is a jack, then you were losing anyway. The really scary cards on fourth street were sevens, eight, and nines, since if he was playing ace-x with one of those cards, he just went from a losing hand to a winning one. If it seems like a stretch to put him on ace-x at this point, remember that in short-handed situations, players almost always play aces, but may or may not play other cards. If you're guessing, putting him on ace-x is always a good first guess.

Having checked up to this point, you might as well continue. A smallish bet won't chase him away, and there's no reason to commit any more chips unless you have to. Checking the hand down would be a good result for you.

**Action:** You check, he bets $300, and you call. The pot is now $2,850.

His bet of $300 doesn't make much sense. It's not large enough to chase you away, and with the potential straight on board, he probably isn't sure he has the best hand at this point either.

**Fifth Street: K♠**

The king on fifth street is a good card for you, for the same reason as the jack on fourth street. If he already had that card, you were probably beaten anyway. It's the cards lower than your ten that are the real swing cards in this situation.

**Question:** *Should you bet on the end?*
**Answer:** No. Just check the hand down if you can.

**Resolution:** You check and he checks. He shows an A♣Q♥, and takes the pot.

# Hand 11-5

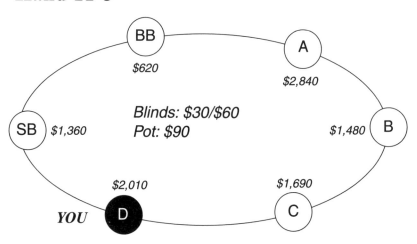

Blinds: $30/$60
Pot: $90

BB $620
A $2,840
SB $1,360
B $1,480
YOU D $2,010
C $1,690

**Situation:** Late in a one-table online tournament. Players A and C are very aggressive.

**Your hand:** A♥T♠

**Action to you:** Players A and B call. Player C folds. The pot is now $210.

**Question:** *Do you fold, call, or raise?*

**Answer:** You could just call but my preference here is to raise, trying to knock out the blinds and perhaps one of the players who are already in. A call in early position from a player who is known to be aggressive means something, but it doesn't indicate any great strength. The call from Player B is a little more threatening, but he didn't raise. Ace-ten is not a great hand at a full table, but it's a pretty good hand for a table of this size. I'd put in a raise of about three times the big blind, say $160 to $200, and see what happens.

**Action:** In fact you just call for $60. The small blind folds, and the big blind checks. The pot is now $270.

**Flop: 6♠4♥4♦**

**Action:** The big blind bets $60. Player A calls. Player B raises to $120. The pot is now $510. *What should you do?*

**Answer:** It was a strange little flop to produce any action, but all three players are in against you, and you only have an ace-high. The big blind might be making a move, but Player A's call is for real, and Player B's raise in the face of a bet and a call indicates that he's not kidding. Don't even think about trying to make a play here. Just get out.

**Resolution:** You fold. The big blind and Player B play the hand down to the end, and split the pot as each holds jack-six.

# Hand 11-6

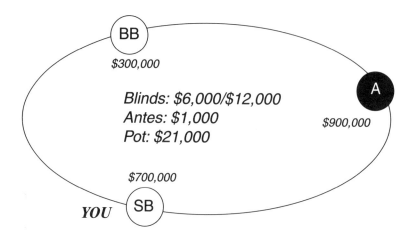

**Situation:** Final table of a major tournament. Three players left. The big blind is a solid player. Player A started out solid, but has gotten more aggressive at the final table.

**Your hand:** A♥J♥

**Action to you:** Player A raises to $60,000. The pot is now $81,000. It costs you $54,000 to call.

**Question:** *Do you raise, and if so, how much?*

> **Answer:** There's no question that you will raise. Ace-jack suited is a very strong hand at a three-handed table, and a raise from the button, which may well be a bluff should not dissuade you. The only real question is how much to raise.
>
> In the tournament from which this hand was taken, the small blind put in $150,000, in effect raising Player A another $96,000. He understood that he had to raise, but the execution was badly flawed. Now the pot is $231,000, and Player A just has to put in $96,000 to call, getting odds of

almost 2.5-to-1. That's a pretty easy call with almost any hand.

When you're debating the amount to raise, be sure to consider who will have position after the flop. *If you have position after the flop, you can make smaller raises and let the hand continue; if you opponent has position after the flop, you must make larger raises in an effort to end the hand now.* You should make a big raise here, in the neighborhood of $240,000 to $300,000. With this bet, you accomplish two things:

1.  You cut down Player A's odds, so with weaker hands he's not getting the right odds to call,

2.  You show clearly that you're very serious about playing the hand.

Good no-limit hold 'em players can smell weakness and attack. If you're a shark by nature, and aren't afraid to lose, it's the best game in the world. If you're not intrinsically a shark, you must at least not act like a minnow.

Another way of playing this hand is to go all-in at this point. That's definitely a play, and I wouldn't criticize a player who went in that direction. Against a top player, a smaller bet is actually scarier; it looks like you don't mind if he calls, hence your hand must be really good. But against an intermediate or a beginner, an all-in bet looks scarier, and is more likely to win the pot.

**Resolution:** You put in only $150,000. Player A calls with an A♠9♠, and sticks around to win the hand with a pair of nines.

# Hand 11-7

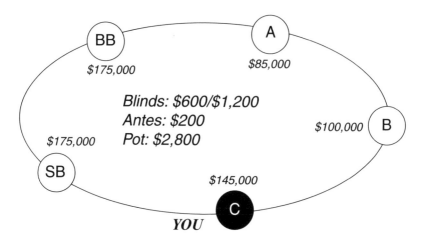

**Situation:** Final table of a major tournament. Player B, the former chip leader, has suffered a number of bad beats lately. His style has been generally aggressive.

**Your hand:** 9♦9♣

**Action to you:** Player A folds. Player B raises to $5,000.

**Question:** *Do you fold, call, or raise?*
  **Answer:** A pair of nines is certainly a good hand at a five-handed table, and either raising or calling is an option. Raising is more likely to eliminate the blinds from the hand. Calling is a play that makes more use of your advantage in position after the flop. I prefer the call since it will enable me to learn a bit more about where I stand before committing any sizeable number of chips to the pot.

**Action:** You call. The blinds fold. The pot is now $12,800.

**Flop:** A♠7♠3♣

**Action:** Player B checks. *What should you do?*

**Answer:** The flop contained only one card higher than your nines, which was good. But that card was an ace, which was bad. But your opponent checked, which was good. So should you bet or check?

Your opponent's check may be a trap, or he may be afraid of the ace as well. If his initial raise was because he has a pair, it's probably a pair higher than your nines because there are more pairs higher than your nines that would force a big bet than there are below your nines. If he did play a pair lower than your nines, a couple of those pairs have just turned into trips. If he didn't have a pair, then ace-x is his next most likely holding. If you bet and you get a reraise, you'll know for sure — your hand is no good and you have to get out. But you don't have to bet. I would check, and see what he does on fourth street.

The downside of checking, of course, is the free card you give your opponent. But you're hoping your position will be adequate compensation. In any event, you're keeping the pot small and avoiding traps.

**Action:** You check. The pot is still $12,800.

**Fourth Street:** 9♠

**Action:** Player B bets $8,000. The pot is now $20,800. *What do you do?*

**Answer:** The nine was certainly a nice card to see. It helped you, and it probably didn't help your opponent. Two spades are an unlikely holding for him pre-flop, because he made a solid bet and we know he didn't have the ace of spades in his hand at the time. If he did hold two spades, he had a chance to make a semi-bluff bet on the flop, but he didn't. It's now much more likely that he held some pair or ace-x, tried to trap on the flop but didn't get any action, and now he's betting to take the pot.

You can't just call here and try to trap. He may very well have one spade, and you can't give him a free shot to win a very large pot from you. Make a roughly pot-sized raise to deny him the drawing odds he would need if he has a flush draw. If he has a pair of aces now he may call. Almost any other hand he will have to lay down.

**Action:** You raise to $23,000. Player B folds, and you win the pot.

Player B had actually been playing with a pair of kings. The ace on the flop won the hand for you by forcing him to check.

# Hand 11-8

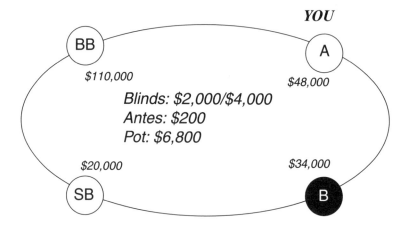

*YOU*

BB
$110,000

A
$48,000

Blinds: $2,000/$4,000
Antes: $200
Pot: $6,800

$20,000

$34,000

SB

B

**Situation:** Final table of a multi-table live tournament. You have been active recently, winning several hands without showing your cards.

**Your hand:** A♥4♣

**Action to you:** You are first to act.

**Question:** *Do you fold, call, or raise?*

**Answer:** An ace is a good hand at a four-handed table, so normally you would want to play in this position. Here, however, there are a couple of counter-arguments against getting involved with this hand.

1.  You have a very weak ace. Any ace that gets involved with you is liable to have you outkicked.

2.  You have been active lately, and as far as the other players know, you may have been pushing the table around with nothing.

3.  There's a very big stack in the big blind. He's the player you least want to get involved with at this table.

An ace and a low card is a tricky hand even when the table is short. If you take the lead, get action, and pair your ace on the flop, you're in danger of losing most (or all) or your chips. If you pair your low card, you still won't have a strong hand, you won't know where you stand, and you'll be in danger of being counterfeited later in the hand. These are hands you want to win before the flop, but the presence of the big stack in the big blind makes that possibility more problematical.

This is a tough problem, and I can't really fault someone for making a raise here. But my preference under this set of circumstances is to let the hand go.

**Action:** You fold.

# Hand 11-9

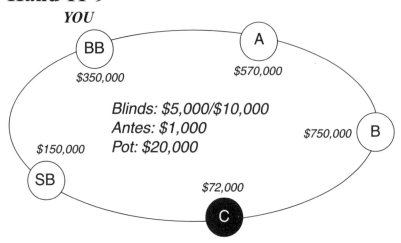

*YOU*

BB
$350,000

A
$570,000

Blinds: $5,000/$10,000
Antes: $1,000
Pot: $20,000

$750,000  B

$150,000

SB

$72,000

C

**Situation:** Final table of a major tournament. Player A has been playing tight, conservative poker. Player C has been aggressive throughout the event but has recently suffered a couple of tough beats.

**Your hand:** A♣J♠

**Action to you:** Player A raises to $35,000. Player B folds. Player C goes all-in for his last $71,000. The small blind folds. The pot is now $126,000. It costs you $61,000 to call.

**Question:** *Do you fold, call, or raise?*
    **Answer:** This is a hand that tricks many players. Ace-jack offsuit is a good hand, and at a short table, in the absence of any other information, you would be delighted to pick up ace-jack. But here you have some additional information. Player A, who's been playing a reasonably tight game, has already raised in opening position. Of course, at a small table that bet doesn't mean as much as it would at a full table. He probably

has some kind of hand, but not necessarily better than your ace-jack offsuit.

What's more interesting is that Player C, who wasn't compelled to make a move at all, has elected to go all-in. In addition, Player C's stack isn't that big, so the pot odds offered to Player A will make for a compulsory call. If the small blind folds and you fold, Player A will need to put in another $36,000 for a shot at a pot of $126,000, which are about 3.5-to-1 pot odds. Any hand that was good enough for a legitimate opening bet will have a mandatory call. So Player C made his move with the knowledge that he would have to show down his hand, and therefore he must have something real.

So how good does your ace-jack look now? Let's remember two key ideas from Volume I, the Gap Concept and the Sandwich Effect.

According to the Gap Concept, when you are thinking of entering a pot behind a player who has already raised, your hand needs to be better than the minimum hand your opponent is likely holding for you to call. Player A might have a good hand, but Player C certainly has a good hand. In fact, your ace-jack is about the minimum hand that justifies Player C's all-in move. (His most likely holding is about a medium pair, which is a favorite against your hand.) Factor in that Player A may have a good hand as well, and this doesn't look like a great call.

Now we have to consider the Sandwich Effect. When there are active players still to act behind you, you need a better-than-minimum hand to compensate for

1. The potential raises you may face, and

2. The uncertainty of not knowing the pot odds you're really getting.

If Player A was making a steal attempt, he'll probably lay down his hand if you enter the pot. But if he had a real hand, he may put you all-in. Your hand needs to be strong enough to call that potential all-in move. When you factor in both the Gap Concept and the Sandwich Effect, your ace-jack just isn't good enough for this situation. You should fold, although it's a close play.

**Resolution:** You fold. Player A calls. Player A shows T♣8♥, while Player C shows 5♠5♦. The flop comes 8♦7♠4♥, but fourth street is a 6♦ and Player C wins with his straight.

There's a footnote to this hand. The hands that were actually shown down were about the weakest you could conceivably be facing, yet you would have been only 40 percent to win had you stayed in the pot with them. Against more reasonable (and more likely) holdings, your winning chances would drop to the low-30s or the high-20s.

# Hand 11-10

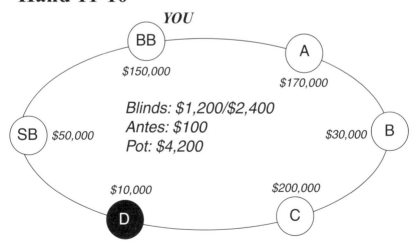

*YOU*

BB
$150,000

A
$170,000

Blinds: $1,200/$2,400
Antes: $100
Pot: $4,200

SB  $50,000

$30,000  B

$10,000

$200,000

D

C

**Situation:** Major tournament, late in the second day. Player C has been aggressive and lucky so far.

**Your hand:** J♦9♦

**Action to you:** Players A and B fold. Player C raises, putting in $8,400. Player D and the small blind fold. The pot is now $12,600.

**Question:** *Do you fold, call, or raise?*
   **Answer:** It costs you $6,000 to call, and there's over $12,000 in the pot, so you're getting 2-to-1 odds to call. That's a mandatory call, even out of position and even with jack-nine suited.

**Action:** You call. The pot is now $18,600.

**Flop:** Q♠8♦4♥

**Question:** You're first to act. *What do you do?*
   **Answer:** You do have an inside straight draw, but other than that the flop has missed you. It may have missed your opponent as well, of course. The shape is good for you, and jacks, tens, and nines might all be outs. Your best chance to win the pot is to bet now. A standard probe bet of about half the pot or a little less is the right move, and offers you good odds. Bet $7,000 to $8,000 and see what happens.

**Action:** In fact you just check. Player C bets $15,000. *What do you do?*
   **Answer:** You fold. You don't have anything, and there are just two cards to come. Your almost an 11-to-1 underdog to fill the inside straight on fourth street, and if you don't fill it there you'll probably be facing a bet which you can't call. There are three jacks and three nines left in the deck, but you can't be sure those are outs since your opponent may have a

queen. And even if Player C missed the flop and thinks he's bluffing, he might still hold an ace or a king and have you beaten. You must fold.

**Action:** You fold.

There's a hidden advantage to being out of position. Acting first allows you to make the first bet, and in fact most pots are won by the player who bets first. That's why a continuation bet or probe bet for half the pot is such a powerful move. Since you're getting 2-to-1 odds on the bet, you only have to win the pot one time in three to break even, and that's assuming you never win any pots where your bet is just called. You can't overdo the move, of course. If you do, players will notice and start raising you whether they hit the flop or not. But a well-timed probe bet has to be a standard part of your repertoire.

# Hand 11-11

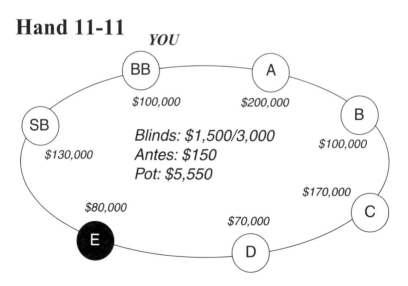

*YOU*

BB
$100,000

A
$200,000

SB
$130,000

B
$100,000

Blinds: $1,500/3,000
Antes: $150
Pot: $5,550

$170,000

$80,000

C

E

$70,000

D

**Situation:** Major tournament, late in the second day. Player A is a very aggressive player. In the past twenty hands, you have made several probe and continuation bets, none of which were called.

**Your hand:** Q♥3♦

**Action to you:** Player A calls. Players B, C, and D all fold. Player E calls. The small blind folds. The pot is now $11,550.

**Question:** *Do you check or raise?*
> **Answer:** Check. You have nothing, but the check is free. Don't lose your head and try to steal the pot at this point. Both of the other players in the pot probably have a better hand than you.

**Action:** You check.

**Flop:** T♠4♦2♦

**Question:** You are first to act. *What do you do?*
> **Answer:** This would normally be an excellent flop for a probe bet. Although you have nothing, there is no reason to believe anyone else has anything either. But you've recently made several probe and continuation bets. Although none were called, you should assume that the other players have noticed this and are ready to jump on you. Since your hand is very weak, lay back and check.

**Action:** You check. Players A and E both check. The pot remains $11,550.

**Fourth Street:** 3♣

**Question:** *What do you do now?*
> **Answer:** Although you only have a pair of treys, you're entitled to bet here. Your two opponents just called before the flop and just checked after the flop, so you have no reason to believe you're beaten. Make a probing bet of about half the pot or a little less, and see if it works. You were cautious

about a probing bet last round, but if the players are going to give you the pot, step up and take it.

**Action:** You bet $6,000. Player A calls. Player E folds. The pot is now $23,550.

**Fifth Street: 2♣**

**Question**: *Should you bet on the end?*

**Answer:** No. This is a standard position that arises constantly. You might have the best hand, but any hand that can call a bet will beat you. So a bet here can only lose money. Just check. If Player A bets, you'll have a tough decision, and you'll have to consider the pot odds carefully. But there's no question that you must check here.

**Action:** You actually bet $20,000. Player A raises you $70,000. The pot is now $113,550. *Should you call?*

**Answer:** You've maneuvered yourself into a position where you have to make a tough decision for nearly all your chips. It costs you $50,000 to call, so the pot is offering you better than 2-to-1 on your money. You can only beat a bluff, but Player A is fully capable of bluffing. Against a conservative player you should fold here. Against an aggressive player, you could consider calling. The pot odds are substantial.

**Action:** You actually fold.

# Hand 11-12

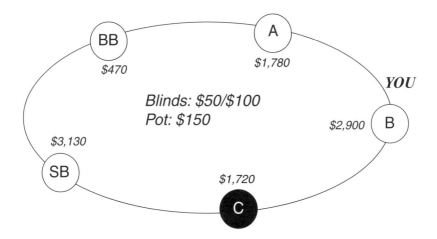

**Situation:** Nearing the end of a one-table online tournament.

**Your hand:** 6♦4♠

**Action to you:** Player A folds.

**Question:** *Do you fold, or try to steal the pot with a raise?*
  **Answer:** Throw it away. It's a very weak hand, and all you know so far is that one player is out. If any of the remaining three call you, you're certain to be a big underdog. What's more, the big blind has only $470, so he'll be eager to go all-in with almost anything. Don't try to run bluffs against a player who's itching to get his chips into the middle. You're not desperate here; your chip position is solid. Let the desperate players make these moves.

**Action:** You raise to $200 in an attempt to steal. Player C and the small blind fold, but the big blind calls. Pot is now $450.

Your steal attempt was misguided in the first place, but you compounded your error by betting too little. Unless you've seen the players behind you folding a minimum raise, you need to bet more, say triple the big blind ($300 here).

**Flop: 8♥3♦2♦**

**Action:** The big blind checks. *What do you do?*
   **Answer:** Actually a pretty good flop for you. It's unlikely to hit your opponent, and you now have an inside straight draw. Of course, you're certainly second-best right now.
      You might as well bet. It's a pretty cheap bet for you since your opponent only has $270 left, and since he checked, there's some chance he'll fold. In addition, sixes, fives, and fours could all be outs. A bet here is of course a semi-bluff.

**Action:** You put him all-in with a $270 bet, and he calls. He turns over J♦8♣, and his pair of eights holds up to win.

Your last bet was sound. It was only the initial decision to go in the pot that was an error.

# Hand 11-13

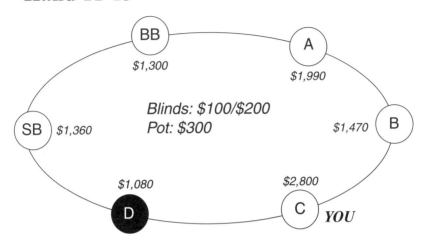

Blinds: $100/$200
Pot: $300

BB $1,300
A $1,990
B $1,470
SB $1,360
C $2,800 *YOU*
D $1,080

**Situation:** Online tournament. Three places will be paid. A loose table has been turning tight. In the last hand, you called and then made a big bet after the flop which wasn't called.

**Your hand:** Q♠T♦

**Action to you:** Players A and B fold.

**Question:** *Do you fold, call, or raise?*

**Answer:** You are in maximum aggressive mode, because the remaining stacks are neither large nor small. With two players already folded, your queen-ten is plenty good enough to make a move. In fact, you could move with considerably less.

How much you raise here depends on what you have done before. In the last hand you called and then moved after the flop. Here, you want to make sure to do something apparently quite different. You're taking their money, *and they know you're taking their money*, but you can't blatantly do the same thing every hand, or they'll get embarrassed and call you whether they want to or not. Remember this, it's a very important concept. You have to steal in a way that allows your opponents a face-saving out, even if they sort of know what you're doing.

So raise a good solid amount here — say to $600.

**Action:** You bet $600, and the rest of the players fold.

# Hand 11-14

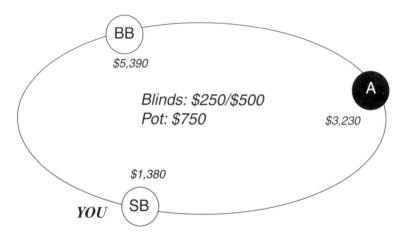

Blinds: $250/$500
Pot: $750

BB
$5,390

A
$3,230

$1,380
YOU SB

**Situation:** Final three players of a single-table online tournament.

**Your hand:** 8♥5♣

**Action to you:** Player A folds.

**Question:** *Do you fold, call, or raise?*

    **Answer:** No question here — you have to shove the rest of your chips in the pot and see if you are called. Once you've posted the small blind, you're down to just $1,130 chips, only about a third of the chips of the player in second place. That means the next set of blinds will essentially wipe you out.

The main reason you should make a move with this unpromising hand (8♥5♣) is that *one player has already folded.* That's valuable information, and if you wait until next hand, when you'll be on the button, you'll have to make a move with two active players already in the pot. You're simply hoping, of course, that the big blind is holding some trash like queen-trey, and decides not to contest the pot.

A secondary reason for moving all-in now is that you already have $250 in the pot, which gives you leverage you won't have from another position.

**Action:** You go all-in, and the big blind folds.

# Hand 11-15

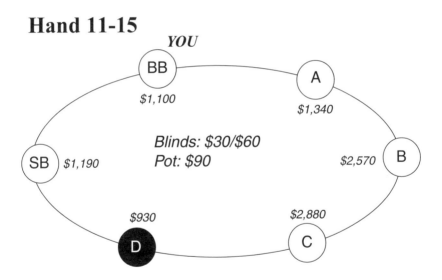

**Situation:** Halfway through a single-table online tournament.

**Your hand:** K♠K♥

**Action to you:** Players A, B, C, and D all fold. The small blind calls. The pot is now $120.

**Question:** *Do you check or raise?*

**Answer:** You'll have to play this hand with the deft touch of a jeweler. You have a monster hand and you're up against just one opponent who may have almost nothing, but who wasn't yet ready to concede the pot. You have to try and make what money you can, which may not be much, while remaining open to the possibility that an ace on the flop could beat you. All in all a tricky situation.

Your first decision is: raise a little or just call? Here you should raise a little, just enough to show him you're serious about the pot, but hopefully not enough to chase him away. You want to build the pot so it becomes a tempting target on the later rounds, and not something he can calmly abandon. You also want to get a little more of his money in the center, so he feels somewhat committed to the pot after the flop. The right raise here is something like $60 to $90. I'd bet the lower amount if he seems like a tight player, the higher amount if he seems a little loose.

**Action:** You actually raise $60, and the small blind calls. The pot is now $240.

### Flop: K♣J♦4♠

**Action:** He bets $60. *What do you do?*

**Answer:** That's an excellent flop for you, obviously. The only downside is the jack, which enables holdings like ace-queen or queen-ten to be drawing at straights. Ace-queen is an unlikely holding since it should have prompted a raise before the flop, but queen-ten would be consistent with a call. However, these are remote worries. You should just call the bet and keep him involved in the hand. At this point, your best guess should be that either he has a pair of jacks and is slow-playing himself, or he's simply making a small bet to find out where he stands.

**Action:** You call. The pot is now $360.

**Fourth Street: A♣**

**Action:** He bets $60. The pot is now $420. *What do you do?*
**Answer:** The ace is both good news and bad news for you. If he's been playing along with an ace and a low card, he now believes that he's hit his hand and he's winning. But the ace could help him if he's been playing with straight possibilities.
   You must charge him here since he could be drawing at a hand that could win. Your problem is that if he has absolutely nothing, any raise on your part could be enough to chase him away. I'd recommend a raise of about $200. That should be enough to keep him curious, but hopefully not enough to chase him away if he has anything at all. If you do get action, you'll have to wonder if he hit his straight, but it won't change your play. He's actually handled this hand very well; his small little bets make your optimal strategy unclear.

**Action:** You actually raise $400 and he folds. You take the pot.

   Your bet didn't leave him an exit strategy. If he called the bet, the pot would be so large that he'd be committed to going all the way on the end, so he quit instead. With very strong hands, you want to bet amounts that still leave him with a good percentage of his chips if he calls and loses. Those bets are much easier to call.

# Hand 11-16

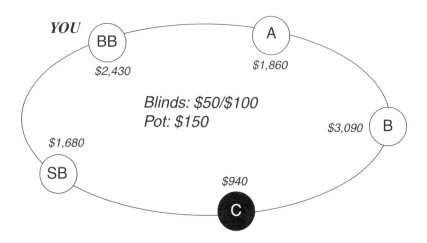

**Situation:** Nearing the end of a single-table online tournament. Five players remain.

**Your hand:** K♥Q♣

**Action to you:** Player A folds. Player B calls. Player C calls. The small blind folds. The pot is now $350.

**Question:** *Do you fold, call, or raise?*
   **Answer:** In a short game, king-queen, suited or offsuit, is now a great hand. You definitely want to play this hand, and you should raise.

**Action:** You raise to $250.

   This is the right idea, but the raise is too small. I would have raised to about $500. You've got two opponents right now, and you'd like to knock out at least one of them. With a small raise, you're giving them great odds to call. In fact, you're practically begging them to call.

**Action:** Player B and C both call for an additional $150. The pot is now $800.

**Flop:** K♦Q♠2♠

**Question:** *Do you bet with your two pair, or check, intending to check raise?*

**Answer:** When you're playing a hand, it's crucial to keep in mind *how your actions appear to the other players*. If you don't, you're going to miss big opportunities, either by winning way too little money on your good hands, or losing way too much on your bad ones.

You took the lead in the first round of betting, despite your bad position, announcing you had a good hand. A good hand usually means one with some high cards. Now a king and a queen come on the flop. If I were one of your opponents. I'm now thinking "Holy smoke! He bet out, and now a king-queen hit the board. Must have helped his hand somehow. Watch out."

If you check, you're not going to get a chance to check-raise, because no one's going to bet. They'll correctly read your check as a trap. If you bet out, say $200 or so, someone might think you're trying to buy the pot and call. It's your best shot to build a pot.

**Action:** You check and Players B and C both check behind you.

**Fourth Street:** 4♣

**Question**: *What now?*

**Answer:** A check will just lead to a couple of more checks, unless someone was sitting there with a pair of fours. Bet a couple of hundred, and see if you get lucky.

**Action:** You bet $200. Both B and C fold.

You made too small a bet on the opening round when you could have built a fair-sized pot with a strong hand. Betting after the flop wouldn't necessarily have made you any more money, but it was the best try.

# Hand 11-17

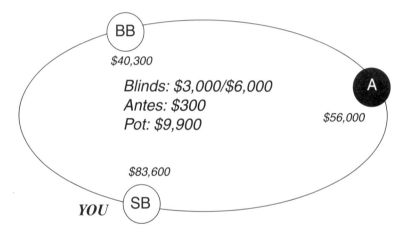

**Situation:** Final table of a multi-table live tournament. All the remaining players have been playing solid, shrewd poker.

**Your hand:** Q♣Q♠

**Action to you:** Player A folds.

**Question:** *Do you fold, call, or raise?*
   **Answer:** A pair of queens is a strong enough hand to slow-play. Just call and try to trap your opponent.

**Action:** You call. The big blind checks. The pot is now $12,900.

**Flop:** K♠6♠4♦

**Action:** *What do you do?*
> **Answer:** You check again, and continue your trap.
> You're only afraid of one card in his hand (a king), and he probably doesn't have that card. If he has a king, you're beaten, and you're going to lose a lot of money on the hand.
> Your hope, of course, is that either the six or four has paired his hand, and he now believes he has the best of it.

**Action:** You check. He checks. The pot remains $12,900.

**Fourth Street:** J♣

**Action:** *What do you do?*
> **Answer:** That's an excellent card for you since it's lower than your pair. It's now time to bet something. If you don't get called there was nothing to be won anyway. A continuation-sized bet will give him good odds to stick around.

**Action:** You bet $6,000. He calls. The pot is now $24,900.

**Fifth Street:** 2♠

**Action:** *What do you do?*
> **Answer:** The deuce puts three spades on board, but you have to discount that possibility. There are many other hands he might hold besides two spades, and in these low-M confrontations you have to ignore the long shots and just keep piling up chips. There are now four cards on board below your queens and just one card above, so make another half-pot sized bet and see what happens.

**Action:** You bet $9,000. He raises all-in, moving his last $28,000 into the pot. The raise to you is $19,000, and the pot is now $61,900. *What do you do?*

   **Answer:** He may have a king, but he might have many other hands you can beat as well. The 3-to-1 odds are just too good under the circumstances, so you must call (against a typical player).

**Action:** You call, and he turns over K♦4♥ and wins the pot.

   He flopped top and bottom pair, and was slow-playing you while you were slow-playing him! By the way, he played the hand perfectly.

# Hand 11-18

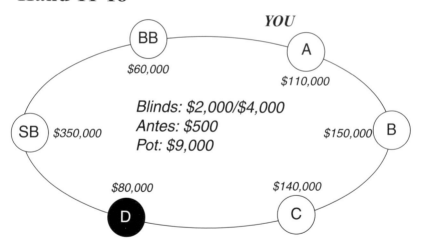

**Situation:** A major tournament, playing down to the last table. The big blind is a conservative player who began the day with a big stack, but who has been steadily whittled down. You have projected a solid image at the table.

**Your hand:** 6♣6♦

**Action to you:** You are first to act.

**Question:** *Do you fold, call, or raise?*
**Answer:** You should raise here, and attempt to win the pot immediately. At a six-handed table, your pair of sixes are probably the best hand right now, but could run into trouble after almost any flop. (The situation is very analogous to holding a medium pair in first position at a full table.) Your job is to discourage some of the high-card hands from playing. A raise of $15,000 to $20,000 seems about right.

**Action:** You raise to $15,000. Players B, C, and D all fold, as does the small blind. The big blind goes all-in, betting his last $56,000 chips. The pot is now $80,000, and it costs you $41,000 to call.

**Question:** *Do you fold or call?*
**Answer:** Let's work this problem out carefully, as it's very typical of a whole class of problems that arise at the end of a tournament. The pot is offering you almost exactly 2-to-1 odds, which is very favorable for you. You know your opponent is a conservative player, and you also know that, although his stack has been whittled down, it's not yet so small that he should be making a desperate move with a very weak hand. (His M is 6.5, and his effective M is 4.) That doesn't mean that he can't be bluffing, only that we have to assign a slightly lower probability to a bluff than usual.
His possible hands fall into three categories:

1.  **A pair higher than yours**. There are six possible ways to hold any pair, and there are eight pairs higher than yours, so there are 48 possible card holdings that leave you about a 4.5-to-1 underdog.

2.  **Two high cards, bet for value**. What hands might a conservative player bet for value in this situation? Ace-

king and ace-queen, certainly, and probably ace-jack and king-queen as well. King-jack and queen-jack are also possible. There are a total of 16 ways to deal any particular non-pair (four suited, 12 offsuit), so these six card combinations total 96 possible hands. Against the hands in this group, you're about a 55-45 favorite.

3.  **Other hands which are either semi-bluffs or legitimate attempts to defend his big blind against a bluff.** He may perceive your bet as a bluff, in which case he might be willing to make a bet with hands like ace-nine, jack-ten, or even a pair of treys. Most of the hands in this group represent two overcards to your sixes, so you're about a 55-45 favorite in those cases. But the possibility of facing a lower pair or even a hand like ace-four suited, with an undercard to your pair, entitles you to boost your chances a little more, perhaps to about 60-40.

Once you know what hands you might be facing, your next step is to assign a probability to each of the three groups. Don't try to be too precise! All you need here is a rough estimate.

For instance, I don't think there's much chance you're facing a hand in the third group because he's a conservative player, and because you've projected a conservative image as well. I'd assign this group a probability of about 10 percent.

Groups 1 and 2 are the important ones, with the most likely hands. There are many more hands in Group 2, but they might not all get bet if they occurred. Would a conservative player really shove all his money in the pot with a queen-jack, for instance? Sometimes, perhaps, depending on his mood, but certainly not always. Let's say that 40 percent of the time you're facing a Group 1 hand, and 50 percent of the time you're facing a Group 2 hand.

Now you're ready for your final, quick calculation.

1.  40 percent of the time you're facing a Group 1 hand, a higher pair, and you win a bit less than 20 percent of these. Let's say you win 8 percent of the time here.

2.  50 percent of the time we're facing a group 2 hand, two high overcards, and you're a 55-to-45 favorite. You win about 27 percent here.

3.  10 percent of the time you're facing a bluff or semi-bluff, and you're 60 percent to win. That gives you 6 percent wins here.

Your total winning chances looks like 41 percent.

$$41 = 8 + 27 + 6$$

You're a 3-to-2 underdog in the hand, but you're getting 2-to-1 pot odds. Easy call.

**Action:** You call, and your opponent shows a pair of kings. You catch a 6♠ on the flop to win the hand.

A couple of final comments on this hand.

Analysis like this looks hard at first but gets easier with practice. The math is not the hard part. What's difficult is being organized and keeping track of the possibilities in your head.

The decisive feature of the hand is the 2-to-1 pot odds being offered. If I don't feel like working my way through calculations, I rely on two quick rules of thumb:

1.  *If I have some kind of hand, and the pot is offering 2-to-1 odds, I probably want to call.*

2. *If I have some kind of hand, and the pot is offering 3-to-1 odds, I definitely want to call.*

# Hand 11-19

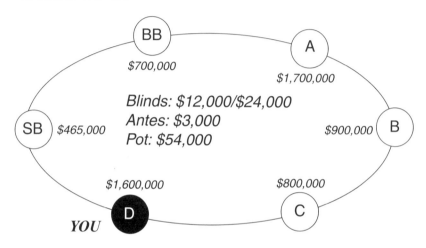

**Situation:** Major tournament, final table. The small blind is a somewhat tight, conservative player.

**Your hand:** 4♦4♣

**Action to you:** Players A, B, and C all fold.

**Question:** *Do you fold, call, or raise?*
  **Answer:** A small pair, with position on two players yet to act, is a strong hand. You should put in a solid raise of about three times the big blind.

**Action:** You raise to $100,000. The small blind goes all-in with his last $450,000 chips. The big blind folds. The pot is now $604,000, and it costs you $350,000 to call.

**Question**: *Do you fold or call?*

**Answer:** This is a very similar problem to the last hand, so you should attack it the same way. The first job is to estimate the pot odds. You need to bet $350,000 to win $604,000. Try to make the arithmetic as simple as you can. Round off the 604,000 to 600,000, drop the thousands, and divide 600 and 350 by 50 to get manageable numbers. You have to put in 7 to win 12, so the pot is offering you 12-to-7 odds, about 1.7-to-1.

Now you have to think about the mix of hands you might be facing. Here things change a bit. Your pair is lower, so there is less chance you're facing a bluffing hand such as a lower pair or something like an ace-trey, simply because there are fewer hands containing a card lower than your fours. Couple that with the fact that your opponent is a known tight player who isn't so short of chips that he has to make a move, and you have to reduce the probability that you're up against a bluff. Under these circumstances, I'd reduce it to zero just to make the math easy.

Now for the real question: How often are you facing a higher pair compared to how often you're facing two overcards? In the last problem, facing an aggressive player, we estimated the chances of facing a pair at 40 percent and the chances of facing two overcards at 50 percent. Against a conservative player, you should adjust the mix in the other direction. Conservative players just aren't as eager to stick all their chips in the pot when holding king-queen or ace-jack, unless time has really run out on them. I'd estimate the balance for this hand at 60 percent pairs, 40 percent overcards. (Remember, we're assuming no bluffs in this situation.)

Using the 60-40 breakdown, your winning chances can be estimated quickly. Against the pairs, you're about a 4.5-to-1 underdog, so you win a little less than 20 percent of the time. 20 percent of 60 percent is 12 percent, so we'll say you win 11 percent here. Against the overcards, you win a little more than half the time. Half of 40 percent is 20 percent, so we'll say you win 22 percent here. Your grand total is 33 percent wins.

$$33 = 11 + 22$$

You're a 2-to-1 underdog in the hand. The pot is only offering you 12-to-7 money odds, so you should fold here.

**Action:** You fold, and the small blind takes the pot.

Compare this hand to the previous one and notice the difference that two small changes made. The pot odds were slightly, but not dramatically, worse. Because we were dealing with a conservative player rather than an aggressive one, we made a small modification in the balance of possible hands. The result of these two changes, however, was to change a clear call into a clear fold. Don't underestimate the importance of pot odds calculations!

# Hand 11-20

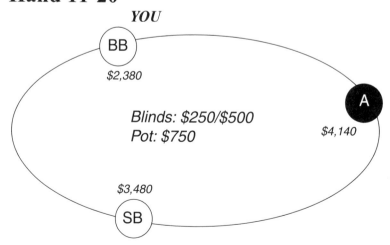

**Situation:** Last three players in a single-table online tournament.

**Your hand:** Q♥6♠

**Action to you:** Player A raises to $1,000 and the small blind folds.

**Question:** *Do you fold, call, or raise?*
    **Answer:** After Player A's bet, the pot contains $1,750, and it costs you only $500 more to call. Those are pot odds of 3.5-to-1. Your hand of queen-six offsuit looks mediocre — well, actually it is mediocre — but those are substantial odds, so you have to ask yourself just how bad this hand really is.

    Against two cards dealt at random from the deck, queen-six offsuit is actually a 51-to-49 favorite! Surprising, but true. Most hands are even worse. The real question is, how confident can we be that we're up against a hand that's significantly better than random?

    By the time we get down to the last three players, we can't be confident of that at all. No matter how bad the hands are, one of the three of us has to win this pot, and our opponent's bet may represent no more than a stealing attempt. At this stage of the tournament, you want to give the pot odds top consideration. 3.5-to-1 are great odds when you're holding a hand that's squarely in the middle of the pack, so call.

**Action:** You call. The pot now contains $2,250.

**Flop:** J♥T♣5♥

**Question:** *Do you bet or check?*
    **Answer:** We completely missed the flop, so the value of our hand has just dropped off the cliff. The texture of the flop is particularly bad. The two medium cards fit a lot of holdings,

and many of the holdings they don't fit (those with aces and kings) beat us. You should be very reluctant to try and steal here. Nothing to do but check and hope you get a free card.

**Action:** You check and Player A checks.

**Fourth Street:** 5♣

**Question:** *What now?*
    **Answer:** Nothing has changed, so you should still check.

**Action:** You check, and Player A bets $1,000. *What do you do?*
    **Answer:** You fold. It's possible you still have the best hand, but there's no reason to bet money on it.

# Hand 11-21

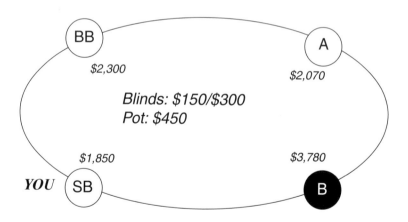

Blinds: $150/$300
Pot: $450

BB $2,300
A $2,070
YOU SB $1,850
B $3,780

**Situation:** End of a single-table online tournament.

**Your hand:** K♥K♦

**Action to you:** Player A folds. Player B, on the button, calls. The pot is now $750.

**Question:** *Do you call, raise, or raise all-in?*

> **Answer:** There's a case to be made here for going all-in. There's now a significant amount of money in the pot to be won right away. You have the short stack at the table, so there's a better chance that an all-in move will be perceived as a desperation play.
>
> But I still wouldn't do it. There's just too great a chance that you'll chase everybody away, and this is a great hand for doubling up. I'd put in about $900. That makes the pot $1,650, and either the big blind or player B can call you for another $600, which looks like pretty good pot odds. It also looks like you're leaving yourself a way to exit the hand later, which projects a little weakness in a subtle way. If either player has some kind of a hand, they're likely to come in against you, which is what you want.

**Action:** You actually go all-in, and the big blind and Player B both fold.

# Hand 11-22

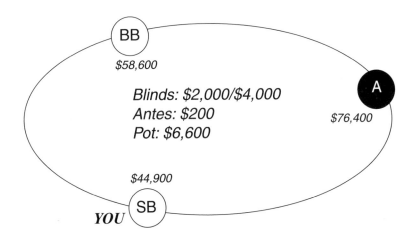

BB
$58,600

Blinds: $2,000/$4,000
Antes: $200
Pot: $6,600

A
$76,400

$44,900

*YOU* SB

**Situation:** Final table of a multi-table live tournament. Both the big blind and Player A have played conservatively up to now. You have been loose and active lately.

**Your hand:** A♣8♥

**Action to you:** Player A calls. The pot is now $10,600.

**Question:** *Do you fold, call, or raise?*
  **Answer:** Your hand is strong enough to raise at a three-handed table, but the call did come from the big stack, so some caution is in order. There's no harm in just putting in $2,000 to see a cheap flop, then deciding if you want to get involved.

**Action:** You call, putting in another $2,000. The big blind goes all-in, pushing his last $56,200 into the pot. Player A folds. *What do you do?*
  **Answer:** First you must resist the impulse to just shove in all your chips because you have an ace, and consider the situation.

  When a player is the first to enter the pot and makes an all-in move, you can assume there's a good chance he's bluffing, or at least playing a hand not as good as your ace-eight. When a player moves all-in to a pot that two players have already entered, that assumption goes out the window. The big blind isn't bluffing in this situation; he expects to be called by someone, and he expects to win anyway. Conservative players try to steal easy pots, not hard pots.

  The most likely hand for the big blind to have is a pair, and probably not one of the very lowest pairs (treys or deuces). Most of the non-pairs that might make this play are hands that have you dominated, so those aren't good news either.

The big blind only raised you the amount of your stack, so the pot now contains $53,300, and it costs you your remaining stack, $40,700 to call. Those are decent odds of about 1.3-to-1. However, look at your chances against the hands you're likely facing:

1.  Against the five pairs between your ace and your eight (KK, QQ, JJ, TT, 99), you're about a 2.5-to-1 underdog.

2.  Against the pairs lower than your eight (77, 66, 55, 44 — we eliminated 33 and 22 as likely hands) you're about a 12-to-10 underdog.

3.  Against the aces that have you dominated (AK through A9) you're almost a 3-to-1 underdog.

4.  Against 88 you're a 2.5-to-1 underdog, and against AA you're a 13-to-1 underdog. (These pairs are only half as likely as the others since you hold one of the cards.)

The only hands where you're getting the right price are the lower pairs, and even there you're only just getting the right price. Fold.

**Action:** You fold.

# Hand 11-23

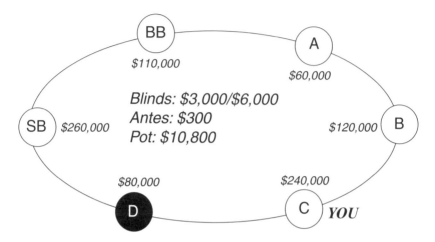

**Situation:** Final table of a major tournament. All the remaining players are strong, experienced veterans.

**Your hand:** A♠K♣

**Action to you:** Players A and B fold.

**Question:** *Do you call, raise to $30,000, or raise all-in?*

**Answer:** This hand came from the final table of a major tournament where the player with the ace-king elected to go all-in. There's nothing horribly wrong with this play, but I don't like it. Here's why.

It's true that most of the time this all-in bet will win the pot. The only hands that will be calling are medium to high pairs, probably ace-queen, and another ace-king. Let's say that your opponents might call with a pair of eights or better, and ace-queen and ace-king. In that case, virtually all of the possible calling hands will be either even money (ace-king), a slight favorite (eights through queens), or a huge favorite (aces or kings). The only hand you're excited to see your opponent call and show is ace-queen. It's true that these hands won't occur often enough to make your play a money-loser. The fact that you'll pick up the blinds most of the time will enable your play to show a profit, on average.

But suppose you just make the normal play, raising to something like $25,000 to $30,000? That's still plenty big enough to take down the blinds when no one else has much. If someone calls you, it's probably one of the medium pairs, so you can try to outmaneuver them after the flop. And if you get raised, it's likely to be by a hand that's a substantial favorite. I like the normal play here, and I think that over time it will show a bigger profit with less risk than the all-in move. But you'll see this all-in move a fair amount, often from players who are afraid (possibly unconsciously) of playing hands after the flop, and are looking to simplify their decision-making.

In the actual hand, the small blind was holding queens. He called, and his hand held up to win the pot. If you call with queens in this position, you can be almost certain that you hold the best hand. The only hands that are favored against you are aces or kings, and players with those hands aren't looking to chase everyone out of the pot with an all-in raise.

# Hand 11-24

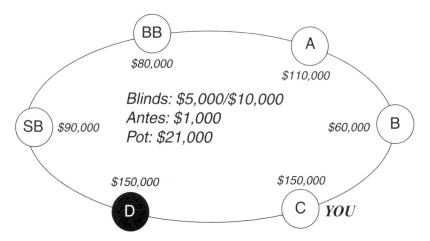

**Situation:** Final table of a major tournament.

**Your hand:** A♥K♦

**Action to you:** Players A and B both fold.

**Question:** *Do you call, raise the pot, or go all-in?*
   **Answer:** In contrast to the last hand, your M is much smaller here (about 7.5, compared to 24 in Hand 11-23). A smaller M creates a better argument for an all-in move, and in fact that's not an unreasonable play. But I still prefer to make a more normal-sized raise, because I really want to encourage action with a hand this good. With ace-jack or ace-ten I would be more happy to just move all-in.

**Action:** You raise to $40,000, Player D on the button raises to $70,000. The small blind and big blind fold. The pot is now $131,000.

**Question:** *Do you fold, call, or go all-in?*

**Answer:** Now you go all-in for your last $110,000. This eliminates the positional value of the button, and gets you full value for your hand. In addition, you may well have the best hand. Since you didn't represent enormous strength with your initial bet, the raise might have come from some hands like ace-queen, ace-jack, or ace-ten, and you're a big favorite against those hands. And of course your opponent may just throw his hand away, which is a great result for you.

The other advantage to playing the hand this way is that you've made it very tough for your opponents to decide what to do, either now or after your first bet. That's a good thing. Many players inadvertently make it easy for their opponents to know what to do.

**Action:** You go all-in, and Player D calls, showing J♣J♠. You catch a king on the flop and hold on to win the hand.

# Hand 11-25

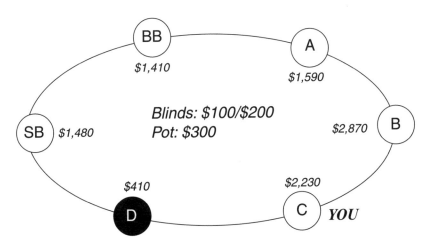

**Situation:** Middle of a one table satellite. Player B is an aggressive player who has accumulated a lot of chips.

**Your hand:** 7♠7♦

**Action to you:** Player A folds. Player B raises to $700. The pot is now $1,000.

**Question:** *Do you fold, call, or raise?*

**Answer:** Since you know Player B is an aggressive player, you have to move all-in here. Your pair of sevens is likely the best hand at this point. Player B probably has two high cards, if that. If he calls you with that hand, you'll be a 13-to-10 favorite, and he may well elect to lay down his hand. Of course it's possible that he has a higher pair, but if you let that fear take you out of the pot, you've wasted the time you've spent observing him. He's aggressive, the table is short, he made a move to take the pot, and you have a real hand. Just go after him.

Many players shrink from going all-in with just a pair of sevens, but to be successful in tournaments you have to be able to make these plays.

**Resolution:** You actually folded, as did everyone else, and Player B took the pot.

# Hand 11-26

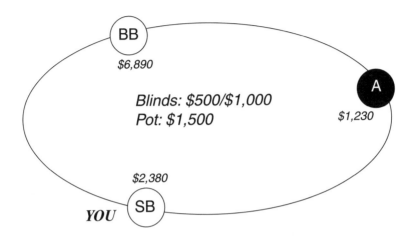

BB
$6,890

Blinds: $500/$1,000
Pot: $1,500

A
$1,230

$2,380

YOU SB

**Situation:** Final three players of a single-table online tournament.

**Your hand:** A♦8♥

**Action to you:** Player A goes all-in for his last $1,230.

**Question:** *Do you fold, call, or raise?*
  **Answer:** Ace-eight is a fine hand three-handed, and you're certainly going to play. Just remember to go all-in yourself, to discourage the big blind from putting his stack to work with a marginal hand. Your best chance of winning the pot is heads-up against Player A.

  There is a second possibility, called the cooperation play. It's used when two players see a chance to move up in prize money by cooperating with each other to knock out a third player. To make this play, just flat call, and hope that the big blind calls as well. Then check the hand down without betting. If the big blind does the same, the chances that Player A is eliminated are maximized.

Cooperative plays are not illegal as long as the players do not openly consult. They simply require each player involved to recognize that their chances individually improve when a third player is eliminated, and make the logical decision to cause that to happen.

**Action:** You go all-in, and the big blind folds. Your A♦8♥ holds up against an A♠6♥.

# Hand 11-27

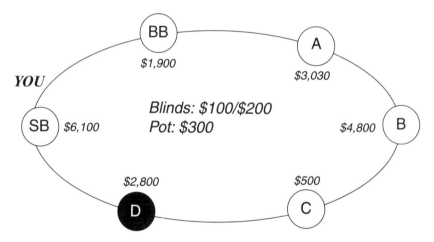

**Situation:** Online tournament after a couple of hours. Twelve players remain at two tables. Player C is a conservative player, but has lost a couple of bad beats. The big blind is a loose player who has been similarly unlucky.

**Your hand:** A♣T♠

**Action to you:** Players A and B fold. Player C goes all-in for his last $500. The pot is now $800. The button folds.

**Question:** *What do you do?*

    **Answer:** By the 10-to-1 rule, you could call this bet with any hand if you were last to act. There is, however, one player still behind you. You have no reason to think he has a hand, but just for insurance, put in a reasonable raise, say to $750. This will show him that you're serious, and will probably get him to throw away some marginal hands that could outdraw you.

**Resolution:** You raise to $750. The big blind folds. Player C shows J♠J♥, and his hand holds up.

    Unlucky, as Player C was desperate and might have been raising with many hands weaker than that.

# Part Twelve

# Heads-Up

# Heads-Up

# Introduction

The English philosopher Thomas Hobbes once characterized life in a mythical state of nature (pre-civilization) as "nasty, brutish, and short." He might well have been describing the final heads-up section of a no-limit hold 'em tournament. The chips are now divided among just two players, but the blinds are generally huge and the starting requirements are generally low. The session typically lasts just a few hands before the players are all-in with some average-plus holdings.

Many players feel at sea in heads-up confrontations. Over the years I've talked to a number of players who reached the finals of their first major tournament either leading or even in the chip count, and then lost in the heads-up session. Invariable they walk away thinking "I blew it. I should have done something different, but I just didn't know what to do." Usually I end up telling them "You played all right, but there really isn't that much you can do. The cards rule in these short little sessions."

Although the cards do rule, there are some simple rules of thumb that will make your play more effective, and some common mistakes you have to avoid. In this section we'll look at the components of heads-up strategy, and examine some actual head-up sessions from beginning to end.

As you read this chapter, keep in mind that quasi-heads-up situations occur at other, earlier points in a tournament. In the most obvious case, you're in the small blind and everyone folds to you. Now there is simply a confrontation between you and the big blind. Much of the advice in this section applies very well in that case.

# Hand Rankings in Heads-Up Play

Before I start describing the strategy of heads-up play, we need to do some preliminary work. To begin, let's create a chart that ranks your hole cards. We want to know which hands constitute the top 10 percent of all hands, the top 20 percent of all hands, and so on. In this chart, hands are ranked by their ability to win an all-in confrontation against a single random hand. There's a lot of key information here, and we'll refer back to it throughout the chapter.

**The Top 10%; (62% or better to win)**
    Pairs: AA-66
    Suited non-pairs: AK - A8, KQ - KJ
    Unsuited non-pairs: AK - AT

**The Top 20% (58% or better to win)**
    All the above plus
    Pairs: 55
    Suited Non-Pairs: A7 - A3, KT - K8, QJ, QT
    Unsuited Non-Pairs: A9 - A7, KQ - KT, QJ

**The Top 30% (55% or better to win)**
    All the above plus
    Pairs: 44
    Suited Non-Pairs: A2, K7 - K5, Q9, Q8, JT, J9
    Unsuited Non-Pairs: A6 - A3, K9 - K7, QT

## The Top 40% (52% or better to win)
All the above plus
Pairs: 33
Suited Non-Pairs: K4 - K2, Q7 - Q5, J8, T9
Unsuited Non-Pairs: A2, K6 - K4, Q9, Q8, JT, J9

## The Top 50% (50% or better to win)
All the above plus
Pairs: 22
Suited Non-Pairs: Q4 - Q2, J7 - J5, T8, T7, 98
Unsuited Non-Pairs: K3, K2, Q7 - Q5, J8, T9

## The Top 60% (47% or better to win)
All the above plus
Suited Non-Pairs: J4 - J2, T6, T5, 97, 96, 87
Unsuited Non-Pairs: Q4 - Q2, J7 - J5, T8, T7, 98

## The Top 70% (44% or better to win)
All the above plus
Suited Non-Pairs: T4 - T2, 95, 94, 86, 85, 76, 75
Unsuited Non-Pairs: J4 - J2, T6, T5, 97, 96, 87

## The Top 80% (41% or better to win)
All the above plus
Suited Non-Pairs: 93, 92, 84, 83, 74, 65, 64, 54
Unsuited Non-Pairs: T4 - T2, 95, 94, 86, 85, 76

## The Top 90% (38% or better to win)
All the above plus
Suited Non-Pairs: 82, 73, 72, 63, 62, 53, 52, 43
Unsuited Non-Pairs: 94 - 92, 84, 83, 75, 74, 65, 64, 54

## The Bottom 10% (32% to 37% to win)
Suited Non-Pairs: 42, 32
Unsuited Non-Pairs: 73, 63, 53, 43, 82, 72, 62, 52, 42, 32

I wouldn't try to memorize this table, but I would look it over a few times to get a general sense of where various hands lie and what hands are roughly equivalent to what other hands. The table should be fairly easy to read. The first group are the hands with winning chances in the top 10 percent of all hands, including the pairs all the way down to sixes, the top ace and king combinations of suited cards, and even the unsuited aces down as far as ace-ten. All of these hands are at least 62 percent to win against a random hand. (The best hand, aces, is 85 percent to win against two random cards. I should say *only* 85 percent, since many players react as though they had a lock when they pick up aces heads-up, whereas in fact they're between a 5-to-1 and a 6-to-1 favorite.)

The next block of hands includes those where you're between 59 percent and 61 percent to win pre-flop, which puts you in the top 80 percent of all hands. The high unsuited kings start to appear in this bunch.

The single key idea to take away from the table is that suits matter a little and high cards matter a lot. Holdings with aces and kings dominate the rankings, while two suited cards are only about 2 percent better in terms of winning chances than the same two cards unsuited.

By the way, the weakest two-card holding heads-up, with the hands played to the end, is trey-deuce offsuit. This differs from the weakest two-card holding at a full table under the same conditions, which is seven-deuce offsuit. Do you see the reason for the difference?

At a full table, playing to the end, many wins for hands of two low cards come when the hands make a straight. (Heads-up, simply pairing one of the low cards might be enough.) In hands where the cards are separated by five spots or more, only one of the cards can be used to make a straight. The weakest hand where the cards are separated by at least five spots is seven-deuce.

Let me emphasize again that this chart ranks hands according to their strength in an all-in confrontation. In many heads-up situations, that's really all you need to know. If both sides have a very low M when the heads-up battle occurs, any contested hand is likely to be an all-in hand.

But if both sides have big Ms, we need to consider another factor called *playability*. Top players consider some card combinations more playable than others. For example, both king-five offsuit and Jack-ten offsuit are in the fourth group (top 40 percent of all hands), but in a hand where there is liable to be betting and maneuvering both before and after the flop, most players consider the jack-ten a more playable holding than the king-five. One reason is the obvious straight possibilities. Another, and more powerful reason, is that the five is more likely to make bottom pair when it hits the flop, while either the jack or the ten have chances to make top pair or middle pair. Hitting the five and making bottom pair might win in a showdown, but you may not want to see that showdown with just bottom pair. That inherent weakness in the high card-low card combinations makes many players more reluctant to get involved with them in a high-M battle.

# Pre-Flop Heads-Up Play

There's nothing clean or neat about heads-up play. There's no hint here of antiseptic modern warfare-at-a-distance with computer screens and drone aircraft as the weapons of choice. Picture instead a couple of Visigoths bashing at each other with maces and battle-axes. It's close-up and dirty, and in order to survive you'll have to fight for each and every hand.

Having said that, let's look at four key principles of pre-flop heads-up play.
1. Any pair is a big hand.
2. Almost all hands are battles of unpaired cards.
3. Domination isn't as bad as you think.
4. You will mostly have the pot odds you need to play.

## One: Any Pair Is a Big Hand

There are 1,326 possible starting hands in hold 'em. (This number isn't hard to calculate. Imagine dealing two cards from a deck of 52 cards. There are 52 ways to deal the first card, and once that card has been dealt, there are 51 ways to deal the second card. 52 times 51 = 2,652. But in this counting, every hand has been counted twice. The hand of

was counted once when the king was the first card dealt, and once when the seven was the first card dealt. So divide 2,652 by 2, and you have 1,326 possible hands.)

Of these possible starting hands, only 78 are pairs, or about 6 percent. (There are six different pairs for any rank of cards, and 13 different ranks.) This number leads to a few interesting conclusions about heads-up play:

1. You'll be dealt a pair once every 17 hands on average.
2. Both sides will be dealt a pair slightly more often than once every 300 hands.
3. Neither side will have a pair 7 hands out of 8.
4. One side will have a pair, but not the other, about one hand in 8.

In short, any pair is a big deal, and deserves to be pushed strongly. Your worst possible pair is deuces, and here's how deuces ranks against some unpaired hands when played to the end:

- Versus AK unsuited: 53.0%
- Versus AK suited: 49.9%
- Versus JT unsuited: 48.7%
- Versus 76 unsuited: 49.4%
- Versus AT unsuited: 52.0%
- Versus K7 unsuited: 52.6%
- Versus Q3 unsuited: 53.8%

The worst possible non-pair holding for deuces to face are the suited connectors between jack-ten and seven-six, since they have straights working in both directions. Amusingly, ace-king is the best suited connector to face, since the straights only work in one direction.

When you have a pair, you should assume you're facing a non-pair and play accordingly. You almost certainly won't be able to read your opponent well enough to distinguish between his holding a pair and his holding two high cards, and he'll be holding a pair so rarely that you'll be costing yourself money if you try.

The only times you can become a big favorite pre-flop in heads-up play is when your higher pair meets a lower pair or two lower cards. Here are a few of examples:

- AA versus 77: 79.7%
- AA versus JT suited: 78.3%

If your pair is in between your opponent's two cards, the presence of his overcard matters a great deal. For example

- 88 versus A2 unsuited: 70.1%

# Two: Almost All Hands Are Battles of Unpaired Cards

Seven hands out of eight the two players are holding unpaired cards. If there is not a card in common (a situation we call *domination*) then *no two unpaired cards are a huge favorite over any other two unpaired cards*.

Here are the probabilities for some matchups of unpaired cards.

**Two higher cards versus two lower cards:**
- AK unsuited versus JT unsuited: 62.6%
- AJ unsuited versus 86 unsuited: 63.1%
- A9 unsuited versus 76 suited: 58.0%
- T9 suited versus 87 suited: 63.5%
- QJ suited versus T2 unsuited: 71.8%

**Highest and lowest versus two middle cards:**
- A2 unsuited versus JT unsuited: 54.5%
- K4 unsuited versus Q5 unsuited: 59.9%
- T7 suited versus 9-8 suited: 56.4%

**Interleaved (first and third versus second and fourth):**
- AQ unsuited versus KJ unsuited: 62.6%
- KT unsuited versus Q4 suited: 61.2%

As you can see, the range is from a little over 70 percent, for a worst-case scenario of two medium-high suited connectors against widely-separated unsuited cards, to lows in the 55 percent to 57 percent range. Most cases cluster in the low 60's.

# Three: Domination Isn't as Bad as You Think

Domination refers to the situation where the two hands have a card in common. If you hold the lower non-common card, you're a substantial underdog, but it's not really as bad as most players imagine. Here are a few concrete examples:

1. QJ suited versus QT unsuited: 73.8%
2. KT unsuited versus K8 suited: 67.6%
3. AT unsuited versus A8 unsuited: 71.2%
4. AK suited versus AQ suited: 71.3%

While these numbers are worse for the trailer than in the previous examples, they're only slightly worse, ranging from the high 60's to the low 70's, rather than the high 50's to low 60's.

# Four: You Will Mostly Have the Pot Odds You Need to Play

In a heads-up confrontation, the player with the button is also the small blind. (His opponent is the big blind.) The small blind/button player acts first before the flop, but last on all subsequent betting rounds.

Whether antes are in play or not, the small blind/button player always has the pot odds needed to at least call pre-flop. For instance, suppose the blinds are $5,000/$10,000 and the antes are $1,000, and both players have good-sized stacks. The pot is now $17,000 and it costs the small blind/button $5,000 to play, so the pot is offering him 17-to-5 odds, over 3-to-1. The worst hand he can hold, trey-deuce offsuit, is only a little worse than 2.1-to-1 against an average hand, so you can literally call with any two cards. (You're not going to stand up to a raise from the big blind with trey-deuce offsuit, but that's a different issue.)

# Position and Bet Sizes in Heads-Up Play

Position is even more important heads-up than at a full table, since it's just a dual-state function. You're either in position for the rest of the hand, or you're out of position. Compare this to preflop betting at a full table, where position is a much murkier concept. Most bets are made without any certainty of what position you'll hold after the flop. For instance, suppose there are nine players at the table, and you're fifth to act, and the first four players fold. If you bet here, what position will you hold after the flop? If you get called by the two players behind you and the blinds fold, you're in bad position — first to act out of three. But if the blinds call while the cutoff and button fold, you have great position — last to act out of three.

Position is especially important when the two competing hands are close in value. In that case, the player who acts last has a sizeable edge. But as we just saw in the previous section, in heads-up play most hands are close together in value! Hence position matters more in heads-up than in any other hold 'em situation.

When you do make a raise, how much should you raise? In Volume I raising on average about three times the big blind was advocated as a standard starting raise, with a range between two and five big blinds, varying as necessary to confuse your opponents. In heads-up play, you don't need to raise quite as much. Part of the reason for the bet size at a full table was to chase away some marginal hands and prevent them from drawing to beat you. With only one opponent, there are no other players to chase away. Now I like a bet range of two to three times the big blind. With two high cards, I strongly prefer a bet of twice the big blind. I'm not committing many chips, and I'm trying to encourage action from a player holding ace-x, king-x, or queen-x, whom I may have dominated. I use a bet of three times the big blind to discourage action and get my opponent to drop.

When the small blind/button player starts off by calling and the big blind wants to raise, he's well advised to make a much larger than usual raise — say four to five times the big blind. The idea is to end the hand quickly when possible and negate the bad position. Good heads-up strategy requires playing as many hands as possible when in position and pushing marginal hands as hard as possible when out of position.

# High-M Confrontations
# Versus Low-M Confrontations

Much of your strategy depends on whether or not the blinds have become large relative to your stack. In online tournaments, particularly sit-and-gos, the Ms are often in the 5 to 10 range when the heads-up period starts. These battles will mostly feature big all-in moves and will end pretty quickly. In live tournaments, however, the blinds may just be a tiny fraction of the stacks, and the Ms might range from 20 to over 100. This situation much more closely resembles normal poker, and requires careful patience and planning.

The notion of "effective M" takes on a slightly different meaning in heads-up play. Since the players are now involved in every hand and sitting out a stretch of hands is not really an option, there is less reason to modify the actual M to reflect strategy changes based on the shrunken table. I just use the actual M when thinking about heads-up play.

## Basic Pre-Flop Betting Strategy

Now let's use the information we already have to construct a basic strategy for pre-flop betting. If you're uncomfortable playing heads-up, as many players are, this strategy will ensure that you're at least making reasonable plays pre-flop while staying out of a lot of trouble. If you want, you can play this strategy mechanically, since in a short heads-up session, in which very few hands are actually shown down, it's unlikely your opponent will get enough feedback to know just what you're doing.

# You are the Small Blind/Button

As the Small Blind/Button, you act first pre-flop and last after the flop. The pot will be offering you better than 3-to-1 odds to get involved, and you'll have a positional advantage throughout the hand. With these edges working for you, play aggressively! Here are your rules:

1.  At least call with any two cards. (If your opponent has been raising regularly from the big blind in response to your calls, then throw away your trash hands — those in the bottom 20 percent of possible hands.)

2.  You have a potential raising hand if you hold any hand in the top 40 percent of all hands and the Ms are low (under 10 for either player). If the Ms of the two players are high (10 or more each), then your standards need to be stricter. In that case, any hand in the top 30 percent of all hands is a potential raising hand. When you have a potential raising hand, raise two-thirds of the time and call one-third of the time. If you have one of the top three pairs (aces, kings, or queens), reverse this mix, calling two-thirds and raising one-third.

3.  If you call and are raised, call with any ace, any pair, or any other hand in the top 30 percent of all hands.

4.  If you call and are raised all-in, call with any hand in the top 20 percent of all hands.

5.  If you raise and are reraised (all-in or not), call with for certain with any pair or any other hand in the top 10 percent of all hands. (Note that 80 percent of all reraises are made with two high cards, hence the rule for calling with pairs.) You may want to call with hands in the top 20 percent of all hands, depending on other circumstances. I would call with

these hands, for instance, if I had money odds of 4-to-1 or 3-to-1. With 2-to-1 odds, I would call if I had any sort of read on my opponent that pointed to a call. If the Ms are very large, I would tighten my restrictions somewhat. Now I would call only with pairs down to sixes, or ace-king, ace-queen, or ace-jack.

The logic of these rules is pretty simple. A raise after your call doesn't necessarily indicate great strength, so you just need a good hand to continue. A raise after you have already raised indicates a very good hand, and restricting your calls to top-10 percent hands gives you a fighting chance of having the best hand in the showdown. Of course, pot odds play a role here as well, and if the pot odds are compelling, you may choose to get involved with weaker hands.

One last important rule: If the Ms are low (say 3 to 5) and you opponent seems to be establishing a pattern of going all-in every hand, just pick a hand in the top 30 percent and call.

# You are the Big Blind

As the big blind, you will have a positional disadvantage for the rest of the hand, so ending the hand quickly is a high priority.

1. If your opponent just calls and the Ms are less than 5, raise all-in with any hand in the top 30 percent of all hands. If the Ms are between 5 and 10, raise, but not necessarily all-in. With big Ms (above 10) increase your requirements to hands in the top 20 percent.

2. If your opponent raises, call with any top-30 percent hand and reraise with any top-20 percent hand. Here, however, you need to be paying attention to what your opponent has been doing. If he hasn't been raising much, then sticks in a strong raise, tighten your calling requirements to a top-20 percent

hand and your corresponding reraising requirement to a top-10 percent hand.

3.   If your opponent raises all-in, call with any top-20 percent hand.

Your raising strategy from the big blind is aggressive, reflecting your desire to eliminate as much post-flop play as possible.

# Some Sample
# Heads-Up Sessions

In Volume I and most of Volume II, we've focused on individual hands and problems. That approach isn't as useful for studying heads-up play, since the play of each hand is typically closely tied to the play that has preceded it. Both players are trying to get inside their opponent's head and reason out each other's strategy. As soon as possible, you want answers to questions like the following:

1. Is he desperate or confident? Tired or energized?

2. Is he happy playing a long session, or does he want the session finished quickly?

3. Is he limping with bad hands, or a mixture of bad and good hands?

4. What hands will he slow-play?

5. What hand does he need to call an all-in move?

6. Is he playing the way he did when the table was three and four-handed, or has he switched to some new strategy just for heads-up play?

Instead of looking at hands in isolation, we're going to watch two heads-up sessions in their entirety, trying to get a feel for the tactics and strategy of these encounters. We'll start with a battle between Phil Ivey and John D'Agostino.

# Heads-Up Session
# No. 1: Ivey Versus D'Agostino

The Turning Stone tournament in 2004 was remarkable in that the entire tournament was broadcast live, a first for poker. Instead of seeing a carefully edited assortment of hands (usually chosen for their big pairs or all-in action), viewers got to see hands that were more characteristic of the nuts and bolts of real poker, where small hands predominated and artful moves decided the winner.

The heads-up finale was a battle between Phil Ivey (a grizzled veteran at 27) and John D'Agostino, a relative newcomer at age 21. Ivey is considered one of the top few players in the world at no-limit hold 'em, and has made the final table of the World Poker Tour on several occasions. In 2003 he was making a strong run at the World Series of Poker before he was eliminated in tenth place on a brutal beat by Chris Moneymaker. D'Agostino was a surprise at Turning Stone only because of his youth. Up until a few years ago, a 21-year old in a major no-limit hold 'em tournament would have been considered easy cannon fodder. Today, the huge growth of online poker has provided a steady supply of players turning 21 with hundreds, if not thousands, of no-limit tournaments under their belt. D'Agostino earned a lot of respect at Turning Stone, and is considered one of the best of this new group.

As the battle starts, D'Agostino has a big chip lead, with about 63 percent of the chips in play. Blinds are $6,000/$12,000, with $2,000 antes.

**Hand No. 1: Blinds $6,000/$12,000, antes $2,000 each**

|  | Stack | Position | Hand |
|---|---|---|---|
| John D'Agostino | $705,000 | SB/B | A♥2♥ |
| Phil Ivey | $417,000 | BB | 7♣3♦ |

382 Part Twelve: Heads-Up

**Action:** D'Agostino puts in $25,000, raising $19,000; Ivey folds

**Result:** Ivey loses $14,000

An ace is a very strong hand heads-up. If you hold an ace, there's about a 90 percent chance that your opponent will not, and the ace can easily win the hand all by itself. D'Agostino's raise is perfectly understandable. Ivey has one of the weakest hands possible, and he properly throws it away.

Ivey commented after the match that his overall plan was to play slowly, hoping to outplay his opponent in many small pots. Although he trails in the chip count, the Ms are pretty large: Ivey's is 19, D'Agostino's is 32. Those are large enough to allow for plenty of moves and maneuvering.

## Hand No. 2: Blinds $6,000/$12,000, antes $2,000 each

|  | Stack | Position | Hand |
|---|---|---|---|
| John D'Agostino | $719,000 | BB | 7♣5♦ |
| Phil Ivey | $403,000 | SB/B | 9♣8♣ |

**Action:** Ivey puts in $30,000, raising $24,000; D'Agostino folds

**Result:** D'Agostino loses $14,000

Ivey thought for a long time before raising, and in fact was very deliberate with all his moves in the session, whether folding, calling, or raising. By maintaining a measured pace, he denied his opponent a chance to get any reads based on the speed of his betting. (Ivey's facial expressions are legendarily inscrutable.)

Ivey's hand, nine-eight suited, was in the middle of the pack. It certainly merited a call, but Ivey has to raise with some medium-strength hands, to disguise the raises with genuinely strong hands. He's picked this hand for one of those raises.

D'Agostino could have won the pot with a reraise, but he had no way of knowing that. His hand is weak, and he can't be criticized for folding.

**Hand No. 3: Blinds $6,000/$12,000, antes $2,000 each**

|  | Stack | Position | Hand |
|---|---|---|---|
| John D'Agostino | $705,000 | SB/B | J♦9♣ |
| Phil Ivey | $417,000 | BB | K♣3♥ |

**Action:** D'Agostino puts in $30,000 raising $24,000; Ivey folds

**Result:** Ivey loses $14,000

This time D'Agostino has a hand that's in the middle of the pack, and elects to put in a raise.

Ivey's fold with king-trey might surprise some players as a king is a good card. However, king-trey only scores in the top 50 percent of all hands on our chart, which makes it a weak candidate for calling a raise according to our basic strategy. In addition, good players are in general much happier playing hands like jack-nine and ten-eight heads-up than they are with the widely separated cards like king-small, queen-small, and jack-small.

While the king-small and other such hands score well in computer matchups where hands are played down to the river, they're less effective on our playability scale, when you will often have to lay the hand down to a bet when your high card doesn't hit. A hand with two closely-connected medium cards gives you more chance of hitting a playable pair, in addition to the long-shot straight possibilities that could end the whole tournament outright.

A further point to note is that Ivey is out of position in this hand, and king-small is a holding that gains strongly with position. In position, there will be situations where the hand is checked down to the river, and the single king actually holds up to win. Out of position, that scenario is much less likely to happen since checks by the first player will eventually be interpreted as weakness and attacked.

### Hand No. 4: Blinds $6,000/$12,000, antes $2,000 each

|  | Stack | Position | Hand |
|---|---|---|---|
| John D'Agostino | $719,000 | BB | A♦8♠ |
| Phil Ivey | $403,000 | SB/B | A♥T♦ |

**Action:** Ivey puts in $36,000 raising $30,000; D'Agostino calls, puts in $30,000 more

An interesting clash of two good aces.

Ivey's raise pre-flop is perfectly justified on the strength of the hand, and also on his previous play. Last time in the small blind/button, he raised with a medium-strength hand. Now he raises with a good hand. His opponent may think he's in perma-raise mode, and decide to fight him right now, which would be great (for Ivey).

With an ace, D'Agostino could certainly consider reraising pre-flop. But ace-eight is what pros consider the crossover hand with aces. If you think your opponent may have an ace of his own, then ace-eight is better than half the aces he might hold. Certainly with a small M, ace-eight is a monster hand and you're happy to commit all your chips with it. But with a large M (here D'Agostino's M is 32) and a big chip lead, you might think about playing the hand slowly and protecting your lead. A reasonable choice by D'Agostino.

**Flop: 5♣4♦3♥**

**Action:** D'Agostino checks; Ivey bets $60,000; D'Agostino folds

**Result:** D'Agostino loses $44,000

D'Agostino checks after the flop, which is a very conservative move. Most players would have led out here to clarify the situation. Ivey very reasonably fills the void with a bet. Now D'Agostino has a real problem. The only aces he can now beat are ace-seven or ace-six. The others either have him dominated or have already made a pair or a straight. In what has become a murky situation, he chooses to protect his chip lead and folds. Tight, but not unreasonable.

**Hand No. 5: Blinds $6,000/$12,000, antes $2,000 each**

|  | Stack | Position | Hand |
|---|---|---|---|
| John D'Agostino | $675,000 | SB/B | J♦4♥ |
| Phil Ivey | $447,000 | BB | 9♣8♥ |

**Action:** D'Agostino folds

**Result:** D'Agostino loses $8,000

A mistake. As I mentioned before, D'Agostino is just about always getting the pot odds he needs to call from the small blind/button, and he will have position after the flop as well. Jack-four is just a slightly below-average hand. (And in fact, here it's the best hand.) Calling is clear.

**Hand No. 6: Blinds $6,000/$12,000, antes $2,000 each**

|  | Stack | Position | Hand |
|---|---|---|---|
| John D'Agostino | $667,000 | BB | T♣7♠ |
| Phil Ivey | $455,000 | SB/B | A♦J♠ |

**Action:** Ivey raises, puts in $30,000, raising $24,000; D'Agostino calls, puts in $24,000 more

Both actions are easy to understand. Ivey continues to raise with strong hands, both to win the money and to prepare for later bluffs. D'Agostino has a medium-strength hand and elects to call. He could fold, but he might be remembering last hand, and wondering if he was pushed around. At any rate, he makes a stand here.

**Flop: T♦9♦4♥**

**Action:** D'Agostino checks

A good play by D'Agostino. He now has top pair, which in heads-up play is the equivalent of flopping a set at a full table. Knowing that Ivey likes to make continuation bets, he correctly decides to trap.

**Action:** Ivey bets $60,000; D'Agostino raises, puts in $190,000

D'Agostino makes his move now, rather than prolonging the trap to the turn. It's a very reasonable decision, especially with a big chip lead. He assumes he has the best hand right now, but he has no way of telling how many outs Ivey has, so he tries to end the hand now.

**Action:** Ivey folds

**Result:** Ivey loses $98,000

A big win for D'Agostino, who now has more than two-thirds of the chips.

**Hand No. 7: Blinds $6,000/$12,000, antes $2,000 each**

|  | Stack | Position | Hand |
|---|---|---|---|
| John D'Agostino | $771,000 | SB/B | A♠T♥ |
| Phil Ivey | $351,000 | BB | J♥6♣ |

**Action:** D'Agostino puts in $30,000, raising $24,000; Ivey folds

**Result:** Ivey loses $14,000

D'Agostino has a strong hand, so he raises. As we've seen, Ivey distrusts hands with a face card and a low card, plus he's out of position, plus D'Agostino says he has a good hand, so Ivey folds.

Notice that D'Agostino elects to raise $30,000, which is 2.5 times the big blind. That's a pretty standard heads-up raise for the player who will have position the rest of the hand. If D'Agostino had checked and Ivey wished to raise, he should raise a larger amount, say three to five times the big blind. As much as possible, the big blind wants to end the hand before the flop, to negate the cost of his bad position.

**Hand No. 8: Blinds $6,000/$12,000, antes $2,000 each**

|  | Stack | Position | Hand |
|---|---|---|---|
| John D'Agostino | $785,000 | BB | 7♠7♣ |
| Phil Ivey | $337,000 | SB/B | A♠8♣ |

**Action:** Ivey calls, puts in $6,000; D'Agostino raises, puts in $36,000 more; Ivey goes all-in, puts in last $323,000; D'Agostino calls, pot is $674,000

**Flop:** K♠8♠4♦

**Fourth Street:** 6♣

**Fifth Street: 8♥**

**Result:** D'Agostino loses $337,000

    A decisive hand unfolds quickly as Ivey gets all-in pre-flop.

    Ivey picks up a good hand, ace-eight, and elects to just call. This is a good move on his part. We've already established that Ivey's strategy is to play a lot of small pots and try to outplay his opponent post-flop. One way D'Agostino could fight this strategy is to blast away with big raises when Ivey just calls. To counter, Ivey needs to establish that he's capable of just calling pre-flop with strong hands, hence the call with a fine hand like ace-eight.

    D'Agostino has in fact picked up a very strong hand, a pair of sevens, so his raise isn't just an attempt to chase Ivey off the hand. But Ivey can't be sure of that, so he's faced with a choice. He could elect to simply call at this point, relying on his positional advantage for the rest of the hand. Instead, he decides to go all-in. He probably expects D'Agostino to fold, which will both win the pot and keep Ivey's hand a mystery. However, D'Agostino is delighted to call. Good play on all sides, but Ivey wins the showdown and survives.

    As a footnote, the pros consider ace-eight to be the minimum ace for making an all-in move because of its status as the crossover hand among the aces. (Less than half of all aces are better than ace-eight, more than half are weaker.)

## Hand No. 9: Blinds $6,000/$12,000, antes $2,000 each

| | Stack | Position | Hand |
|---|---|---|---|
| John D'Agostino | $448,000 | SB/B | J♠5♠ |
| Phil Ivey | $674,000 | BB | K♠7♣ |

**Action:** D'Agostino calls, puts in $6,000; Ivey checks

Note that D'Agostino chooses to call with jack-five suited, but earlier he had folded jack-four offsuit. Suited cards win about 2 percent more often than the same cards unsuited.

Ivey elects to check with his king-seven. It's a better-than-average hand, but not a powerhouse. Here he's out of position, so he elects the smaller play.

**Flop: Q♠Q♥9♣**

**Action:** Ivey checks; D'Agostino checks

The flop missed both players. Ivey checks, keeping the hand small. D'Agostino by now understands that Ivey is frequently checking good hands, and declines to attempt a steal.

**Fourth Street: K♥**

**Action:** Ivey checks; D'Agostino bets $15,000; Ivey calls

Ivey makes top pair. It's probably good, but he gives D'Agostino a chance to make a big move at the pot. D'Agostino in fact makes a minimal move at the pot, and Ivey just calls.

**Fifth Street: 7♠**

**Action:** Ivey checks; D'Agostino checks

In his live commentary, Howard Lederer called Ivey's check on fifth street an "offensive check," meaning that while Ivey thinks he probably has the best hand, he's playing the hand in such a way that he can't lose a lot. With the chip lead, Ivey doesn't want to lead out and have to face a giant reraise with a potentially dangerous hand. It's a good observation, and consistent with Ivey's overall game plan. D'Agostino meanwhile has nothing, and Ivey's call on fourth street indicated that he's probably not going away, so D'Agostino is content to show the hand down.

**Result:** D'Agostino loses $29,000

## Hand No. 10: Blinds $6,000/$12,000, antes $2,000 each

|  | Stack | Position | Hand |
|---|---|---|---|
| John D'Agostino | $419,000 | BB | T♥8♣ |
| Phil Ivey | $703,000 | SB/B | T♣2♠ |

**Action:** Ivey calls, puts in $6,000; D'Agostino checks

Note that Ivey simply does not fold pre-flop. In this case, he would call even if he knew D'Agostino's hand, since he's only a 2.5-to-1 underdog, and he's getting better than 3-to-1 from the flop. It's hard to keep shoving your money in with hands like ten-deuce, but it's the right play heads-up, especially for a player of Ivey's caliber.

**Flop: K♥6♥3♦**

This is an excellent flop for a cheap steal — three widely separated cards and only one high card. In position, Ivey has the best stealing chances.

**Action:** D'Agostino checks; Ivey bets $16,000; Ivey makes his move — D'Agostino folds — and it works.

**Result:** D'Agostino loses $14,000

Ivey's move here was routine for a good player. It's plays like this which give top players an edge in high-M heads-up confrontations. The counter-move is to lead out with a bet into that flop, which then leads to a head game between the two players, as each tries to play chicken with the other. Weak players tend to lose heads-up confrontations by not betting frequently enough. You have to be willing to both lead and reraise with nothing on a regular enough schedule to keep your opponent guessing.

## Hand No. 11: Blinds $6,000/$12,000, antes $2,000 each

|  | Stack | Position | Hand |
|---|---|---|---|
| John D'Agostino | $405,000 | SB/B | A♦5♦ |
| Phil Ivey | $717,000 | BB | A♣6♠ |

**Action:** D'Agostino raises, puts in $30,000, raising $24,000; Ivey raises, puts in $80,000, raising $56,000

Ivey departs from his conservative game plan by sticking in a good-sized reraise, a little more than twice D'Agostino's raise. If D'Agostino comes back over the top, Ivey would lay this hand down. It's also a move designed to end the hand quickly since Ivey is out of position.

DiAgostino's laydown of the ace-five is both correct from a practical sense (since we know he's beaten) but also correct theoretically. As I mentioned before, ace-eight is usually the minimum ace I want for an all-in move pre-flop.

**Action:** D'Agostino folds

**Result:** D'Agostino loses $38,000

## Hand No. 12: Blinds $6,000/$12,000, antes $2,000 each

|  | Stack | Position | Hand |
|---|---|---|---|
| John D'Agostino | $367,000 | BB | T♠6♥ |
| Phil Ivey | $755,000 | SB/B | 9♦6♣ |

**Action:** Ivey calls, puts in $6,000; D'Agostino checks

**Flop:** 5♦4♣2♠

**Action:** D'Agostino checks; Ivey bets $20,000; D'Agostino puts in $70,000, raising $50,000

A good move by D'Agostino. Ivey has been taking over the betting in this last run of hands, and D'Agostino needs to fight back at some point. This flop probably didn't help Ivey much, so why not now? In addition, the raise is actually a typical no-limit semi-bluff. It's designed to win the hand now, and if it doesn't, the tens, sixes, and treys all look like outs.

**Action:** Ivey folds

**Result:** Ivey loses $34,000

## Hand No. 13: Blinds $6,000/$12,000, antes $2,000 each

|  | Stack | Position | Hand |
|---|---|---|---|
| John D'Agostino | $401,000 | SB/B | ?? |
| Phil Ivey | $721,000 | BB | ?? |

This hand wasn't broadcast, but D'Agostino folded pre-flop, losing $8,000. Folding on the button pre-flop is a mistake, as we now know.

## Hand No. 14: Blinds $6,000/$12,000, antes $2,000 each

|  | Stack | Position | Hand |
|---|---|---|---|
| John D'Agostino | $393,000 | BB | T♥6♣ |
| Phil Ivey | $729,000 | SB/B | A♠3♠ |

**Action:** Ivey calls, puts in $6,000

With ace-small suited, Ivey could raise. But he has two good reasons for calling:

1. As part of a balanced strategy, keeping his opponent guessing, and

2. Limping with good hands to prevent random reraises, thus keeping most pots small.

If D'Agostino raises at this point, Ivey will most likely just call.

**Action:** D'Agostino checks

**Flop: J♣7♥3♥**

**Action:** D'Agostino checks; Ivey checks

**Fourth Street: A♥**

**Action:** D'Agostino bets $20,000

The ace is a two-way scare card, putting an ace and a three-flush on board. D'Agostino's bet represents either or both possibilities. From Ivey's quiet play so far, he has no reason to think that the ace has made Ivey's hand.

**Action:** Ivey puts in $65,000, raising $45,000

Ivey has top and bottom pair, but the three-flush on board is dangerous, so Ivey plays to end the hand now.

**Action:** D'Agostino folds

D'Agostino took a few seconds before folding, which is good technique. He's showing Ivey that he wasn't bluffing with zip. (We know he was, of course.) You don't need to play Hamlet here, just think a bit and then muck your hand.

**Result:** D'Agostino loses $34,000

**Hand No. 15: Blinds $6,000/$12,000, antes $2,000 each**

|  | **Stack** | **Position** | **Hand** |
|---|---|---|---|
| John D'Agostino | $359,000 | SB/B | 9♠8♠ |
| Phil Ivey | $763,000 | BB | K♣J♦ |

**Action:** D'Agostino calls, puts in $6,000; Ivey checks

Ivey has a good hand and could raise here, perhaps twice the big blind. If your opponent has either a king or a jack, you rate to get involved in a hand where you have him outkicked. Ivey remains consistent to his smallball strategy and just checks.

**Flop: T♦7♠5♦**

**Action:** Ivey checks

A good player in aggressive mode could bet half the pot to see what happens. However, Ivey's out of position, and he doesn't want to create a big pot lacking position, so he checks. He probably wouldn't mind checking the hand all the way down, hoping the king would hold up by itself. Big stack plus bad position dictates caution.

The king makes a difference here. If Ivey's hand were just queen-high or jack-high, I'm pretty sure he would bet, seeing that as his only chance to win the pot. But you don't need to bet to win a pot if there's a good chance you'll win it anyway in a check-down.

**Action:** D'Agostino bets $25,000

Ivey shows reluctance to bet, so D'Agostino makes a classic semi-bluff, which in fact takes down the pot.

**Action:** Ivey folds

**Result:** Ivey loses $14,000

## Hand No. 16: Blinds $6,000/$12,000 antes, $2,000 each

|  | Stack | Position | Hand |
|---|---|---|---|
| John D'Agostino | $373,000 | BB | Q♥9♥ |
| Phil Ivey | $749,000 | SB/B | 9♦4♦ |

**Action:** Ivey puts in $35,000, raising $29,000

Ivey continues to mix up his play. He's raised with strong hands before, now he raises with a weak hand. He will, however, have position later in the hand. I wouldn't make this move myself, however. I think nine-four suited is just a little too weak for the way I like to play heads-up.

**Action:** D'Agostino calls, puts in $29,000

D'Agostino actually has quite a good hand for heads-up play, so he cheerfully calls.

## Flop: J♣9♣4♣

A good flop for both players. D'Agostino hits middle pair, while Ivey hits bottom two pair. However, there are three clubs on board, and neither player has a club. Each must suspect that the other has conceivably a flush or at least a flush draw, which should lead to cautious betting.

**Action:** D'Agostino checks; Ivey bets $60,000

Ivey figures he certainly can't slow-play with three clubs showing, but he does have two pair and the clubs may be scary for his opponent as well, so he makes an effort to win the pot. If D'Agostino's check really indicated weakness, Ivey should win the pot right now.

**Action:** D'Agostino calls $60,000

A good call by D'Agostino. Middle pair is a big hand heads-up, he does have an overcard, and Ivey probably hasn't made a flush. He's not prepared to raise, but he does have to call.

From Ivey's point of view, D'Agostino's check and call with three clubs showing must indicate real strength. It's unlikely he will put any more money into this pot, despite his two pair.

**Fourth Street: Q♣**

A huge card which kills all the action. D'Agostino gets two pair, but there are now four clubs on board and he doesn't have a club. Since Ivey led out into a three-flush last turn, there's a higher-than-usual chance that he's now made a flush. The same logic also prevents Ivey from betting.

**Action:** D'Agostino checks; Ivey checks

**Fifth Street: 6♠**

**Action:** D'Agostino bets $50,000

An excellent bet by D'Agostino. Ivey's check on fourth street has led him to the conclusion that his two pair are probably good. The pot is now $206,000, so D'Agostino's bet is giving Ivey 5-to-1 odds to call. Those odds will be hard to resist. First-rate play from D'Agostino.

**Action:** Ivey folds

And fine play from Ivey as well. The way the hand has played makes it just too unlikely that D'Agostino is bluffing. Odds of 5-to-1 aren't good enough if you think your winning chances are just 10 percent.

**Result:** Ivey loses $103,000

## Hand No. 17: Blinds $6,000/$12,000, antes $2,000 each

|  | Stack | Position | Hand |
|---|---|---|---|
| John D'Agostino | $476,000 | SB/B | 7♠2♠ |
| Phil Ivey | $646,000 | BB | A♥K♠ |

**Action:** D'Agostino calls, puts in $6,000; Ivey raises $35,000

A correct call by D'Agostino given the pot odds. Ivey continues to balance his play. Last hand he raised preflop with a bad hand, this time he raises with a good one.

**Action:** D'Agostino folds

**Result:** D'Agostino loses $14,000

The blinds now increase to $8,000/$16,000, still with $2,000 antes. The Ms drop a little as a result: D'Agostino's M goes down to 17, Ivey's goes down to 23.

## Hand No. 18: Blinds 8,000/16,000, antes $2,000 each

|  | Stack | Position | Hand |
|---|---|---|---|
| John D'Agostino | $462,000 | BB | 7♠5♥ |
| Phil Ivey | $660,000 | SB/B | 9♦8♠ |

**Pre-Flop:** Ivey calls, puts in $8,000; D'Agostino checks

**Flop:** 8♦3♠2♥

**Action:** D'Agostino checks; Ivey bets $25,000; D'Agostino folds

**Result:** D'Agostino loses $18,000

Ivey just calls with a slightly below-average hand, and D'Agostino, with a weak hand, checks. D'Agostino misses the flop, checks with nothing, and Ivey takes the pot.

## Hand No. 19: Blinds 8,000/16,000 antes, $2,000 each

|  | Stack | Position | Hand |
|---|---|---|---|
| John D'Agostino | $444,000 | SB/B | Q♣9♦ |
| Phil Ivey | $678,000 | BB | 9♣6♦ |

**Action:** D'Agostino puts in $48,000, raising $40,000; Ivey calls

This looks like a weak call. Ivey will be out of position with a bad hand. With a big stack, he should just let this one go. D'Agostino hasn't been raising that many hands, so Ivey needs to give him credit for at least a decent hand here. Now is not the time to make a stand.

**Flop:** A♣Q♦5♣

**Action:** Ivey checks; D'Agostino checks

D'Agostino's hand is certainly good enough to bet, but he may be planning a trap on the turn. Note that he doesn't have to worry much about giving a free card here. If Ivey has an ace in his hand, then D'Agostino is already beaten and doesn't need to worry. The only situation where a free card will beat him is if Ivey holds a single king, and a king comes on fourth street.

**Fourth Street: T♣**

**Action:** Ivey checks; D'Agostino bets $40,000; Ivey puts in $148,000, raising $108,000

It's hard to believe this play could work. D'Agostino showed strength pre-flop, and three overcards to Ivey's nine have since appeared. Folding seems pretty clear.

**Action:** D'Agostino goes all-in

D'Agostino moves in very quickly, which may have indicated to Ivey that he was facing a genuinely big hand (which he wasn't). This was just a bad hand for Ivey from beginning to end, and now the players have switched stacks.

**Action:** Ivey folds

**Result:** Ivey loses $206,000

**Hand No. 20: Blinds 8,000/16,000, antes $2,000 each**

|  | Stack | Position | Hand |
|---|---|---|---|
| John D'Agostino | $650,000 | BB | 9♠8♥ |
| Phil Ivey | $472,000 | SB/B | 9♣8♦ |

**Action:** Ivey calls, puts in $8,000; D'Agostino checks

Amusing — both sides have the same hand! Howard Lederer, in his commentary, opined that the side with position was about a 2-to-1 favorite in this situation, which seems about right. This hand illustrates with brutal clarity just how important position really is.

**Flop:** T♣6♣4♣

**Action:** D'Agostino checks; Ivey bets $25,000; D'Agostino folds

**Result:** D'Agostino loses $18,000

## Hand No. 21: Blinds 8,000/16,000, antes $2,000 each

|  | Stack | Position | Hand |
|---|---|---|---|
| John D'Agostino | $632,000 | SB/B | T♠8♣ |
| Phil Ivey | $490,000 | BB | 9♥8♦ |

**Action:** D'Agostino puts in $50,000, raising $42,000; Ivey calls

Two hands ago, Ivey called a big bet out of position with nine-six. Nine-eight is a somewhat stronger hand, so this is a marginally better play.

**Flop:** A♣9♣2♥

**Action:** Ivey checks;

Ivey has flopped middle pair, which as I said before is a very strong hand heads-up. He checks to induce D'Agostino to bluff at the pot.

**Action:** D'Agostino bets $50,000; Ivey calls

Ivey is happy to call here.

**Fourth Street: J♣**

**Action:** Ivey checks

The check is to induce a bluff, but D'Agostino has seen Ivey check many good hands so far, and doesn't bite.

**Action:** D'Agostino checks

**Fifth Street: A♥**

The ace on the river is a bad card for D'Agostino. It's hard to represent an ace when two have already appeared on board. Ivey is pretty certain he has the best hand here, but as on several previous occasions, he's content to check the hand down rather than get involved in a monster pot.

**Action:** Ivey checks; D'Agostino checks

Ivey wins with a pair of nines.

**Result:** D'Agostino loses $110,000

**Hand No. 22: Blinds 8,000/16,000, antes $2,000 each**

|  | Stack | Position | Hand |
|---|---|---|---|
| John D'Agostino | $522,000 | BB | K♣Q♣ |
| Phil Ivey | $600,000 | SB/B | 9♥8♠ |

Ivey holds nine-eight for the sixth time in 22 hands!

**Action:** Ivey calls, puts in $8,000; D'Agostino raises $40,000

D'Agostino's hand is very strong for heads-up, and at this point he should be thinking of charging Ivey more to play. By now, Ivey has clearly shown that he's interested in calling a lot of bets and playing a lot of hands. A bet of $60,000 to $70,000 here, in the neighborhood of four times the big blind, would be reasonable given what D'Agostino knows of Ivey's tendencies. It's also the right play given that D'Agostino is out of position, and would prefer to either end the hand quickly, or force Ivey to pay more to keep his positional advantage.

**Action:** Ivey calls

Ivey is in position with a medium-strength hand. He can't be sure yet what D'Agostino's bet means. I would call with his hand in position, but not out of position.

**Flop:** 9♦4♠2♣

**Action:** D'Agostino bets $80,000

This is a continuation bet, although a bit on the large size. There's a very good chance he could win the pot right here, and he has two overcards to the board, for six likely outs. There's also a danger, however. An $80,000 bet doesn't look like a bet from someone angling for a call. This will not escape Ivey's notice.

**Action:** Ivey goes all-in

Ivey pulls the trigger with top pair. It's a very strong hand heads-up, and D'Agostino's overbet doesn't smell like the betting of someone with a strong overpair. A strong overpair seeks a call, and D'Agostino seemed to want Ivey to go away.

Of course, a strong player must be capable of overbetting a pot with an overpair from time to time. But heads-up sessions aren't of infinite duration, and in a short contest, you have to give greater weight to more likely explanations, rather than get caught in the convoluted maze of "He knows that I know that he knows that I know …" sort of thinking. Ivey knows that the most likely explanation for D'Agostino's bet is that D'Agostino wants Ivey out of the pot, so he goes with that explanation.

**Action:** D'Agostino folds

**Result:** D'Agostino loses $138,000

**Hand No. 23: Blinds 8,000/16,000 antes $2,000 each**

|  | Stack | Position | Hand |
|---|---|---|---|
| John D'Agostino | $384,000 | SB/B | J♠6♥ |
| Phil Ivey | $738,000 | BB | K♠4♠ |

**Action:** D'Agostino folds

**Result:** D'Agostino loses $10,000

Howard Lederer, commenting on the tape, said "D'Agostino need to get his bearings after two big beats." That's probably what happened. Jack-six, in position and getting better than 3-to-1 odds, is certainly good enough for a call.

**Hand No. 24: Blinds 8,000/16,000, antes $2,000 each**

|  | Stack | Position | Hand |
|---|---|---|---|
| John D'Agostino | $374,000 | BB | 9♣2♣ |
| Phil Ivey | $748,000 | SB/B | 9♦7♣ |

**Action:** Ivey calls, puts in $8,000; D'Agostino checks

**Flop:** 3♣2♥2♦

**Action:** D'Agostino bets $40,000

I don't like this bet, for several reasons.

1.  D'Agostino clearly wants to get more money in the pot
    quickly, but I think that's the wrong approach given how
    the last few hands have gone. Ivey just won two big pots
    to retake the lead, and last hand D'Agostino declined to
    even call. Ivey must feel he's on top of the situation
    now, and he'll be looking to push D'Agostino around,
    probing for signs of weakness. D'Agostino has flopped
    a monster hand which is completely disguised, so he
    needs to be patient and milk the situation for whatever
    he can get. D'Agostino should check, and if Ivey moves
    at the pot, just think a bit and call. If a big card comes on
    the turn or the river and hits Ivey, D'Agostino could win
    a big pot here, but he needs to be patient.

2.  In one of the heads-up hands played just prior to Hand
    No. 1, D'Agostino held a nine and the flop came 9-9-5.
    D'Agostino bet his trips strongly throughout and Ivey
    called the hand down to see what D'Agostino was doing.
    (That hand actually gave D'Agostino his early lead.)
    Ivey certainly remembers that hand, and since an
    identical situation has now arisen, D'Agostino should
    take a different tack, and not merely repeat his earlier
    strategy.

3.  Ivey has been more and more aggressive lately.
    D'Agostino should give Ivey's aggression a chance to
    continue. Just play passively and let Ivey take the lead.

You should never get too discouraged playing heads-up, because any random bit of luck can let you double up no matter how badly the previous hands have gone. Patience is a huge asset in poker.

**Action:** Ivey folds

**Result:** Ivey loses $18,000

Ivey doesn't have a strong hand, of course, but he may also remember how costly the earlier hand was with a pair showing. For a combination of reasons, he could easily let the hand go.

### Hand No. 25: Blinds $8,000/$16,000, antes $2,000 each

|  | Stack | Position | Hand |
| --- | --- | --- | --- |
| John D'Agostino | $392,000 | SB/B | Q♦6♥ |
| Phil Ivey | $730,000 | BB | A♣K♦ |

**Action:** D'Agostino calls, puts in $8,000; Ivey raises $45,000

Ivey doesn't like to slow-play his ace-high hands out of position. He prefers to push them and win the pot right away.

**Action:** D'Agostino folds

**Result:** D'Agostino loses $18,000

### Hand No. 26: Blinds $8,000/$16,000, antes $2,000 each

|  | Stack | Position | Hand |
| --- | --- | --- | --- |
| John D'Agostino | $374,000 | BB | 5♠5♣ |
| Phil Ivey | $748,000 | SB/B | J♦J♣ |

After a lot of maneuvering, we finally reach a hand where the result is almost preordained. Trailing 2-to-1 in chips, it's virtually certain that D'Agostino will get all his chips in the pot with a pair, and Ivey will be happy to play with him holding a high pair. After that it's just a question of whether D'Agostino can hit a five or some flukey straight or flush draw.

**Action:** Ivey puts in $48,000, raising $40,000

As a technical point, we should note that Ivey's hand was strong enough to just limp. He may have sensed that D'Agostino was getting impatient and wanted to play. He might also have wanted to avoid the chance of getting beaten on the flop if D'Agostino is holding a random king or queen. (If D'Agostino is holding an ace, he'll get involved whether Ivey bets or not.)

**Action:** D'Agostino goes all-in; Ivey calls

**Flop:** 8♥7♠2♦

**Fourth Street:** Q♣

**Fifth Street:** 3♥

**Result:** Ivey wins

All in all, a very long, interesting, and well-played heads-up session. Despite my occasional criticisms, this battle reflected well on both players. Heads-up sessions can appear confusing to the novice, with plenty of what at first seems to be random punching and counter-punching. Behind the scenes, a hidden story emerges, dominated by hand rankings, position, and the events of the immediate past.

# Pre-Flop Strategy When
# First to Act: Ivey vs D'Agostino

Let's briefly take a look at how the players bet when they were first to act in the hand.

**Ivey Acted First:**

| Hand | Action |
|------|--------|
| JJ | Raise 2.5 BB |
| AJo | Raise 2 BB |
| ATo | Raise 2.5 BB |
| A8o | Call |
| A3s | Call |
| T2o | Call |
| 98s | Raise 2 BB |
| 98o | Call |
| 98o | Call |
| 98o | Call |
| 97o | Call |
| 96o | Call |
| 94s | Raise 2.5 BB |

A few ideas stand out as we look at Ivey's hands, arranged in order.

1. He never folded because of the pot odds.
2. With his strong hands he mostly raised, but mixed in a few calls.
3. With his weaker hands he mostly called, but mixed in a few raises.
4. His raises were in a very narrow range of 2 to 2.5 times the big blind.

It was a strategy designed to mix up his hands and keep the pot small, and it was very consistently implemented throughout the session.

**D'Agostino Acted First:**

| Hand | Action |
|---|---|
| ATo | Raise 2 BB |
| A5s | Raise 2.5 BB |
| A2s | Raise 1.7 BB |
| Q9s | Raise 2.5 BB |
| Q6o | Call |
| J9o | Raise 2 BB |
| J6o | Fold |
| J5s | Call |
| J4o | Fold |
| T8o | Raise 2.7 BB |
| 98s | Call |
| 72s | Call |
| (unrecorded) | Fold |

D'Agostino raised more consistently with his better hands, and his bet range was a little larger than Ivey's, but not much. Both of these are good strategic moves when you believe you're the underdog. He did fold three hands during the session, which were mistakes given the combination of pot odds and position.

Notice that for both players, the raises used were smaller than the raises you would see at a full table.

# Heads-Up Session No. 2: You the Reader

In this session the Ms are much lower, as is typical of many online tournaments. We've changed the layout a little bit to put you, the reader, into the hands. You're starting with a 3-to-1 chip lead, but your M is only 14, while your opponent's M is only 3.5. You'll be able to see your hands, but not your opponent's.

### Hand No. 1: Blinds $3,000/$6,000, antes $300 each

|  | Stack | Position | Hand |
|---|---|---|---|
| Opponent | $41,700 | BB | ?? |
| You | $138,300 | SB/B | Q♥8♥ |

**Action:** You raise to $15,000; opponent folds

**Result:** (Opponent loses $6,300)

Queen-eight suited is a pretty good hand heads-up, ranking in the top 30 percent of hands. Combined with position, it's definitely worth a raise, and your opponent elects to fold.

### Hand No. 2: Blinds $3,000/$6,000, antes $300 each

|  | Stack | Position | Hand |
|---|---|---|---|
| Opponent | $35,400 | SB/B | ?? |
| You | $144,600 | BB | Q♦7♠ |

**Action:** Opponent goes all-in; You fold

**Result:** You lose $6,300

Here's a mirror of the previous problem. This time you have just a slightly weaker hand than before, but your opponent elects to put you all-in. Do you call?

My own standards are pretty strict. I'm certainly not in a desperate situation with my 3-to-1 chip lead. In that case, I want a hand that's both reasonably strong and getting good pot odds to call. Right now the pot contained $9,600 and your opponent just moved in with his last $32,100, making the pot $41,700. Since $3,000 of that bet was a call of your blind, you'll need to put in $29,100 to call. The pot is offering you a bit better than 1.5-to-1 to call.

Here are the facts I'd be weighing in my mind:

1. The Ms are relatively low, dictating aggressive play on both sides.

2. I don't know much about my opponent yet. However, it's just the second hand of the session, and he's already moved all-in. I'll give him credit for a better-than-average hand, but I can't yet credit him with much more than that.

3. The pot is giving me about 1.5-to-1 odds.

4. My hand is in the top 50 percent of all hands — just slightly above average.

Under the circumstances, I don't need a premium hand to call this bet. The real question is just how weak a hand I'm willing to play. Here I look carefully at the hand strength and the pot odds. With a slightly above average hand like queen-seven, I like to see pot odds in the range of 1.6-to-1 or 1.7-to-1. If my hand were in the top-40 percent group, I'd be happy calling with 1.5-to-1. For a top-30 percent, I'd need even less, say 1.4-to-1 or perhaps even 1.3-to-1. (Keep in mind that these are not absolute numbers. They're heavily influenced by the first two points, namely that the Ms are already quite low and my opponent is moving all-in on the second hand. If the all-in move came with high Ms, or from an opponent who had played conservatively for awhile, I would certainly want a stronger hand or better odds.)

We should note here that some players adopt a perma-raise strategy in heads-up, basically going all-in on every hand. (For very weak players it's not a bad strategy.) If your opponent is playing this way, you'll have to just take a reasonable hand and call. For me, a top-40 percent hand is plenty for this purpose. Here, we don't have enough data yet to know if that's the case, but we'll have to remain very alert to the possibility.

## Hand No. 3: Blinds $3,000/$6,000 antes $300 each

|          | Stack      | Position | Hand |
|----------|------------|----------|------|
| Opponent | $41,700    | BB       | ??   |
| You      | $138,300   | SB/B     | 8♦6♦ |

**Action:** You call $3,000; Opponent goes all-in; You fold

**Result:** You lose $6,300

Both the call and the fold are correct, for the reasons just discussed. Eight-six suited is only in the top 70 percent bracket of hands, and just isn't strong enough to call an all-in raise getting those odds.

Our evidence is growing, however, that our opponent is in permanent raise mode. That queen-seven offsuit that we threw away last hand is looking better now. Had these two hands occurred in reverse order (throwing away eight-six to an all-in, *then* being raised all-in with a queen-seven), I'd have given very serious consideration to calling.

The astute reader might well ask at this point "Isn't this very skimpy evidence for calling an all-in move?" The answer is "Yes, it's actually very very skimpy." But it's all the evidence you have! You're not in the enviable position of a judge weighing pounds of evidence while deciding to issue a search warrant. You're more in the position of a soldier on the battlefield, trying to decide in a second or two whether

412 Part Twelve: Heads-Up

that moving shadow is friend or foe. I'll put a little twist on
Amir Vahedi's favorite saying: "In order to live, you must be
willing to pull the trigger."

Now the blinds increase to $4,000/$8,000, with $400
antes. The Ms shrink again. Your M declines to just over 10,
while your opponent's drops to just under 4.

**Hand No. 4: Blinds $4,000/$8,000, antes $400 each**

|  | Stack | Position | Hand |
|---|---|---|---|
| Opponent | $48,700 | SB/B | ?? |
| You | $132,000 | BB | K♣7♥ |

**Action:** Opponent folds

**Result:** Opponent loses $4,400

As before, he should call. If he called, you should have
raised. Even an all-in raise would not be a bad move. When
a player who's been raising steadily slows down, it's more
likely an indication that his hand is weak rather than strong.
(A player who makes several raises, doesn't get called, and
then picks up a big hand, is likely to continue raising with it
because his previous raises provide cover and indicate that
he's likely still bluffing.)

Since our opponent folded a hand with good pot odds, we
now have to revise our opinion of his style. He must have some
standards, although we don't yet know what they are, and our fold
of the queen-seven is looking more reasonable once again.

**Hand No. 5: Blinds $4,000/$8,000, antes $400 each**

|  | Stack | Position | Hand |
|---|---|---|---|
| Opponent | $43,600 | BB | ?? |
| You | $136,400 | SB/B | Q♠8♦ |

**Action:** You raise $12,000; Opponent goes all-in for $35,200; You call $23,200

**Opponent shows:** 3♦3♠

**Board:** A♠T♣5♣T♥9♥

**Result:** You lose $43,600

Queen-eight offsuit was in the top 40 percent of all hands, so a raise is reasonable. After your opponent's all-in move, the pot contains exactly $60,000, and it costs you $23,200 to call, so your pot odds are just over 2.5-to-1. Those are huge odds for a heads-up call. You're only getting the wrong price for your call if he has precisely one of three pairs: aces, kings, or queens.

Here's an important note: Even if he has you dominated with ace-queen or king-queen, the price is still right. (As we saw earlier in the chapter, domination situations tend to be 70 percent or so pre-flop. That's all right when you're getting 2.5-to-1 pot odds.) Most poker players who aren't adept in math seem to think that domination is a disaster which makes you a 3-to-1 underdog, but the truth isn't nearly that bad.

With the loss, however, your opponent pulls almost even in stack size.

**Hand No. 6: Blinds $4,000/$8,000, antes $400 each**

|  | Stack | Position | Hand |
|---|---|---|---|
| Opponent | $87,200 | SB/B | ?? |
| You | $92,800 | BB | 5♣3♥ |

**Action:** Opponent goes all-in; You fold

**Result:** You lose $8,400

A clear decision here, as you're unlucky enough to pick up a hand in the bottom 10 percent of all hands.

## Hand No. 7: Blinds $4,000/$8,000, antes $400 each

|  | Stack | Position | Hand |
|---|---|---|---|
| Opponent | $95,600 | BB | ?? |
| You | $84,400 | SB/B | 8♣4♣ |

**Action:** You call $4,000; Opponent checks

**Flop:** Q♥7♣3♦

**Action:** Opponent checks; You bet $8,000; Opponent folds

**Result:** Opponent loses $8,400

Your call before the flop was clear, despite your weak hand. After the flop you have nothing, but your opponent checks to you, indicating weakness. Although you didn't show strength before the flop, you make a large probe bet for $8,000, one-half of the pot. This is an extremely attractive bet from a risk-reward ratio. If your opponent folds this bet half the time, you'll make a steady profit. Even if he only folds one-third of the time, you'll break even. Your opponent actually does fold, and you pick up the pot.

What should you do if you're in the position of your opponent in this example? That is, you've missed the flop and you check, and now he bets half the pot at you? You actually have a few options.

1. Against a player who can do this on a regular basis, you'll have to pick some spots and just move in with a big raise. (In a small-M game, that might well mean an all-in move.)

2.   Alternatively, you could just call with any ace or king, and call the hand down. A significant portion of the time, even a single high card is good enough to take the pot in heads-up play.

3.   You could also just call on the flop, then bet if he checks on the turn.

These plays take courage in the absence of a genuinely strong hand, but you can't allow your opponent to nibble away at you for free. Just remember that the continuation-type bet offers such favorable odds that many times players will be making it with no hand at all.

## Hand No. 8: Blinds $4,000/$8,000, antes $400 each

|          | Stack    | Position | Hand  |
|----------|----------|----------|-------|
| Opponent | $87,200  | SB/B     | ??    |
| You      | $92,800  | BB       | J♠6♠  |

**Action:** Opponent folds; Opponent loses $4,400

Opponent folds pre-flop, which is a mistake as we now know. He's made this mistake twice in eight hands, which is a pretty steady dribble of equity. Your long-term prospects in the session should be good, if an accident doesn't happen along the way.

Note: Folding pre-flop on the button is actually all right if your opponent has shown he will raise you most of the time when you just call. Now your strategy changes: You fold your weakest hands (bottom 30 percent is a good number) and play actively with the rest.

**Hand No. 9: Blinds $4,000/$8,000; antes $400 each**

|  | Stack | Position | Hand |
|---|---|---|---|
| Opponent | $82,800 | BB | ?? |
| You | $97,200 | SB/B | K♣J♦ |

**Action:** You raise to $12,000; Opponent calls $8,000

**Flop:** Q♠8♠2♥

**Action:** Opponent checks; You bet $12,000; Opponent calls $12,000

**Fourth:** K♦

**Action:** Opponent checks; You bet $18,000; Opponent goes all-in for $54,400; You call $36,400

**Opponent shows:** Q♥8♣

**Fifth Street:** 4♠

**Result:** You lose $82,800

King-jack offsuit is an excellent hand (top 20 percent) so your pre-flop raise is correct. He calls, indicating some kind of hand.

The flop is non-descript and he checks, so your post-flop bet is also quite reasonable. It's another continuation bet, this time a little less than half the pot. But your opponent calls again, which is certainly suspicious. You should be thinking at this point that he must have something. A pair is possible, and a flush draw is also possible, given what he may believe to be his implied odds.

Once the king hits, you have top pair, and you're committed to the hand. Top pair is a monster hand heads-up, and the pot already contains $56,000. While you can certainly still lose, this is a great situation heads-up. In fact, your opponent had been slow-playing top two pair, a nice move on his part. That's effectively the whole tournament, as the hand consumed most of your chips.

### Hand No. 10: Blinds $4,000/$8,000, antes $400 each

|  | Stack | Position | Hand |
|---|---|---|---|
| Opponent | $165,600 | SB/B | ?? |
| You | $14,400 | BB | 8♠3♦ |

**Action:** Opponent bets $10,000, putting you all-in; You call your last $6,000

**Opponent shows:** A♣Q♠

**Board:** 8♦4♥4♠3♣Q♦

**Result:** You lose $14,400

When your opponent pushed you all-in, you had a terrible hand but fantastic pot odds. You needed to bet $6,000 to see a pot of $22,800, almost 4-to-1 odds. As the hand played out, you hit both your hole cards, but the treys were counterfeited, and your opponent drew out on the river. *C'est la vie.*

# Part Thirteen

# Final Thoughts

# Final Thoughts

# Introduction

In this last chapter I want to cover a couple of topics that don't fit easily into the other chapters. I also want to spotlight an amazing hand that illustrates many of the ideas I've been developing in both Volume I and Volume II.

In addition to regular tournaments with their graduated prize structures, there are now many satellite tournaments, both live and online, which are designed to qualify players to other events. The endgame of these tournaments poses some unique problems, and hand valuation can change dramatically. Study the examples in the first part of this chapter for some key insights.

When you get close to the money in major events, deal-making becomes commonplace, and can be treacherous for the novice. In the second part of the chapter, I've laid out some rules of thumb that will keep you out of trouble.

The last section covers one of the most interesting sequence of hands in the last couple of years. Watch, learn, and enjoy.

# Multi-Qualifier
# Satellite Tournaments

With entry fees in major events ranging from $5,000 to $25,000 these days, a mini-industry of satellite tournaments has arisen, to give players a shot at the big money for a modest investment. In return for a relatively small entry fee, you get a chance for a free entry to a major event, plus some money toward expenses. In many cases the satellite tournaments are open-ended. All comers can play, and the organizers will give away as many free entries as they can, based on the number of participants. Satellite tournaments are a great deal for players, and in fact many top players enter satellites routinely as a way of reducing their overall expenses on the circuit. (When I won the World Series in 1995, I had qualified from a live super-satellite with a $100 entry fee. In the past two years, both Chris Moneymaker and Greg Raymer qualified from online satellites.)

The early part of a satellite tournament works just like any other tournament. You play your cards, make moves, and accumulate chips. The endgame, however, is quite different. The top few finishers get an identical big prize, while no one else gets anything. Being on the bubble is no longer a difference between zero and a modest prize; it's the difference between everything and nothing.

Endgame decisions in these multi-qualifier events can become quite unusual and counter-intuitive. Consider the following simple situation.

**Example No. 1. Six players remain in a satellite qualifying tournament. The final four places advance to the big tournament. Fifth and sixth places receive nothing. Of the last**

six players, Players A, B, C, and D all have 4,500 chips. Players E and F have 1,000 chips each.

**Question:** *At this point, what is the probability that each player will qualify?*

**Answer:** This is pretty easy to calculate if we make a couple of observations.

First, notice that when we get down to four players, each of the remaining players will have a 100 percent chance of qualifying. Therefore at any earlier point, the sum of all the probabilities of qualifying must add to 400 percent (not 100 percent).

Second, whatever the chance of qualifying may be, Players A, B, C, and D must all have the same chance, and Players E and F must also have the same chance. (To make the problem easier, we'll ignore for now that whoever is on the button next hand will have a slightly better chance than the others, and so forth.)

Third, the chance of qualifying at any particular time is approximately proportional to the chip counts of the players.

Now let's put all these observations together with a little simple algebra. Let's say that E's chance of qualifying is "x." Then F also has "x" chance of qualifying, while A, B, C, and D all have 4.5 times "x." So we can write down a little equation:

$$x + x + 4.5x + 4.5x + 4.5x + 4.5x = 400$$

So 20x = 400, and x = 20. Therefore players E and F each have a 20 percent chance of qualifying, and Players A, B, C, and D all have 4.5 times as much chance, or 90 percent each. And the probabilities all add to 400 percent, as they should if four people are going to qualify.

These numbers all make sense. E and F are clearly big underdogs to make it, but they're not out of the running. A, B, C, and D are huge favorites, but not certain to get in.

Having established each player's chance of qualifying a priori, let's now sit them down at the table and watch what happens.

**For the next hand, the players are arranged as follows:**

|            |          |         |
| ---------- | -------- | ------- |
| **Sm Blind**  | **Player C** | **$4,500** |
| **Big Blind** | **Player D** | **$4,500** |
| **1**         | **Player E** | **$1,000** |
| **2**         | **Player F** | **$1,000** |
| **3**         | **Player A** | **$4,500** |
| **4 (You)**   | **Player B** | **$4,500** |

**The blinds are $100/$200. Players E and F fold. Player A goes all-in. You are Player B. You pick up**

*Is your hand good enough to call?*

**Discussion:** Your first reaction should be annoyance, since Player A clearly doesn't understand that the idea for the leaders is to gang up on Players E and F, not to bash each other. Just his bad luck that he happened to pick the wrong hand to go all-in on ... or did he?

Before you reflexively shove all your chips in the pot, contemplate your winning chances against some hands that he might have, while remembering that, if you fold, you're still about 90 percent to qualify.

1.  Versus KK: 81.1%
2.  Versus 99: 80.1%
3.  Versus 22: 81.2%
4.  Versus AK: 92.0%
5.  Versus AK suited: 87.2%
6.  Versus A2: 92.0%
7.  Versus A2 suited: 87.3%
8.  Versus JT suited: 78.1%
9.  Versus Q3: 87.4%
10. Versus 72: 87.3%

(In all these examples the hands have no suit in common with your aces.)

You're obviously 0 percent to qualify if you call and lose. Even if we assume that you're 100 percent to qualify if you call and win (not quite, but close), the only hands you're happy to see if you call are ace-x unsuited, which makes you about 92 percent to win. On all other hands you're better off having folded.

So when you're a big favorite to qualify anyway, you have to fold your aces in response to an all-in bet that can knock you out of the tournament. This extreme example leads to a general insight about how to play the endgame of all these events:

*Correct strategy for the leaders is to avoid confrontations with each other and cooperate to eliminate the small stacks.*
Can the leaders violate this strategy to their own advantage? In this example Player A, presumably with a pretty good hand, went all-in against Player B who was forced to fold any hand, even aces. Did A make the right move under the circumstances?

In a theoretical world where A is certain that B, C, and D all understand the logic of the situation, A's move was correct. (In fact, he could have made the move with any holding at all as long as E and F have already folded.) In any real-world situation, A's move is a major blunder, since it's highly unlikely that B, C, and D will all know to hold back from a call with a huge hand. In the real world, the aces call.

You won't have to play many of these types of events before you'll see incredible blunders made in the endgame play. Let's take a look at a few situations from real-life and see how they should be handled.

**Example No. 2. Near the end of a satellite tournament. Five players remain vying for four qualifying spots. The blinds are $150/$300. The players and their chip counts are as follows:**

| | |
|---|---|
| SB (You) | $6,000 |
| BB | $1,100 |
| Player 1 | $4,800 |
| Player 2 | $4,400 |
| Player 3 | $3,700 |

**You are the small blind. Players 1, 2, and 3 all fold. You hold 9♦6♣.** *What should you do?*

**Answer:** The game plan is to attack the small stack relentlessly, especially as the small stack moves through the blinds. With a stronger hand you could just move all-in. With a weak hand like 9♦6♣, you should be a little more cautious and tricky. I would recommend a simple call. If the big blind willingly puts you all-in, you'll have the pot odds to call anyway. If not, you will move all-in after the flop, no matter what comes. Since most flops miss most hands, the big blind will often have a harder call after the flop than before. Remember that while you'll settle for an all-in confrontation that could simply end the tournament right here, you're even happier if you can just nick him for another $300 and keep him pathetically weak.

**Example No. 3. Same situation as before. Blinds are still $150 and $300. Now the players and chips are arranged as follows (before posting the blinds):**

|  |  |
|---|---|
| SB | $650 |
| BB | $3,500 |
| Player 1 | $4,550 |
| Player 2 | $5,000 |
| Player 3 (You) | $6,300 |

**Players 1 and 2 fold. You have**

**and call. The small blind goes all-in, moving his last $500 into the pot. The big blind calls. *What do you do?***

    **Answer:** You should call, after which you and the big blind should check the hand down to the end. The best chance of eliminating the small blind and ending the tournament comes when as many hands as possible are in action against him. You would make the same play with any two cards; the idea is just to reduce the chance that the small blind survives the hand. The longer the small stack survives, the greater the chance that he catches a hand or two and rejoins the main pack. Drive a stake in his heart while you have the chance.

    This strategy may look obvious, but you'll see many tournaments where, in similar situations, one of the players catches a hand on the flop, drives out the other active player with a bet, and then loses to the small stack!

# Making Deals

A deal (or a "hedge" as it's sometimes called) is just an arrangement between two or more players to divide the prize money in some fashion that's different from the stated prize payout. For example: three players remain in the tournament, all with roughly equal chip counts. The prizes for the last three places are $1,000,000 first, $400,000 second, and $200,000 for third. One player goes to the other two and says "$800,000 is too big a swing for a coin flip. Let's all take $500,000, finish the tournament, and give the extra $100,000 to the winner." If the other two players agree to this arrangement, they have in effect changed the prize distribution from a 10-4-2 distribution to a 6-5-5 distribution.

A more complicated arrangement might take into account some perceived skill differential between the players. For example, let's say one participant in the first example was a known world-class player with some big tournament wins under his belt, while the other two were nervous newcomers. The pro might counter with a different offer: "I'll take $600,000, and you two get $400,000 apiece. Then we play for the last $200,000." Depending on their state of mind, the amateurs might find this an agreeable offer. Then again, they might not. Negotiations can continue for some time while the players hammer out what seems to be an equitable deal.

So let's suppose you venture off to your first big tournament, and with good luck and favorable winds, you cruise into the final table. What do you need to know about good deal-making?

Your first job is to determine whether deals are officially sanctioned and administered by the tournament organizers, or are private matters between the players. Some organizers will honor deals made by the surviving players, and redistribute the prize money accordingly. Some online sites will even stop play in the tournament for a period of time while the players conduct open negotiations through the chat box. You can get a good feel for the deal-making process by watching the final table of some big online tournaments and observing the negotiations in action. (I'm talking here about tournaments with prize funds of several hundred thousand dollars and more, not sit-and-gos or small-stakes multi-table events.)

Until recently, major tournament organizers regarded facilitating deals as a pretty routine matter, just one of the services they offered to the players who had paid a lot of money to come to their events. The television era has changed that practice to some degree. Television producers like to emphasize the huge size of first prize and accentuate the drama involved in the competition for gigantic sums of money. Televised tournaments don't like to see deals between players, and the organizers of televised tournaments will not generally assist in the deal-making process. The players can still make them of course, but they are a private matter and unenforceable. For the players, this introduces some risk. If you have a choice, you definitely want to make your deal through the organizers.

When you get to the final table of a tournament and you're in a situation where you have to make a private deal or none at all, be careful. Here are a few guidelines:

1. **You're not as big an underdog as you think.** As in most negotiations, the first deal you're offered probably won't be very good. Don't be afraid to ask for more. Remember that as the blinds get high and the Ms shrink, the tournament becomes more and more of a crapshoot. Your more experienced opponents know this, which is why they're dealing. Don't let them push you into a bad deal just because they have fancy reputations.

2. **In the long run, the cards are fair**. If you can't make a deal that seems fair to you, just walk away and play. Over time,

this won't cost you any money. In 1995 when I won the World Series of Poker, I offered deals to all my opponents at the final table, and they all walked away! (I thought the deals were fair, but they wanted the $1,000,000 first prize.)

3.  **Being on television doesn't make you a stand-up guy.** Just because you've seen someone on TV, don't assume you're all right making a deal with him. Try to get a line on your opponents before the final table starts. Is so-and-so good for his word? Is he trying to support a couple of ex-wives? Did he lose all his money last week in the big game at Bellagio? These things are good to know.

If the organizers will honor and enforce deals, you're in a very safe situation. If not, and the deal is strictly a private matter between two players, then *caveat emptor.*

In the gaming world, even the most harmless-sounding offers can go horribly astray. Consider the following cautionary tale.

I once knew an excellent player who was temporarily down on his luck. He wanted to enter a big tournament but he didn't have the cash for his entry fee. He decided to franchise himself, so he went around to his friends offering to sell bits and pieces of his interest in the tournament at par value. (This was in ancient times when you actually had to solicit people you knew; nowadays players put themselves up for sale on eBay.) His friends were enthusiastic and sales went well. Accounting, however, was not my friend's strong suit. By the time the tournament rolled around, he had managed to sell 150 percent of himself!

At this point, a conscientious player would have returned some of the sales, admitting his error; embarrassing but prudent. An unscrupulous player would have gone in the tank and pocketed his profit; sleazy but solvent. My friend took a third way: He won the tournament! (It took years, but he eventually paid back all his investors.)

# Putting It All Together

To understand just how marvelously complicated and subtle no-limit hold 'em can be, we're going to conclude the book by looking at a series of three hands. These hands were played in the Plaza tournament held in June 2004, just after that year's World Series of Poker. The field was small (only 68 players), and the format was unusual in that the blinds and antes increased very slowly throughout the event. Even at the final table, the Ms of most of the players were in the range of 40 to 200, meaning that players were under no pressure to get their chips in the center of the pot. There was a lot of tough, interesting poker, featuring plenty of slow-playing, careful maneuvering, and post-flop play. The following three hands, however, illustrate the artistry which is possible at the highest levels of poker.

**Hand No. 1:** This hand occurred on the first day of play and occasioned little notice at the time. Only in retrospect was it seen as important. Layne Flack, Freddy Deeb, and Daniel Negreanu were all in action at the same table. A relatively big pot developed between Layne Flack and Freddy Deeb. On the river, the pot had grown to about $5,000, and Layne Flack made a small bet of $1,000 into the pot. Deeb folded, believing he was being trapped, and commented "I wish you had bet more." (Implying he wouldn't have feared calling a larger bet, which might easily have been a bluff.)

**Hand No. 2:** This hand occurred when the final table had been reduced to six players. At this stage the blinds were $600/$1,200 and the antes were $200. The starting pot was $3,000. Here were the players, their approximate chip counts, and their hands, if relevant:

| Small Blind | Daniel Negreanu | $65,000 | K♣T♠ |
| Big Blind | Dan Alspach | $60,500 | A♠J♥ |
| Player 1 | Gavin Smith | $161,400 | |
| Player 2 | Layne Flack | $153,900 | 8♣5♣ |
| Player 3 | Ted Forrest | $185,800 | A♦4♦ |
| Player 4 | Freddy Deeb | $82,900 | J♦8♠ |

**Gavin Smith**. Folds under the gun.

**Layne Flack**. Calls with his 8♣5♣ suited in second position. Even at a short table, eight-five suited isn't much of a hand with four players yet to act. But Flack is one of the most talented and aggressive young players on the circuit, and he doesn't mind pushing at pots with hands like this. Notice that only one of the four players who remain to act has a stack that's comparable in size to Flack's. That's a favorable situation, since ultimately Flack has the threat of putting any of the short stacks to a decision for all their chips.

**Ted Forrest.** Calls with his A♦4♦. A reasonable decision. Forrest is known as an aggressive player (as are most of the players at this table) but calling here with ace-x suited would be completely reasonable even for a conservative player.

**Freddy Deeb**. Deeb is a very strong player, aggressive and tricky, with great tournament results. Calling with J♦8♠ is a loose move, but no one has shown great strength yet and he will have position on the other players after the flop.

**Daniel Negreanu.** Daniel had the best results in the world in 2004, winning the all-around title at the World Series of Poker, in addition to finishing first at this event in June and the Borgata tournament in September. He's very strong, very aggressive, and extremely dangerous (as you will see). The pot has grown to $6,600 with the three calls, and in the small blind, it costs

Negreanu only $600 more to stay involved. Getting 11-to-1 on his money, Negreanu's king-ten offsuit is a much better hand than he needs. In fact, he could play with almost any two cards.

**Dan Alspach**. Alspach's ace-jack offsuit is the best hand at the table right now, but of course he can't know that. With four callers already, he has to suspect that he's facing at least one pair and perhaps two. There could also possibly be a better ace at the table somewhere. Since he'll have poor position after the flop, he prudently just checks.

The pot is now $7,200 before the flop, with five of the six players still active. The flop came

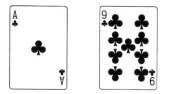 

**Daniel Negreanu**. With his K♣, Negreanu now has the nut flush draw, but with the ace on board and four other callers in the pot, he almost certainly doesn't have the best hand yet. He sensibly checks.

**Dan Alspach**. Alspach has top pair, aces with a jack kicker. That's normally a strong holding, but not here. With three clubs showing and four other callers, at least one or two players must have flush draws, and there's a reasonable chance that someone has already made his flush. A beginner could lose a lot of money with Alspach's hand; Alspach checks instead.

**Layne Flack**. Flack has a flush, but he also has problems. When he made his initial call, he almost certainly didn't expect four other players to go in with him. His first problem is to find out where he stands on the hand. If someone else has a flush, it's almost certainly better than his. (The only cards that are available to make a lower flush are the 7♣4♣3♣2♣, and even most aggressive players would toss suited cards that low.) Even if no one has a flush yet, one or two players may have a flush draw, and since players tend to play high cards, those draws will probably beat him if they come through.

Flack needs to bet here. Slow-playing is now too dangerous. A pot-sized bet will chase out some of the drawing hands, while allowing someone with a set to stick around and lose all his money. If someone does call, Flack's job will be to decide if he's calling with a made flush, a draw against the odds, or a losing set. Accordingly, Flack bets a little more than the pot, $9,000, making the total pot $16,200.

Note that had he flopped a straight instead of a flush, and the board wasn't suited, he'd have a weaker hand but a much stronger position. It would then be more likely that he had both the best hand at the table and a hand that couldn't be caught. That's characteristic of most of these calls with low suited cards. Flopping the straight will almost certainly win, while flopping the flush leads to a dangerous, double-edged situation.

**Ted Forrest**. Forrest has a pair of aces but no clubs, so his position is dangerous. He knows Flack is perfectly capable of betting at the flop with nothing, so he decides it's worth a call to see if Flack's bet plus his call chases away the other three players. If so, he has a chance. If not, he's almost certainly beaten. He calls. The pot is now $25,200.

**Freddy Deeb**. No clubs, no pair, no draw, and plenty of action so far. Deeb folds.

**Daniel Negreanu**. Negreanu's nut flush draw was just helped by Forrest's entry into the pot. Now it costs him $9,000 to see a pot of $25,200, so he's getting almost 3-to-1 odds. His odds of hitting the flush on the turn are about 4-to-1 against, and 2-to-1 against

434 Part Thirteen: Final Thoughts

on the turn and river combined. However, given the action in the hand so far, his implied odds may be considerably better than that. He reasonably calls. The pot is now $34,200.

**Dan Alspach.** So far he's seen a pot-sized bet followed by two calls. Although the pot is offering almost 4-to-1 odds, he's facing three opponents and the distinct possibility that he's drawing dead to a flush. He's currently the small stack at the table, but his M is still a very healthy 20, so he has plenty of maneuvering room left. If he calls here, he's getting involved in a hand which could potentially cost him all his chips. He prudently folds his aces.

Three players are still alive and the pot is $34,200.

The turn is the K♠.

**Daniel Negreanu.** Negreanu doesn't believe that the king has put his hand on top; it has merely provided him with extra outs. Besides the clubs which are outs against any hands he's facing, the two available kings will provide outs against any pair of aces or any two pair hands. The three available tens will at least be enough to beat a pair of aces.

Negreanu at this point elects to make a very bold play. He leads out with a bet of $24,000, which leaves him with only about $31,000 in his stack. It's a no-limit semi-bluff, a bet which, coupled with his call on the flop, indicates a very strong hand. The bet gives him two ways to win; he may win right here if both opponents lay down whatever they have, and he has plenty of outs to win on the river if he gets called. Right now, however, his bet is representing an already-made flush, so his two opponents have to be very careful. The pot now contains $58,200.

**Layne Flack.** Flack knows he may be beaten, but he may not. The pot is offering him 2.4-to-1, and he has a made flush. The combination of his hand and the pot odds makes a call mandatory, so he calls. The pot now contains $82,200.

**Ted Forrest**. With three clubs on board and a big bet and a call in front of him, Forrest knows that his pair of aces will not be enough to take down the hand. He's looking at pot odds of 3.4-to-1, but odds won't do you any good if you're putting dead money in the pot. Forrest folds.

The pot is now $82,200, and only Negreanu and Flack remain. The river card is the T♣.

**Daniel Negreanu**. Negreanu has made the nut flush, and with no pair showing, he knows he has the winning hand. His only question is: "How big a bet can I make and still get paid off?" With his stack at $31,000, Negreanu elects to bet $14,000. It's a bet so small that the pot odds virtually compel a call. The small bet creates the impression that he's trying to preserve at least half his remaining chips, and thus hopefully some appearance that he's not holding the nuts. The pot is now $96,200.

**Layne Flack**. With four clubs now on board, Flack is losing if his opponent holds the K♣, Q♣, or J♣, but he can win against all other holdings. He's sure Negreanu has a real hand, but the pot is offering him almost 7-to-1, so on the off chance that Negreanu has been playing with pocket aces or kings, or has just hit a straight, he calls.

Negreanu shows the K♣ and takes the pot.

**Hand No. 3.** The third hand in our trilogy occurred after the field had been reduced to just the final two players. The blinds were now $800 and $1,600 with $300 antes, so the initial pot was just $3,000. The table appeared as follows:

| | | | |
|---|---|---|---|
| Sm Blind/Button | Daniel Negreanu | $337,700 | A♥7♦ |
| Big Blind | Freddy Deeb | $342,300 | A♣K♦ |

Although we're in the heads-up part of the tournament, both players have Ms above 100! Very unusual for a major poker tournament, and both Negreanu and Deeb have responded with cagey, cautious play.

**Daniel Negreanu**. Just calls with his ace-seven offsuit. It's a strong hand for heads-up play, and Negreanu could certainly raise. Both players have set a pattern of just calling with their better hands, looking to trap their opponent and win a big pot down the road. So far that hasn't happened, and the two players have remained within a few thousand chips of each other throughout the session.

**Freddy Deeb**. Elects to raise $7,000 with Big Slick. That's obviously a fine raise with a strong hand, and it has the added virtue that Deeb has just been checking his good pre-flop hands for quite awhile, so Negreanu may not know how to interpret the bet.

**Daniel Negreanu**. Calls the bet.

The pot is $17,800 before the flop. The flop is

**Freddy Deeb** Deeb has hit top pair with top kicker. On the videotape, Howard Lederer commented that it was a great flop for Deeb, but it was hard to see how he could get any action on the hand, since Negreanu doesn't have anything. Deeb continues to play the hand in a straightforward manner, and bets $16,000, almost the size of the pot. It's a straight value bet, and it also denies proper drawing odds for any flush draw. Deeb knows that this flop will have missed most hands, so if the bet gets no action, there was probably no action to be had.

**Daniel Negreanu**. Calls Deeb's $16,000 bet.

Lederer's comment was that Negreanu could not be calling for value; he had to be planning to take the pot away from Deeb somewhere down the road. With ace-seven offsuit, and only one heart, his outs, assuming he thinks he's beaten right now, are pretty slim. He might think the three aces are probably outs (although we know they're not) and he needs two running hearts for the nut flush, about a 25-to-1 shot. No one calls a pot-sized bet on the basis of such a puny collection of outs. Clearly Negreanu has something else in mind.

The pot is now $49,800. The turn is 4♠.

**Freddy Deeb**. Deeb's first problem is deciding what kind of hand Negreanu might have, if he has a hand at all. At this point Negreanu has called a big bet before the flop, and a pot-sized bet after the flop. Even for an aggressive, trappy player, that's hard to do with complete trash. Let's run through some possible hands as Deeb might have done, and see what holdings appear to make sense.

1. **AA or KK.** Since Deeb has one of each card, it's very unlikely that Negreanu has either big pair. Good players sensibly proceed on the assumption that if you're unlucky enough to run into one of these pairs while you hold a good hand yourself at heads-up, you're supposed to lose all your chips.

2. **High pairs: QQ, JJ, TT**. These holdings account for the call after the flop, since a player with one of these hands would

438 Part Thirteen: Final Thoughts

hold on for at least one bet in the face of what might well be a bluff. What's unclear here is the call before the flop. These are hands that have to fear overcards, so you want to reraise with these hands preflop. Negreanu just called, which makes these holdings less likely.

3. **Medium pairs: 99, 88, and 77** These are the rest of the pairs down to the six on the board. Each is a definite candidate hand given the betting so far. They're good enough to have called on the flop, and they're not strong enough to make raising on the flop a mandatory play. Since only one overcard to these pairs has flopped, the post-flop call is reasonable.

4. **The killer pairs: 66 and 22**. A pair of sixes fits all the betting action so far. A pair of deuces is more problematic, since most players would fold deuces to a big pre-flop raise. Either hand is a potential disaster for Deeb.

5. **The small pairs: 55, 44, and 33**. These are now unlikely holdings. Any of these pairs might have called the pre-flop bet. Calling after the flop, with two overcards and a flush draw on board, is pretty dicey. Mark all these pairs as dubious.

6. **Two hearts**. Since Deeb doesn't have a heart in his hand, all the high hearts are still out there, and a bunch of plausible holdings fall in this group. A♥K♥ and K♥Q♥ fit the betting perfectly. Each hand could be bet for value before the flop, and are now so strong (top pair plus flush draw) that Negreanu could now be trapping. K♥J♥ and K♥T♥ also work. As the side card with the king gets lower, the pre-flop call gets a little more unlikely. Two lower hearts without a king are much more unlikely; now both calls become dubious and the combination even more so.

7. **Ace-x**. The only plausible holdings here are ace-six and ace-deuce. Each might have called before the flop based on the strength of the ace, and each might have called after the flop based on the pair. Holdings where the ace is the A♥ are a bit more likely than the others.

8. **The two pair hands**. For Negreanu to now hold two pair, he had to start with king-six, king-deuce, or six-deuce. None of these hands are likely to have called the bet before the flop, although all could certainly have called and trapped after the flop.

So what, by this analysis, does Negreanu have at this point? Most likely one of four groups of hands:
1. King-x of hearts (A♥K♥, K♥Q♥, K♥J♥, K♥T♥)
2. A medium pair (99, 88, 77)
3. Trips (66 or 22)
4. Ace of hearts and a pair (A♥6x or A♥2x)

(We know, of course, that Negreanu doesn't have any of these hands. His call after the flop was a complete bluff. However, it would be very difficult for Deeb to make that assessment at this point. Even though he knows a bluff is possible, his thinking has to be directed toward the types of hands that Negreanu could call for value.)

Currently Deeb is beating all of these hands except the trips or the A♥K♥ (which is a tie). Should he bet or check and trap? I think betting is best here, although either move is reasonable. At this point the hands in the second and fourth groups have only a couple of outs, and will fold to a bet. The trips will likely raise. But the hands in the first group will be denied the odds they need for drawing. If Negreanu has one of those hands and calls, he'll be making a mistake. Checking gives those hands a free card, which could be very costly.

Deeb actually checks.

**Daniel Negreanu**. At this point Negreanu likely realizes that he can only win on a bluff. If Deeb has a hand, which he has been representing all along, then aces are probably Negreanu's only outs. (We know they're not outs at all, of course.) With so few real outs, checking here to get a free card is pointless; the free card isn't likely to matter, while the check represents weakness which might encourage Deeb to call a bet on the end. Negreanu realizes he has to project strength and bets $30,000, a little over half the pot.

**Freddy Deeb**. Calls.

But why call? Why not raise? A raise of twice Negreanu's, $60,000 or so would knock out the draws and settle the hand with a nice profit. It's possible Deeb was planning an even more elaborate trap on the river. But not raising now creates two possible dangers: It may give Negreanu a winning hand (not possible here, but only we know that), and it may allow Negreanu to represent a winning hand. In all, a very dangerous call.

The pot is now $79,800. The river is the 4♥.

**Freddy Deeb**. The four of hearts is an exceptionally bad card for Deeb, elevating another group of hands into the lead. Now Deeb bets $65,000, probably a bad move given what he now suspects. If Negreanu was playing a hand in Group 2 or 4, he'll lay his hand down and lose no more money. If he was playing a Group 1 or 3 hand, he'll raise. A better play was to check, then make a decision if Negreanu bets.

**Daniel Negreanu**. Negreanu understands that he almost certainly has to raise to win the hand. But how much to raise?

Beginners like to make a huge raise, hoping to scare the opponent out of the pot. But Negreanu has already seen (in Hand

No. 1) that Deeb respects the small, deadly raise on the end, and can lay down a hand despite good pot odds. What's more, he knows that Deeb knows (from Hand No. 2) that Negreanu is fully capable of making that raise with a good hand. So Negreanu calls Deeb's $65,000 bet and raises only another $100,000. Negreanu's play leaves Deeb looking at a pot of almost $310,000 and needing to put in just another $100,000 to call.

**Freddy Deeb**. What to do? Negreanu's bets make perfect sense if he flopped a set of trips. They also make sense if he started with two high hearts, including the K♥. No other holdings fit the bets very well. Has Negreanu really bet his whole tournament on a stone bluff? (We, of course, know that he has. But giving an opponent credit for such a move in the heat of battle is very difficult.)

If Deeb folds, he'll have lost almost $120,000 on the hand. Since the players started with about $340,000 apiece, he'll be trailing Negreanu by more than 2-to-1 in the chip count, $460,000-to-$220,000. But if he calls and loses, the gap will be $560,000-to-$120,000, more than 4.5-to-1. Deeb thinks for awhile and decides to give it up.

All in all, an amazing hand. Poker has been a steady presence on television for about two years now (I'm writing this in the Spring of 2005), and if I had to cast a vote for the most interesting and ingenious hand in this period, this one gets my vote. What's particularly fascinating is not just the courage to make such a play at a critical time, but the logic and preparation behind the play. When beginners try to bluff, it's often a desperate, spur-of-the-moment decision when a promising hand has gone bad. These bluffs are fairly easy to pick off because the sequence of bets doesn't make sense. The real keys to a great bluff are threefold:

1. Do all the plays make sense in the context of the hand you're representing?
2. Will your opponent understand what you're representing?

3.   If your opponent understands, will he fold?

In this play, Negreanu knew from previous observation that (2) and (3) were in place. Deeb knew that Negreanu could make a small bet with the nuts, and Negreanu knew that Deeb had in the past folded to a small bet on the end. All that remained was to create a series of bets that reasonably well represented either trips or a flush. Negreanu's play shows poker thinking (and poker courage) at its very best.

# Conclusion

Now that you've finished *Harrington on Hold 'em; Expert Strategy for No-Limit Tournaments; Volume II: The Endgame,* you should have a much clearer idea of how to conduct the later stages of a no-limit hold 'em tournament.

**Successful move making depends on observations**. Whether your moves have a high or low probability of success depends on the betting patterns of your opponents. The more closely you can observe those patterns, the better you will be able to choose moves appropriate to the situation, and the higher your batting average of success will be. Beginners tend to pick moves out of the blue, to see if they might work. Don't fall into this trap. The experienced player observes his opponents closely to pick moves carefully tailored for the occasion.

**Your M determines your strategy**. A big M allows you to play in many different ways — conservative, super-aggressive, or anywhere in-between. You can make small probing bets or plan and execute big moves, switching from style to style as the occasion allows. As your M shrinks, your options contract. When your M gets low enough, your decision is not whether to go all-in, but only when.

**You must be aware of the Ms of everyone at your table**. While your M will govern your strategy, *their* M will govern their strategy. Pay attention to the status of everyone else, and you'll have a much clearer idea of what their plays actually mean.

One final thought before signing off on *Volume II.* Poker is, more than any other game, an arena where experience counts. Reading and studying, while valuable, can only carry you so far.

## 444 Conclusion

To go the rest of the distance, you have to play, play, and then play some more, until your instincts are as finely honed as your logic. Hopefully, with the aid of the ideas in Volume I and Volume II, the journey will be a little easier.

With our look at the general principles of no-limit tournament hold 'em completed, the next book will focus on practical applications. *Volume III* will be a workbook of about 120 problems, mostly drawn from major tournaments and large online events. The format will be that of a quizbook, and the reader will have the choice of simply reading the book from beginning to end, or treating it as a large quiz and scoring himself. The quiz answers will be grouped into categories so the reader can see in which areas he excels and in which areas he needs improvement.

# Index